It's French-English Dictionary

<<Where are all the accents?!>>

<<Et puis quoi?>>

Grappling with French language

John Wright asserts his right to be identified as the creator of the design of the format of the contents contained within this work

© John Wright 2021-2022

This book is sold subject to the condition that the format within it shall not, by way of trade or otherwise, be copied unless the prior written consent of the author or any publisher to whom he delegates authority has been obtained, and without a similar condition including this condition being imposed on the subsequent purchaser

Yes, I studied 'A' level French many years ago. But reading French books is a mental stretch, resulting in this "impure" and alternative French-English DICTIONARY. No cedillas, no accents, no 'roofs'. If you want to improve your skill, there's no secret formula. Just keep practising and you'll get better. Even now, I still read French slowly. BUT...the point is that I read French.

Having read several French books in the process of creating this dictionary, I fully understood them (even Diderot's "Le neveu de Rameau", a series of essays by a French philosopher). The Dictionary has deliberate gaps so it will develop as you read and can add in new words. This edition has been extended as a result of further reading, with some corrections to definitions and 'fine tuning', and includes a number of idioms and phrases, common verbs (etre, faire, passer, prendre, savoir etc) and prepositions (en, y, dans, tout)

There is some predictability when reading French: e.g. words that end 'ment' are usually male nouns; words ending 'ure' usually female nouns. The French arrangement of words (sentence 'construction') follows order, unlike us British who are not as careful with words. In this dictionary you will only rarely find multiple uses of one word but it will always have its own line, not a huge block. Also, there is no English-French section if you want to find the French equivalent of an English word. The reader will notice that many French words are followed by abbreviations in brackets (like nm, nf, adj etc) and the translations have abbreviations (e.g. Mus, Bot, Zool, Fig, Expl etc). There follows a list of common abbreviations to eliminate confusion. So, key point to remember: throughout the dictionary, you will find spare lines between some definitions which are for you to exploit by adding words you encounter as you widen your reading of French literature.

This fourth edition follows on from previous editions in fine-tuning what is intended to be a user-friendly and unoverwhelming compendium to the user's reading of French, whether it be a journal, literature or whatever. It is not an expert piece of work. It's aim is to be practical and useful to those who have a basic grasp of French and want to enjoy reading French without needing to consult a tome which puts their arm tendons at risk.

June 2022 – John E Wright

Abbreviations and Meanings

Geol	geological	nm	noun masculine
Geog	geographical	nf	noun feminine
Med.	medical	nmpl	noun masculine plural
Fig	figurative	nfpl	noun femine plural
Cine	cinema	nmf	noun masculine or feminine
Theatre	theatre	s.o	someone
Pol.	political	s.t	something
Agric.	agricultural	qch	something
Hort	horticultural	qn	someone
Naut	nautical	adj	adjective
Mil	military	Mech	mechanical
Biz	business	Jur or Jud	jurisprudence or judicial (legal)
Comm	commercial	Zool	zoological (e.g. birds, animals etc)
Merc	mercantile	Bot	botanical (e.g. plants, flowers)
Naut	nautical	Expl/Vulg	expletive or vulgar, swearing etc
Coll	colloquial or slang	Pej	pejorative (i.e. insult)
Eccl	ecclesiastical	RCC	Roman Catholic Church
Arch	architectural	Anat	anatomical
Hist	historical	Lit	literature
Antiq	antiquity	Cul	culinary

A

	a-coup		jolt, hitch
	abaissa		lowered, reduced, pulled down
s'	abaisser		to demean oneself
s'	abandonner	a	to let oneself go, give way to despair, become addicted to, neglect oneself
	abat-jour (nm)		lampshade
	abattant (nm)		leaf, flap, lid
	abattement (nm)		despondency, reduction, allowance (tax)
	abattre		to cut off, knock down, pull down, dishearten s.o
s'	abattre sur		to pounce, swoop down
	abattu		dejected, depressed
	abbe		abbot, priest (RCC)
	abeille (nf)		honey-bee, drone
	abime		abyss, chasm, gulf
	abimer	(dans)	to damage, be lost (in)
	abject(e) (adj)		despicable, abject
	abjurer		to recant
	abnegation (nf)		self-sacrifice
	aboiement		barking, ranting
aux	abois (nmpl)		at bay, in dire straits
des	abonnes		subscribers (to papers, works)
tout d'	abord		at first, initially
d'	abord		first, at first, first of all
	abordable		accessible
	aborder		to land, approach s.o, accost, tackle (question)
	abouti		successful
	aboutir	a	to end up in /at, lead to, end in
	aboyer		to bark, shout
	abreger		to precis, shorten, abridge, abbreviate
s'	abreuver		to drink
	abri abritat		shelter
s'	abriter		to take shelter
	abroger		to repeal (law), abrogate
	abrupt		steep
	abruti		stupid (adj); moron (n)
	abrutissement		exhaustion, mindless state
	absent(e)		absentee, missing person
	abside		apse (arch)
	absolu		undisputed, absolute, uncompromising
	absolutisme		absolutism (being arbitrary and despotic)
	absorption		taking, absorption, take-over (Comm)
s'	absoudre		to forgive (s.o s.t), absolve s.o
	absurde		nonsensincal, absurd
	abuse (nm)		abused person, fooled person

	abuser		to fool
	abuser	de (l'alcool)	to exploit abuse, (drink to excess)
	abuser		to take advantage of (s.o), misuse
	abusif -ive (adj)		excessive, unfair, wrongful, improper, over-possessive
du meme	acabit		of that sort
	acariatre		cantankerous, bad-tempered
	accablant		overwhelming, overpowering
	accabler		to overwhelm, overpower
	accaparant(e) (adj)		very demanding
	accaparer		to hoard, monopolise, preoccupy, take up
	acceder		to reach, acquire, obtain
s'	accelerer		to quicken, accelerate
	accelerer		to speed up (work), accelerate
s'	accentuer		to become more pronounced
	accepter		to come to terms with, agree, accept
un	acces	de	a fit, outburst, attack, approach, access
	accessit		honourable mention
	accessoire		secondary, accessory
	accidenter		to bump (vehicle)
	acclamer		to cheer, acclaim
	accolade		embrace, accolad
	accoler		to join side by side, bracket
s'	accomoder	de qch	to make the best of s.t
	accompagner		to go with, accompany
	accord	de gre a gre	mutual agreement
se mettre d'	accord		to come to an agreement
d'	accord		OK, alright, fine
tomber d'	accord		to come to an agreement
etre d'	accord		to agree
	accord	a	consent (to), agreement, understanding, chord (Mus)
	accordage (nm)		tuning
s'	accorder	avec	to agree, come to an agreement, fit in (with)
	accorder		to attribute importance, grant (favour), tune (Mus)
s'	accoter		to lean
	accouchement		delivery (birth)
	accoucher	de	to give birth
	accoucheur -euse		an obstetrician (-euse) midwife
s'	accouder		to lean on one's elbows
	accoudoir (nm)		arm-rest
	accouplement		coupling, mating
	accouru		came running
	accoutrement		outfit
	accoutume(e) (adj)		customary, usual

	accoutumer		to get (s.o) used to, accustom (to)
	accroche		slogan, hook (idea)
	accroche-coeur (nm)		kiss-curl
s'	accrocher		to cling to
	accrocher		to hook, catch (s.t), fasten (belt)
	accrocheur -euse		eye-catching, persistent, catchy
s'	accroitre		to grow, increase
	accroupie(s)		squatting
s'	accroupir		to squat, crouch (down)
	accueillir		to receive, greet, welcome
	acculer	qn a qch	to drive s.o to/against s.t
	accuser	(a qn de qch)	to define, accentuate, show up (accuse s.o of s.t)
	acere		sharp, cutting, scathing, trenchant, keen
	achalande		well-stocked (shop)
	acharne		fierce, relentless
	acharnement		relentlessness
s'	acharner		to pursue, lay into
s'	acheminer		to forward, despatch, set out for
cela ne s'	achete	pas	it's s.t money can't buy
cela ne s'	achete	pas	it's s.t money can't buy
s'	acheter	qch	to buy oneself s.t
s'	acheter	qn	to buy oneself s.t
s'	achever		to draw to a close, end
	achever		to conclude, finish, complete, end
	acier		steel
	acompte		a down-payment, instalment, deposit, advance (on salary)
(s')	acoquiner		to get on well/be 'thick' with s.o
	acore		sweetener
	acquerir		to purchase, gain, acquire, undergo
	acquis		established, accepted (fact), acquired (knowledge)
	acquisivite		desire to acquire
	acquitter		to settle a debt, pay, acquit (s.o)
	acra/akra		fried Haitian malanga (root veg)
	acre		sharp, caustic, acrid
faire	acte	de presence	to put in an appearance
	actes (nmpl)		proceedings (Jur)
	actif -ive (nfm)		working person, assets (nm)
	actife (nm)		assets (of biz)
	actionner		to activate, operate, sue (Jur), turn on
en	activite		active, working, in operation
	actuel -elle (adj)		present, current, topical, actual
	acuite		acuteness, intensity, shrillness, Keenness, seriousness
	addition		the bill (restaurant), addition

une	adepte		a follower
	adequat(e) (adj)		appropriate, suitable, adequate
	adequation		appropriateness
	adhesion (nf)		support, membership
	adjoint(e)		assistant
	admettre		let, admit
	administre (nf)		constituent
	administrer		to manage, run (biz), dispense (justice), produce (proof), govern (country)
	admiratif -ive		admiring
	admirer		to admire
	admonester		to admonish
s'	adonner		to devote oneself to
	adosser	(a/contre)	to lean (on/against)
	adoucissement		softening, alleviation
	adresse		dexterity, skill, tact, address
s'	adresser	a	to apply to s.o, speak to s.o
	adresser		to aim, address (letter, remark)
	advenir		to occur, come about
	adynamie		adynamia (Med) I.e debility due to disease, lack of vital power
	aerien -ne		aerial, atmospheric, overhead (cable), elevated (railway), air, floating, exquisite
	aerogare		air terminal
	aerolithe		aerolite (a meteorite, meteoric stone)
	affable		courteous, affable
	affabulation		fabrication
	affaiblir		to weaken
avoir	affaire	a	to be dealing with
	affaire		business, concern, deal, case, crisis, scandal, affair, matter
J'en fais mon	affaire		I'll deal with it
s'	affairer		to bustle about
les	affaires		business
	affale		slumped, lowered (Naut)
	affame		starving, famished
	affame(e) (nmf)		starving child
	affamer		to starve
	affectation (nf)		appointment, allocation, posting, affectation
	affecter		to assign, allocate, pretend, touch/move s.o
	affectif -ive		emotional
	affectionner		t be very/particularly fond of
	affectueux -euse		affectionate, fond

s'	affermir		to become stronger
	affiche		poster (of play)
	afficher		to display, show, declare
	affilee		straight
	affiner		to refine, sharpen (senses), ripen (cheese)
	affinite		affinity
	affirmer		to maintain, assert, affirm, declare
	affleurer		to be level, make s.t flush with, surface, crop up (Fig)
	affligeant		distressing, pathetic, depressing
s'	affliger		to be grieved/distressed about s.t
	affliger		to afflict, strike, distress
	affluence		crowd
	affluer		to flock, pour in
	affole(e)		thrown into a panic
	affolement		panic
	affoler		to drive crazy, throw into panic
	affranchir		to (set) free, stamp (letter)
	affreter		to charter
	affreux -euse		ugly, hideous, dreadful, awful
	affrontement		clash, confrontation
	affronter		to confront
	affubler	a qn de qch	to dress s.o up in s.t
	affubler		to saddle s.o with (Coll), deck s.o out in, dress s.o up in
	affut		gun carriage, hide, look-out place
	afin	de	in order to, so as to
	agacant		annoying, irritating
	agacement (nm)		irritation, annoyance
	agacer		to annoy, irritate s.o
	age		old, elderly
	agenais(e)		s.o from Agenois (old French region)
	agenouiller		to kneel (down)
	agent	de change	stockbroker
	aggiornamento		modernisation
s'	agglomerer		to gather together, be grouped together
	aggravation	(de)	worsening, aggravation, increase in (de)
s'	aggraver		to worsen
s'	agir	que	to must do as; it's that one must...(do s.t)
s'	agir	de	to do with, be about, be a matter of
	agir		to act, take proceedings, behave, take effect
qu'il s'	agisse	de	either, whether it's about.../a question of
	agissements		activities, doings
	agitation		restlessness, commotion, unrest, agitation
	agite		rough, choppy (sea), restless (night, patient), excited, fidgety, troubled (mind)

s'	agiter		to be agitated, fidge
	agonie (nf)		death throes, slow death
	agonisant(e)		dying
	agrandir		to make s.t larger, magnify, enlarge
	agreable		pleasant, nice, agreeable
	agrege		holder of the agregation award (5 year role teaching at highest level in snr school/uni)
	agrement		pleasure, amusement, approval, consent
	agrementee	de	approved, embellished by
les	agrements		pleasures, amusements, amenities, charm
	agres (nfpl)		apparatus
s'	agripper	a	to cling to, grab
	aguerri		seasoned (pro), hardened
etre aux	aguets		to be on one's guard, watch like a hawk, lie in wait
	aguichant(e)		alluring
	aguicher		to lead (s.o) on, attract, allure
	ahuri(e)		bewildered
	ahurissant(e) (adj)		incredible, staggering
s'	aider		to make use of
	aieul		grandfather, ancestor
	aigle		eagle, lectern
	aigrelet(te)		shrill, rather sharp, rather sour
	aigrette	garzette	little egret (Zool)
	aigrette		crest, egret (Zool)
	aigreur		bitterness (Fig), sharpness, sourness
	aigrir		to turn sour/bitter
	aigu(e) (adj)		Keen, sharp, pointed, keen, acute, high-pitched, criticical, treble (Mus)
cabine d'	aiguillage		signal-box (railway)
	aiguille		needle, hand (watch), peak (Geol)
	aiguilleur		points-man (railway)
	aiguillonner		to spur, goad, stimulate
	aiguise		sharpened
	aiguiser		to sharpen, heighten, whet (appetite), arouse, hone, stimulate
	ailes		wings
d'	ailleurs		besides, moreover
par	ailleurs		in addition
	ailleurs		elsewhere, somewhere else
	ailleurs (nm)		elsewhere, an aside
s'	aillir		to jut out, protrude
	aimant		magnet
	aimer	mieux	to prefer
s'	aimer		to love each other
	aimer		to like, make love

	aine(e)		older, oldest, elder
pour	ainsi	dire	so to speak, as it were
	ainsi		like this
	ainsi		thus, so
	air		melody, tune atmosphere, appearance, spirit, air
	airain		bronze
	aire		sphere, area, strip (Veh), bay (Comm)
	aisance		ease, freedom of movement
bien	aise		Well-pleased
	aise		easy, free (manner), well-to-do, well-off, ease, comfort
	aisselle (nf)		armpit
	ajouter		to add
	ajouter	foi a	lend credence to
	ajuste		adjusted
	alarmant(e)		alarming
(variable)	aleatoire		risky (random, variable)
	alentours (nmpl)		surrounding area
	aleser		to bore (metal)
	alesoir (nm)		reamer (a machine tool with fluted bit to enlarge or make conical hole)
	algarade (nf)		quarrel
	aliene(n)		mad/insane person
	aliener		to give up, alienate
	aligner		to put (s.t) in a line, line (s.t) up, align, give a list of
	aliment		food
un travail purement	alimentaire		a job done purely to make a living
	alimentaire (adj)		dietary, food
	alimentation (nf)		diet, feeding, food
	alimenter		to supply, feed
	allaiter		to suckle, breast-feed
etre plein d'	allant		to be full of bounce, have plenty of drive
	allant (adj)		active, lively
	allee		path, drive, road
	allee		avenue, drive, path (in garden)
	alleger		to lighten, relieve
	allegre		lively, cheerful, light-hearted
	alleguer		to invoke, claim, allege
	aller	a qn	to suit someone
le pis	aller		the last resort
s'en	aller		to go away, leave

	aller		to go, be (NB: it's also a linking verb, e.g: aller passer)
	alliage		alloy
	allier		to combine, unite, alloy
	allonge		extension
	allongent		lengthen
s'	allonger		to get longer, stretch out
	allonger		to lie down
	allouer		to allocate, allot, grant, allow
s'	allumer		to catch fire, light up
	allumer		to light, strike, switch on, turn on, arouse
	allumette		match, matchstick
	allumeur -euse		tease, lamplighter, distributor
	allure		walk, bearing, style, pace, behaviour, look
	allusion (nf)		allusion (reference to)
	allusion (nf)		allusion, hint
de bon (mal)	aloi		genuine (ungenuine, false)
	aloi (nm)		worthy
	alors que		while
	alourdir		to weigh (s.o) down, make (s.t) tense
	alteration (nf)		impairment, spoiling, deterioration, change, distortion
	alterer		to change (for worse), impair, spoil (food), tamper with s.t, twist (truth), make s.o thirsty
	altier -ere		haughty
	amant		lover
	amarre(s)		rope(s), mooring(s)
	amarrer	(a/sur)	to moor (Naut), tie (to)
	amas		mass, heap, pile
	amasser		to amass (riches), collect (memories)
	ambassade		embassy
	ame		soul, spirit (departed), heart, feeling, bore (of gun)
fut	amenage		was furnished, fitted out
les	amenagements		fittings, fixtures, installation
	amenager		to convert, do up, develop, fit out, create, lay out, equip, adjust, arrange, make up
	amende		a fine
	amener		to bring
	amenite (nf)		affability, friendliness
	amer(e)		bitter

	amertume		bitterness (Fig)
	ameublement		furnishing, furniture
c'est un	ami	de simplicite	he likes simplicity
	ami(e)		friend, dear (Coll)
	amiable		privately negotiated
	amical(e) (adj)		friendly
	amicalement		kindly, warmly, in a friendly way
	amitie		friendship
	amnesique (adj)		amnesic
	amnistier		to grant amnesty to/for
	amoindrir		to diminish, lessen, weaken
	amollir		to soften, weaken
	amoncellement		heap
	amonceller		to heap up, accumulate, pile up
	amont		upstream
	amorce (nf)		beginning, initial section, initiation, bait, cap
	amorcer		to begin (building, negotiations), bait (trap), prime (pump) entice
	amorphe (adj)		lifeless, apathetic
	amorte (nf)		bait, detonator, primer, beginning, initiation, hint
	amortir		to deaden, muffle (sound), break (fall), deaden (pain), absorb (shock), pay off debt/redeem
	amour-propre		self-respect, pride, vanity, self-esteem, conceit
	amphore (nf)		jar, amphora
	ampleur		width, fullness, volume (voice), extent (disaster)
	amplitude		amplitude
	ampoule		light bulb, phial
	ampoule		turgid
	amputer		to cut (s.t) drastically, cut off, amputate
s'	amuser		to play, enjoy oneself, have a good time
	amuser		to entertain, distract, amuse
	amuseur (nmf)		entertainer
trois fois par	an		three times a year
	analogue		similar to, analogous, analog
	ananas		pineapple
	ancien -enne (adj)		former, old, antiquarian, senior
a l'	ancienne		in the traditional way
	andrinople		andrinople fabric (with identical floral borders on each side of the cloth)
	aneantir		to destroy, dash
	aneantissement		annihilation
	anemier		to weaken (fig), make anaemic
	anerie (nf)		silly remark, rubbish (coll), silly blunder
	aneroide		aneroide (for a barometer - gravity-based, not mercury)

	ange		angel
	angelot		cherub
	anglaise		slanted handwriting, ringlet
	angle		corner, angle (of wall)
	angoisse		anxiety, anguish, angst
	angoumoisin		s.o from Angoumois
	anguille		eel
	animal(e) (adj)		animal, savage, brutish
	animer		to give life to s.t, to stir up (feelings)
	annaliste		annalist?
	anneau		ring, link (of chain), coil (of snake)
	annihiler		to destroy, cancel out
	annonce		announcement, advert, sign
	annulaire		ring finger, third finger
	anodin(e)		safe, mild, innocuous, innocent, anodyne, insignificant, harmless
	anonymat		anonymity, confidentiality
	anonyme (adj)		impersonal, anonymous
	anormal(e)(aux) (adj)		unusual, abnormal, unfair
	anse (nf)		a cove (geog), handle (of jug, basket)
a l'	antenne		on the air, to the air (TV, radio)
	anterieur		previous, front, anterior
	antienne		refrain
	antiquaires		antique dealers
	antique (adj)		age-old, old-fashioned, antiquated
	antiquisant		antiquity (Roman/Greek)
	antre		den, lair
	apaisement (nm)		calming down, calm
s'	apaiser		to become calm, abate
	apanage		privilege, monopoly
(diner d')	aparat		(banquet, formal dinner) state, pomp
	aparte		private conversation
	apatride		stateless (person)
s'	apercevoir	de qn	to realise, notice, become aware of s.t
	apercevoir		perceive, catch a glimpse of, see
	apercu (nm)		glimpse, taste, outline, insight
	aperitif		drink (stimulates appetite), apperitif
	apesanteur (nf)		weightlessness
	apeure(e) (adj)		scared, timid, frightened

	apitoiement (nm)		pity
	aplanir		to level, smooth away, iron out, make s.t flat
	aplati		flattened
	aplomb		balance, self-assurance, perpendicularity, aplomb
	apogee		zenith, height, apogee
	apostrophe (nm)		remark, heckle, shouting out, apostrophe
	apostropher		to shout at
	apparante		related
d'	apparat		sumptuous, ceremonial
	apparat (nm)		grandeur, pomp, ceremony
	appareil		device, equipment, apparatus, machine
	apparemment		seemingly, apparently
s'	apparenter	a	to have s.t in common with
ne plus s'	appartenir		to not have one minute for oneself
	appartenir		to be owned (by), belong (to)
s'	appartenir		to live for each other
	appat		bait, lure
	appauvrissement		impoverishment
	appel		call, appeal
	appele		conscript (Mil)
	applaudissements		applause, clapping
	applique(e) (adj)		studious/hard-working person
s'	appliquer (ait)	a	to take great care, apply o.s to, apply to (s.t/s.o)
	apport (nm)		contribution, input, supply
	apporter		to bring, provide (proof)
	apposer		to affix (stamp), stamp
	apposition		fixing, placing
	apprendre		to learn, hear of, get to know (of s.t), apprise
qch qui s'	apprendre		s.t which is learned
faire l'	apprentissage		to train as, complete apprenticeship in/as
	appret		affectation, dressing, finishing, size
s'	appreter	a faire	to get ready to (do)
	apprit		learned
	apprivoiser		to tame, win (s.o) over

	approchant(e)		similar, close, approximate	
s'	approcher		to get closer, approach	
	approfondir		to deepen, increase (one's sadness), go deeply into s.t	
	appropriation		appropriation, embezzlement	
s'	approprier		to take the credit for, seize, steal, appropriate	
	approvisionne		stocked	
	appui		support, rest	
	appui-tete		head-rest	
s'	appuyer		to lean, rest	
	appuyer		to support, prop up	
	apre (adj)		bitter, harsh, fierce	
	aprement (adj)		fiercely, bitterly	
d'	apres		according to	
	apres	de	near, by, close to	
	aprete		roughness, sharpness, bitterness, harshness	
	apte	a	capable of, qualified for, suited for	
	aquarelles (nfpl)		watercolours	
	aquilin		aquiline (nose)	
	araignee (nf)		a spider	
	arbalete		crossbow	
	arbitre		referee, arbiter, arbitrator, adjudicator	
	arborer		to sport, wear, parade, bear	
	arbuste (nm)		bush, shrub	
	arc		bow, arch	
s'	arc-bouter		to brace oneself, buttress o.s	
	arc-en-ciel		rainbow	
	arcadien		arcadian	
	arceaux		arches	
	archet		bow (violin, cello)	
	archeveque		archbishop	
	ardent(e) (adj)		burning hot, passionate, eager, ardent, fervent, blazing fire	
	ardu(e) (adj)		taxing, difficult, arduous, steep	
	arete		ridge, line, edge	
les	aretes		bones	
d'	argent		silver	
	argente(e) (adj)		silvery, silver-plated	
	argenterie (nf)		silverware, silver	
	argile		clay	
	argileux -euse (adj)		clay-ey, clayish	
	argot (nm)		slang	
	argotique		slang	

	argouisier		sea-buckthorn (Bot)
	argumentation (nf)		line of argument
	armateur		ship-owner
	armature		frame, armour
	arme		weapon, arm
	arme	blanche	weapon with a blade
	armee (nf)		army, bunch
	armoires		cupboards
	armoiries (nmpl)		arms
	armorie(e) (adj)	de	with the family/company coat of arms, crested
	armure		form of protection (Fig), armour, sleeving
	arpentent		walk
	arpenter		to walk, pace, survey, measure
	arpenteuse -eur		(land) surveyor
	arquebuse		arquebus (Mil.)
	arquer		to bend, curve, sag, walk
	arrache		scratch, tear
	arrachement		parting, wrench
	arracher		to uproot, tear down, tear (one's hair out)
s'	arracher	aux entreintes	to tear oneself away from embraces
s'	arracher	les yeux	to fight like cat and dog
s'	arracher		to fight over, scramble for
s'	arranger		to manage, tidy oneself up
	arret	de mort	death sentence
en	arret		at a standstill
	arret	maladie	sick leave, sick note
	arret (nm)		cancellation, halt, stopping, stop, cessation
	arretation		arrest
s'	arreter		to come to a standstill, stop, dwell on s.t
	arreter		to stop (s.o, s.t), arrest (growth), fix/fasten (shutter), close, settle (an a/c)
Rien ne pourra l'	arreter		Nothing can stop him/her
en	arriere	de	behind
	arriere (nm)		arrears (pl)
	arriere-cuisine		scullery
	arriere-plan		the background
	arriere-saison (nf)		late autumn

	arriere-salle			back-room (cafe/restaurant)
	arrierer			to defer (payment)
s'	arrimer		a	to bind itself to
	arrimer			to stow (s.t) away, dock (in space)
	arrivage			delivery, consignment
s'etre	arrive			to have happened
s'	arrondir			to fill out, become rounded
	arrondissement			largest civil sub-division of French dept
	arroser			to water, baste, wash down
	arrosoir (nm)			Watering-can
	arsenal -aux			paraphernalia, gear, arsenal
	art			craft, art
	artere			artery
	artichaut			artichoke (n); fickle (adj)
	article			critical point, clause (of treaty), article, commodity, item, news posting
	articule			jointed, articulated
	artifice			trick, pretense, contrivance
	artilleur			gunner, artillery man
	artiste			artist, performer
	ascendant		(sur)	ascendancy (over)
	ascese			(form of) ascetism
s'	asembler			to gather, assemble
	asile			sanctuary, shelter, retreat
	aspect			side, aspect, appearance
	asperge			asparagus
	asperite (nf)			bump, protusion, harshness
	asphyxie			death by suffocation, suffocation (Med), asphyxia (Med), paralysis
s'	asphyxier			to suffocate to death, paralyse
	aspirant (n)			candidate, suction, extractor (adj)
	aspirer			to breathe in, inhale, suck up, vacuum, pump (s.t) up/out, aspirate
	assagir			to quieten, quiet (s.o) down
	assagissement			quietening, calming
	assaillir			to attack, plague, set upon, assail

	assassinat (nm)		murder, assassination
	assaut		attack, assault
	assembler		to collect, gather, convene, assemble
	assez		rather, fairly, enough, quite
	assidu		diligent, unceasing (care), assiduous
	assiette		plate, seat (horse), foundation (of road)
	assimiler		to learn, adopt, assimilate
	assise		stratum, bed, foundation
	assise(s)		seat(s), seating, hardcore, foundation, basis, stratum (geol)
les	assises (nfpl)		conference, meeting, assizes, court
	assistance		onlookers, audience, presence
	assister	a	to be present at, be at, witness, attend
s'	associer		to join with, join forces with, share in
	associer		to associate, unite, join
	assoiffer		to make (s.o) thirsty
	assombrie		darkened
	assombrir		to darken, obscure
	assommer		to club (s.o), knock (s.o) senseless, bore s.o to tears, to stun s.o, to fell (an ox), stagger, overcome
	assortir		to match
s'	assoupir		to doze off, drop off to sleep, calm (pain)
	assoupir		to soften (s.t) up, soften, loosen, relax, make (s.t) less strict, make (s.t) supple, make (s.t) more flexible
	assourdir		to deaden/muffle (sound), deafen
	assourdissant		deafening
	assouvir		to satisfy, assuage
	assouvissement		satisfying, satisfaction
s'	assujettir		to submit to s.t
	assujettir		to subject (s.o) to a rule, subdue
	assure		sure, certain, confident, steady
s'	assurer		to make sure/certain of s.t
	assurer		to fix, secure, ensure, make s.t firm
	astre		star
	astre	du jour/de la nuit	sun (literature)/moon
	astreindre	qn a qch	to force s.t on s.o, bind s.o to s.t
	astreindre		to compel, oblige
s'	astreindre		to make oneself do, force o.s to do, subject o.s to s.t
	astreinte (nf)		constraint, daily fine for delay (Comm), periodic penalty (Jur)
	astuce		manoeuvre, pun, trick, cleverness, shrewdness
	atavisme (nm)		atavism (I.e. recurrence of hereditary characteristics or diseases which have skipped one or more generations, reversion to type)
	atelier		workshop, studio

		athee		atheist, atheistic
		atone (adj)		apathetic, lifeless, expressionless, atonic (Med)
		atonie (nf)		sluggishness, apathy, lifelessness, atony (Med)
		atout (nm)		trump card, asset, trump
	de l'	atre		of the earth
		atrocement		dreadfully, terribly, horribly, atrociously
		attabler		to sit down to table
		attachant(e)		charming, engaging, sweet (coll)
	s'	attacher		to cling, stick, attach oneself to
		attacher		tie, chain, tether, stick, fasten
		attaquer		to attack, criticise, assault, tackle (subject)
		attarde	a	delayed at
	s'	attarder	(sur)	to stay, linger, dwell on
		atteindre		to reach, attain, suffer from (health), hit (target)
		atteint (adj)		affected
		atteinte (nf)		reach
	hors d'	atteinte		out of reach, beyond
	s'	atteler	a faire	to get down to doing
		atteler		to yoke (oxen), harness (horses)
		attenant		adjoining, adjacent
	en	attendant		nonetheless, in the meantime, all the same
	s'	attendre	a	to expect s.t
	s'	attendre	a mieux	to expect better
		attendre		to wait, wait until, wait for, be ready for, expect
		attendri		compassionate, fond, tender, tenderised (Cul)
	s'	attendrir		to feel moved, become tender
		attendrir		to touch, move, tenderise
		attendrissement		tenderness, emotion
		attendu		given, considering
		attendu(e) (adj)		expected
		attendus (nmpl)		grounds (Jur)
		attentat		assassination attempt
	en	attente		pending, waiting
		attente (nf)		expectation, anticipation, wait(ing)
		attenter	a	to cast a slur on, infringe, offend against, be an affront to
		attentif -ive		special, careful, attentive
		attention (nf)		attention
		attenuer		to tone down, soften, lessen, weaken, reduce, mitigate
		atterrer		to overwhelm, shatter, astound

		atterrir		to land, touch down
		atterrissage (nm)		landing
		attiedir		to warm, cool (desire)
		attirail		gear, paraphernalia
		attirance		attraction
		attirant		attractive
		attirer		to draw, attract
		attitude		pose, posture, attitude
		attouchement		touching
		attrait (nm)		appeal, lure, attraction
		attraper		to catch, pick up
	s'	attribuer	qch	to claim (s.t)
	s'	attrouper		to gather (around)
		au-dedans		inside
	l'	au-dela		the hereafter, beyond
		aube		dawn
		auberge		hostel, inn
		aubergiste		innkeeper
		aucun		no, any, none, anyone, any, some
		aucunement		in no way, by no means, not at all, not in the least
		audience		hearing (jud), audience
		auge		trough, plate, U-shaped valley (Geol)
		auguste		venerable, noble, august
		aujourdhui		nowadays, today
		aumone		hand-out, alms, pittance
		aumonier		chaplain
	a l'	aune	de	by the yardstick of
		auparavant		previously, beforehand, at first
		aupres	de	close to, near to/by, compared with
		auquel		which
		aura		aura
		aureole		halo, ring
		aussitot	(que)	immediately, directly (as soon as)
		autant	dire que	you might as well say that, in other words
	d'	autant	plus	all the more so
		autant	de...que	as much...as, as much as
		autarcie (nf)		autarchy (absolute power, dictatorship)
		autel		altar
		auto-critique (nm)		self-criticism
		autodafe		book-burning, autodafe (ceremony accompanying sentence and execution of heretics by the Inquisition)
		autodenigrement		self-denigration
		autodidacte		self-taught, self-educated

parc	automobile			fleet of cars
	automutilation			self-harm
s'	autoriser	de qch pour faire		to use s.t as an excuse for doing
	autoroute			motorway
	autour	de		around, round
nul	autre	que		none other than
	autre			other, different, what is more...
	autrefois			formerly, in the past
	autrement	dit		in other words
	autrement			differently, otherwise, in another way
	autruche			ostrich
	autrui			others, other people
	auvergnat			of the Auvergne
s'	avachir			to sag, let oneself go (Fig), flop, slump
qu'il n'en	avait	l'air		than it looked
en	aval			downstream
	avaler			to swallow
	avance (nf)			advance, projection, lead
	avancee (nf)			overhang, advance
s'	avancer			to move forward, head towards, advance
	avancer			to put forward, advance
les	avanies			insults
	avant	peu		before long
(d')	avant			first, beforehand, before, previous, ahead
	avant-bras			forearm
	avant-gout			foretaste
	avant-guerre (nm)			the pre-war period
	avant-hier			the day before yesterday
etre a son	avantage			to show oneself at one's best
	avantageux -euse			good value, favourable, advantageous, attractive
	avare			miser
	avare (adj)			stingy
	avarice (nf)			meanness with money, miserliness
	avarie			damage
	avenir			future
	aventure			risky, ventured, risked
d'	aventure			by chance
	aventure (nf)			affair, adventure, venture
	aventurer			to risk, venture
s'	averer			to prove to be, transpire, turn out to be
	averse			downpour, shower
	avertir			to inform, notify, warn s.o of s.t

		avertissement		warning, reprimand
		aveu(x)		confession(s)
		aveugle (adj)		blind, sightless, blinkered, blank, blocked up
		aveugle (nmf)		blind person, implicit trust
		aveugler		to block up, stop up, blind, dazzle
	s'	avilir		to degrade, demean oneself
		avilir		to degrade
		avilissement		degradation
		avine		drunken, intoxicated
		avis		opinion, judgment, advice, counsel, notice
		avise (adj)		prudent, sensible
	s'	aviser	de faire qch	to venture to do s.t
		aviser		to catch sight of (s.o), perceive
		aviso (nm)		escort vessel
		aviver		to kindle, intensify, stir up
		avoir		to get, catch, have, wear, have (s.t) on, feel
		avoir (nm)		credit note, credit, assets (pl), holdings (pl)
	s'	avoisiner		to be near/adjacent to s.t, border on s.t
		avoue (nm)		solicitor, attorney
		avouer		to confess, admit, acknowledge
	grands	axe (nm)	de circulation	major routes
		axe (nm)		axis, spindle
	l'	ayant (nm)	a droit	the rightful owner/claimant, interested party (Jur.), beneficiary
		azote (nm)		nitrogen
		azotique (adj)		nitric

B

	babil		chattering, babbling
	babiole		trinket, trifle, 'nothing'
	bac	a sable	sandpit
	bac (nm)		tub, tray, vat, ferry
le	badinage		banter(ing)
	bafouer		to ridicule, jeer at s.o
	bafouiller		to mumble
	bagatelle		trifle, minimal, triviality, physical love (euphemism)
	bagnole		old banger, clunker
	bagout		gift of the gab, volubility, glibness
(se)	baguenauder		to stroll, saunter about
	baguette		rod, baton, stick
	bahut		sideboard
	baie		berrry, bay, opening (Arch)
	baigner		to bathe, steep (in s.t), soak, water (district)
	baignoire (nf)		bath, bath-tub, conning tower (Naut)
	baignoire-sabot		walk-in bath, seated bath
	bailler		to yawn
c'est un bon	baiseur -euse		he/she's a good f*!k (crude)
se	baisser		to stoop, bend down
	baisser		to lower, open, let down
	bal		ball(room), dance(hall)
	balade		walk, stroll, ride, drive
se	balader		to go for a walk/stroll/ride, tour
	balafre		scar, slash, gash
	balancement (nm)		swing(ing), rocking, sway(ing), balance
	balancer		to waver, swing, balance
	balancier		pendulum (clock)
	balayer		to sweep out, blow away
	balbutiant(e)		stammering, babbling, in its infancy
	balcon		balcony
	baleine		whale
	baliverne (nf)		nonsense
	ballant(e) (adj)		dangling
	balle		ball
	ballet	bleus	paedophile ring (young boys)
	ballon	d'eau chaude	hot water bottle
	ballon (nm)	(verre)	ball, balloon; (brandy/wine glass)
	ballotage		absence of an absolute majority in 1st round of an election (pol)
	ballotter		to toss, shake about, roll around, swing to n fro

	balourd		awkward/clumsy person
	banal		commonplace, banal, unremarkable
voiture	banalisee		unmarked car (police)
	banaliser		to trivialise, make (s.t) commonplace
	banc		bench
	bande	dessinee	comic strip (e.g Tintin, Asterix)
par la	bande		on the grapevine (Fig), on the side (Fig)
	bande (nf)		group, strip, band
	bandeau		headband, blindfold
	bandouliere		shoulder-strap
	banlieue		suburbs
	banqueroute		bankruptcy
	banquette		bench, seat
	baobab		baobab tree (they live for centuries!)
	baoum!		boom (onomatopaeic sound)
	baraque(e)		hefty
les	baraquements		shacks, hutted camp (Mil.)
	baratineur -euse		smooth talker, liar
	barbarisme		incorrect use of a word/idiom, Barbarism
	barbe		beard
	barbele		barbed wire
	barbon		(old) fogey (Coll)
	barboter		to paddle, dabble, nick, filch
	barbouiller		to smear, daub, scribble, scrawl
	barda (nm)		baggage, gear, kit
	barette		bib, flank, mudflap (car)
	barge	a queue noire	black-tailed godwit (Zool)
	barge	rousse	bar-tailed godwit (Zool)
	bargue		(jewelled) ring, band
	barguigner		to bark(?)
	baril		barrel, cask, keg
	bariole(e)		motley
	baroud		fighting
	baroudeur		fighter, warrior, adventurer
	barque (nf)		(small) boat
	barrage		dam, roadblock, barracade
	barre (nf)		bar, rod of metal, barrier, line, clash
	barreaux		bars, rungs (ladder), rails
	barrer		to obstruct, dam
	barrette (nf)		(hair-)slide, bar-brooch, ribbon

	barriere (nf)		fence, gate, crossing, barrier
plus	bas		lower
en	bas		(down) below
la	bas		there!
	bas-relief		low-relief, bass-relief (sculptures etc)
	bas, basse		low, low-lying, bass (Music), lowly, bottom, base, coarse, vulgar
	basane		swarthy, tanned
	bascule		rocker, see-saw, rocking, weighing machine
	basculer		to topple over, tip into, knock (s.o) off balance
la	base		the rank and file
	base		foundations (building), base, basis, foot (of mountain)
	basilic		linked to basil plant or the Basilica
les	basques		skirts (of garment), tails (jacket)
	basse-cour		farmyard, poultry (adj)
	bassesse		lowness, mean, contemptible
	bassin		pond, pool, reservoir, tank, dock, basin (geol), bowl, pan
	basson		bassoon
	bastingage (nm)		(hand) rail, topside, bulwark
	bastion		stronghold
	bat-flanc (nm)		wooden partition, stall partition
	batailler		to fight, battle
	bati		developed, built
	batiment		building, vessel, ship
	batisse		building, house
	batiste		lawn, cambric (fine kind of linen cloth – batiste)
	baton		stick, staff, rod, truncheon, 10,000 Francs
	battant		hinged section (door/window), leaf (table)
	battement (nm)		beating, beat, flutter, fluttering
	battine		ankle boot
	battre	monnaie	to mint coins
se	battre		to fight
	battre		to beat, flog, thrash
	baudrier (nm)		shoulder-strap, harness
	bavard		talkative, gossip
	bavardage		chattering, gossip, idle chatter
	bavarder		to chatter, gossip, talk, blab
	baver		to dribble, drool, leak
	beant(e)		gaping
	beat		blissfully happy, blissful

	beatement		blissfully, rapturously
	beatitude		bliss, beatitude (Theo)
	beau-frere		brother-in-law
	beau-pere		father-in-law
	beau, bel, belle, beaux		beautiful, nice, good, lovely, fine, noble, successful, great, tidy
	beauceron		s.o from the Beauce (in France)
refiler le	bebe		to pass the buck (Fig)
	bebe		baby
	bec		beak
	becasse		woodcock, feather-brain (Coll), silly goose (Coll)
	becasseau	cocorli	curlew sandpiper
	becasseau		sandpiper
	beche		spade, lip (of jug), spout (coffee pot)
	becher		to dig, criticise
	bedounant		pauncy
	beer		to gape
	begayer		to stutter, stammer
etre	begue		to stammer, stutter
	begueule		trickster, con
	beguin (nm)		crush, bonnet
	bel et bien		indeed
	belement		bleating
	belier		ram, battering ram (Mil)
	belitre		beggar, good-for-nothing
	bellatre		handsome, hunk
	belle-maman		mother-in-law
	belliqueux -euse		quarrelsome, warlike, bellicose
	benefice		profit, gain, living, benefice
	benefique		beneficial
	benet		simple, simple-minded
	benir		to bless
	benito		blessed, consecrated
	bequille		crutch
	berce		rocked, soothed
	berceau		cot, cradle
	bercer		to lull, soothe
	berceuse (nf)		lullaby
	berge		bank (of river – steep)
	berger		shepherd

	bergerie			sheep pen
	bernois			of Bern (town)
la	besogne			work, task, job
	besoin			necessity, need, want, requirement, poverty, indigence
	bestiaux			cattle, livestock
	bete			stupid, simple; animal (Zool), insect/bug
Peux-tu etre	bete			How silly can you be!
	betise			stupidity, nonsense
	beton (nm)			concrete
	betonner			to concrete
	beuglant			bellowing
	beuverie			drinking session
	bevue			mistake, blunder
regards en	biais			sidelong glances
	biais (nm)			bias, way, dodge
	biaiser			to hedge (risk)
	bibelot			ornament
	biberon			(baby's) bottle
	bicetrien			Bicetre (in Paris) was hospital for the mentally ill
ma	biche			doe (Zool); honey, pet (terms of affection)
	bidasse (nm)			soldier
faire le	bide			to be a flop
	bide			stomach
	bidon (nm)			can, drum, flask, stomach, hogwash (Fig)
	bidonnage			joking around, hilarity
(se)	bidonner			to laugh, fall about
son	bien			his property
c'est	bien		a cela	that's it
	bien		que	although
	bien			good, thoroughly, carefully, definitely, very, at least, very much, well, comfortably, tastefully, completely, properly, correctly
	bien-fonde (nm)			validity, legitimacy (Jur)
	bienfaisance			charity
	bienfaisant			beneficent, charitable, beneficial
	bienfait			benefit, kindness, gift, blessing, service
	bienfaiteur			benefactor
	bienseance			propriety, seemliness
	bienseant			seemly
	bientot			soon
	bienveillance			kindness, benevolence
	biere			beer, coffin, casket
	bigleux -euse			poor-sighted
	bijou(x)			jewel, gem, jewellery

	bijoutier (nm)		jeweller
	bilan		assessment, balance sheet, outcome, toil
	billes		bills
	billet	doux	a love-letter
	billet (nm)		short letter, note, notice, invitation, bank-note, bill
	billetiste (nmf)		writer of short articles, ticket clerk
	billevesees (nf)		nonsense
	billot		block (for beheading)
	biner		to hoe
	bipede		biped (animal with 2 feet)
	bisannuel -elle		biennial (Bot)
	bisburner		to twist
	biscaien		Biscayan (from Bay of Biscay)
	biscornu (adj)		quirky
(en)	biseau		bevel (edge); at an angle
	bisou		kiss
	bisou (nm)		kiss
	bissac		(huntsman's) pouch
	bissextile (adj)	annee	leap year
	bistouri		scalpel
	bite, bitte		bit, bitt, pr*?k (Expl)
	bitterois(e)		native of Beziers
	bivouaquer		to take shelter, bivouac
	bizarrerie		oddity
	bizuter		to bully, rag
	blafarde		pale
	blague		joke, fib
	blanc (nm)		blank, gap, lull, white(ness), household linen
	blanc, blanche (adj)		blank, white
	blanche (nf)		brandy (eau de vie), smack (Coll), minim (Mus), white ball (billiards)
	blancheur (nf)		whiteness, innocence
	blanchir		to turn white, whiten, bleach, light up, grow light (sky), go grey
	blason		coat of arms, heraldry
	ble		corn
	Bledines		branded jars of baby food
	blesser		to wound, injure, hurt, offend
	blessure		wound, injury
	bleuir		to turn (s.t) blue
	bleusaille (nmf)		rookie'

	bleute(e)		bluish
	blinde		armour-plated, armoured
	blini		blini (pancake)
a	bloc		tightly, fully
	bloc (nm)		notepad, block
	blocs		lumps (of wood)
	blocus (nm)		blockade
	blondeur		fairness (hair)
	bloquer		to jam, lock, block the way, blockade, freeze
se	blottir		to nestle, snuggle up against s.t/s.o
	bobine		spool, reel, coil
	bobos		sores
	boire		to drink
	bois		wood
	boise (adj)		wooded
	boisseau		bushel
	boisson		drink, beverage
	boite	de vitesses	gear-box
aller en	boite		to go to a nightclub, go clubbing
	boite		box, office
	boite		box, tin, can, firm, office, club, school
	boiteux -euse		lame (person), lame, wobbly, rickety, shaky
en avoir ras le	bol		to be fed up
	bol (nm)		luck, bowl
	bolide		meteor, racing car
	bombardes		bombards (old style ammo)
	bomber		to swell with pride, bulge out
	bond		bound, leap, jump, bounce, spring
	bonde(e) (adj)		packed
	bondir		to leap, react furiously, hit the roof (Fig)
par	bonheur		happily
	bonheur		happiness, success, good luck, good fortune
	bonhomie (nf)		good nature
	bonhomme		good-natured (adj); old chap/man (n)
	bonification		bonus, improvement (of land)
	bonne		the maid
	bonnement		simply
	bonnet		brimless cap, hat
	bonnetade		a greeting by raising your hat

	bonte		goodness, kindness
	boqueteau(x)		copse(s)
	borborygme		stomach rumble
	borborygme		gurgling, mumbling, rumbling
au	bord	de	on the verge/edge of, at the side of
a	bord		on board (ship), aboard
	bord		edge, border, brink, verge, rim
	bordant		bordering
	bordee		volley (of abuse), broadside
	bordel		brothel, shambles
	border	(de)	to line with, border, run alongside, tuck in, edge, take up the slack (Naut)
	bordure		border, edge, kerb
s'etait	borne		he had limited himself to
	borne		limited, narrow-minded
	borne (nf)		boundary stone, post, bollard, limit
se	borner	a faire	to content oneself with doing
se	borner		to restrict oneself
	borner		to mark (out) the boundary, limit, stake (claim), be limited or restricted
	bortsch		Bortsch (a beet soup)
	bosse		a bump, lump, swelling, unevenness
	bossele(e) (adj)		dented, bumpy, battered
	bossu(e)		hunchbacked
	bottes		boots (high)
	bouche	a fer	piece of ordnance (Mil) (a heavy mounted gun)
la	bouche		opening, aperture, mouth
	boucher		to fill up, block (up), clog
	boucher -ere (nmf)		butcher
	bouchon (nm)		cork, stopper, plug, cap, lid
	bouchone	de paille	straw cork
	boucle		ring, buckle, loop (of river), bend (in road)
	boucler		to curl, fasten, surround, lock
	bouclier (nm)		shield
	bouder		to sulk, refuse to have anything to do with s.o
	boudeur -euse (adj)		sulky
	boue		mud, sediment, sludge
	bouee (nf)		rubber ring, spare tyre, buoy
	boueux -euse		muddy, sludgy
	bouffant(e)		puffy
	bouffee		a puff (smoke), hot flush (med), outburst (anger), fit (of pride)
	bouffir		to swell, puff up/out, scoff (food)
	bouffon		clown, jester, buffoon, comical
les	bougardes		large villages, townships
	bougeoir		candleholder, candlestick

	bouger		to move, budge
	bougie		candle, spark-plug
	bougonnement (nm)		grounding
	bougonner		to grumble
	bougre		chap, bloke
	bouillant		fiery (temper), boiling
	bouillie		porridge(gruel), baby food
	bouillir		to boil, seethe (Fig)
	bouillon (nm)		bubble, broth
	bouilloner		to bubble, be lively
	boule (nf)		bowl, know, lump, ball
	boule (nf)		lump, leadweight, bowl, knob, boule
	bouleau		silver birch (tree)
	bouledogue (nm)		bulldog
le	boulet	(de canon)	ball and chain, (cannon) ball
	boulette (nf)		pellet, blunder
	boulevard		avenue, boulevard, farce (Theatre)
	bouleversement		upheaval, upside down
	bouleverser		to upset, overthrow, distress, disrupt, move s.o deeply
	boulon (nm)		bolt
	boulonner		to bolt (down), work hard
	boulot		work, job
	bouquet		cluster, clump (of trees), bouquet (flowers)
	bouquin		book
	bouquiniste		second-hand bookseller
	bourbilloner		to whirl, swirl
	bourde		blunder
	bourdonnant		buzzing (in ears), droning
	bourdonnement (nm)		buzzing, drone, humming, tinnitus
	bourg		town
	bourgade (nf)		small town
	bourgeois		commoner
	bourgeoisie		middle-class, the middle class
	bourgeon (nm)		bud (Bot), pimple
	bourgeonner		to bud, burgeon, get pimples
	bourlinguer		to travel round a lot, sail the seven seas
	bourrasque		squall
	bourreau		the hangman, torturer, executioner
	bourrelier		saddler
	bourrer		to stuff, cram (cupboard) fill (pipe)
	bourru (adj)		surly
	bourse		purse, pouch, grant, scholarship

	boursuflure		swelling, blister (paper)
	bouscarle		warbler (Zool)
	bousculade		jostling, crush, rush
	bousculer		to jostle s.o, knock into s.o, hustle s.o
	bousiller		to ruin, wreck, smash up, do (s.o) in, waste
venir a	bout	de	to overcome, get through
au	bout	de compte	ultimately
le haut	bout	de la table	the head of the table
	bout		a tip, bit, end, bottom, extremity, piece, toe
	bout	pour bout	end for end
au	bout	de	at the end of
	boutade		flash of wit, whim
	bouton (nm)		spot, pimple, bud
	bovin(e)		bovine
	boyau		narrow passage, bowel, gut
avoir de la	branche		to have a lot of class
	brandir		to hold up (s.t), brandish, throw out
en	branle		impetus, impulse, swing (motion)
	branler		to shake, nod, move
	braque		crazy
	braquer		to turn, fix, aim, point (gun)
	bras		arm arm-rest, handle (of pump)
laisser sur les	bras		to be left lumbered with
	bras-le-corps		bodily, head-on (Fig)
	brasser		to boss (s.t) around, shuffle, gather up
	brasseur	d'affaires	business tycoon
	brasseur -euse		brewer
	bravache		blustering (adj); show-off (n)
	brave		courageous, good, worthy, brave, nice
	braver		to face s.t bravely, to brave, defy
	braves	gens	good, honest, worthy folks
	brebis		sheep
	breche		breach, opening
	bredouillant		empty-handed
	bredouiller		to mumble
	brelan (nm)		3 of a kind
	breloque		charm (on a bracelet)
	bretelle (nf)		strap, slip-road, sling

	bretelles		suspenders
	breveler		to patent
	breviaire		breviary (eccl)
	bribes (nfpl)		snatches, bits and pieces
	brider		to bridle, curb, control
	brigand		crook, ruffian
	brillant (nm)		brilliant (diamond), brilliance, sparkle, glitter, brightness, shine
	briller	par son absence	to be conspicuous by one's absence
	briller		to shine, sparkle, gleam, be shiny, burn brightly
	brin		bit, fragment, strand, blade (grass), wisp (straw), sprig
	brindille		twig, sprig
	brique		carton, brick (Constr), 10,000 Francs
	briquet		cigarette lighter
	briquetier		bricklayer
	brisant (adj)		high explosive
	brise		breeze
se	briser		to be smashed, shattered
	briser		to break, smash, wear s.o out
	brisure		brokenness
	broc		pitcher, large jug
	brochet		pike
	brodequin		a (laced) boot, buskin
	broder		to embroider
	broie		grinds
	broncher		to flinch, budge, move
	bronches (nmpl)		bronchial tubes
	brosser		to brush, scrub, paint
	brosses		brushes
	brouhaha		uproar, hum (of conversation)
	brouillard		fog, mist, haze
	brouille (nf)		quarrel, discord
se	brouiller		to fall out, become blurred, become confused, become cloudy, scramble
	brouiller		to mix up, muddle, jumble, scramble, blur, smudge, fall out (Fig)
	brouillon (adj)		untidy, disorganised, muddled
	brouillon (nm)		rough draft
	broussaille		brush, bushy (of beard)
	brouter		to browse, graze (on grass)
	broutille (nf)		trifle (i.e. nothing)
	bruant (nm)		bunting (Zool)

	bruire		to russle, rumble, hum
	bruisse		murmur
	bruissement		rustle, rustling, humming, murmuring
	bruit	de fond	background noise
	bruit		noise, clatter, din, fuss, sound
	brule-gueule (nm)		short-stemmed pipe
	bruler	les etapes	to go too far too fast
	bruler		to burn, be on fire, consume (energy)
	brulure (nf)		burn, mask
	brumaille		mist
	brume		mist
	brumeux – euse (adj)		hazy, misty, foggy
	brune		dark-haired, brown, brown ale
	brunir		to tan, burnish, brown
	brusque		sudden, curt, sharp(bend), abrupt, off-hand
	brusquer		to be brusque/curt with s.o, treat s.o harshly
	brut		rough, unrefined, raw, dry
	bruyamment		noisily, loudly
	bruyant		noisy, loud, boisterous
	buchant		slogger
	bucher		to slog away
	bucheron		lumberjack
	buee		steam, vapour, mist, condensation
	buffet		sideboard, dresser, buffet
	buissons		bushes
	bulle (nf)		bubble, balloon
	bureau		desk, office, study
	burg		burg
	buste		chest (of person), bust
	but		object, aim, purpose, target, goal
	butait		struck, knocked against
	buter		to trip, stumble, abut on s.t, make (s.o) even more stubborn, prop up, bump (s.o) off (Fig)
	butin(s)		haul, loot (booty, spoils)
	butiner		to glean, pick up, gather pollen from
un	butor		a lout, oaf
	buvette (nf)		refreshment area, pump room
	buveur		alcoholic, drinker

C

	c'est		qu'il est	it's just that he, it is
	ca		et la	here and there
	ca		va	Is that a deal? How are things? Alright, it's alright
	ca		y est	there, that's it, is that it?...
	cabane			hut
	cabanon			hut, shed, (country) cottage
	cabaret			inn
	cabaretier			innkeeper
	cabas (nm)			shopping bag
	cabestan			capstan
	cabine			booth, cubicle, cab
	cabinet			office, chambers, surgery, agency, practice, firm
	cabochard(e)			pig-headed, stubborn
	cabosse			battered
	cabosser			to dent
	cabotin			3rd rate actor, show-off
se	cabrer			to rear (horse), jib, zoon
	cabri			kid (Zool)
	cabriole			somersault, caper, cavorting
	cabriolet			convertible, cabriolet
	cache (nf)			hiding place, hide
	cache (nm)			mask
	cache-nez			scarf, muffler
	cache(e) (adj)			hidden, secret
se	cacher			to be hidden, lie in hiding, hide, lie low
	cacher			to conceal, hide
	cachet			fee (artiste), seal, mark, stamp
	cacheter			to seal (up)
en	cachette			in hiding, on the sly
	cachot			dungeon
	cachottier -ere			secretive person
	cacique (nm)			leading figure
	cadavarique			deathly (pale)
	cadavre			corpse, body, carcas
	cadenasser			to padlock
	cadet -ette			the younger, youngest, junior, cadet (Mil)
	cadran (nm)			face, dial (watch)
	cadre			frame
	cadrer			to centre, fit, tally, restrict (Fig)

	caduc		nullified (legacy), out-of-date, old-fashioned, deciduous (Bot)
un coup de	cafard		a fit of depression
un coup de	cafard		a fit of depression
avoir le	cafard		to be down in the dumps (Fig)
	cafard(e) (adj)		shifty
	cafard(e) (nmf)		hypocrite, sneak, tell-tale, tattletell
	cage		stairwell, shaft, hutch, cage
	cage (nf)	d'escalier	stairwell
	cageot (nm)		crate
	cagneux -euse (adj)		crooked, bow-legged
	cahiers (nmpl)		journal (mag.)
	cahotant(e) (adj)		bumpy, jerking, lacking coherence
	cahute		shack
	caillesse (nf)		stones
	caillout(x)		pebbles, stones, borders
	caisse		crate, chest, box, cashbox, till, fund, case, drum (Mus)
	caissier -ere		cashier
	caisson		ammunition chest
	cajoler		to make a fuss over, bring (s.o) round
	cajolerie (nf)		cuddle
	cajoleur – euse		affectionate
	calamistre(e)		brilliantined, waved, curled
	calciner		to char, scorch
	calcul		calculation, arithmetic, reckoning
	caleche (nf)		barouche, calash
	calembour		pun
	calendrier		schedule, calendar
	calepin		notebook
	caler		to stall, give up, wedge, steady, support, set, fill (you up)
a	califourchon		astride (a chair, a wall etc)
	calin		affectionate, cuddly; cuddle, lovemaking (fig)
	caliner		to cuddle
	calligraphier		to write in a decorative hand
se	calmer		to calm down, die down, quieten, cool, subside, ease, wear off
	calomnier		to slander
	calorique		calorie
	calotte		(Jew's) skull-cap
	calque		tracing, exact copy
	calus (nm)		callus

36

	calvitie		bald patch, balness, bald head
	cambouis (nm)		dirty grease
	cambrioler		to burglarise, burgle, rob
	cambrure (nf)		curve, bending
	camee (nm)		cameo
	camelote		junk
	camion		truck, lorry
changer de	camp		to change sides
etre dans le	camp		to be in shot (cine)
tout fout le	camp		everything's falling apart
	camp		side, camp
	campagnard		rustic, country
	campagne		countryside, country, campaign
	campanile		bell-tower
	campanule (nf)		bellflower/campanula (Bot)
	campee(s)		camped
	campement (nm)		camp, camping
	camper		to portray, depict, camp
	canaille		scoundrel, rabble
	canal (nm)		channel, canal
	canalisation (nf)		pipe, mains (pl), channelling
	canape		sofa, couch, settee, canape (Cul)
	canard	siffleur	widgeon (Zool)
	canard		duck, rag (Coll), newspaper, false rumour, darling, wrong note
	cancan		gossip
	cancre		dunce
	candeur		ingenuousness
	cane		a female duck
	caniche		poodle
	canif		penknife
	canne		reed, walking stick, cane
	cannelure (nf)		flute
	cannonier		gunner
	canon		gun (big), cannon, canon (Rel)
	canot (nm)		boat, dinghy
	cantatrice		opera singer, (professional) singer
	cantine		canteen, cafeteria
	cantique (nf)		canticle, song

a la	cantonade			to no-one in particular, to anyone and everyone
se	cantonner			to confine oneself to, restrict oneself to
	caoutchouc			elastic band, rubber band, rubber
	cap (nm)			hurdle, cape, course
	capable			right person, capable
	capital			fundamental, essential, principal, assets, capital (£)
	capitale			capital city, capital letter
	capitonnage			padding
	capote	(anglaise)		hood (car), top, great-coat; (condom)
	capricieusement			whimsically, freakishly, capriciously
	capter			to get, pick up (signal), capture
	capucin			monkey, Capuchin friar (eccl)
	caquet			cackle, cackling (of hens)
	car (n)			coach, bus
	carabine			rifle
	caractere			character, letter, graphic sign, feature, disposition, characteristic, nature
	caracteristique (adj)			characteristic
	carafe			carafe, head, 'nut' (coll)
	caravanserail			caravanserai (large, unfurnished Eastern inn)
	carboniser			to char (wood), carbonise
	carburat			fuel
	carburer			to vaporise (fuel), work (slang), go well (slang)
	carcan (nm)			straitjacket, rigidity, vice, yoke, iron collar (Hist)
	caresser			to stroke, caress, cherish, toy with
	cariatide			caryatid (instead of a column, a woman statuesque/statue in drape)
	carillon			chimes, bells
	carmes			Carmelites
	carmin			cochineal, carmine, crimson (make up)
	carnation			skin tone
	carnaval			carnival
	carnet			notebook
	carnissier -ere			carniverous, ferocious
	carotte			carrot
	carre (adj)			square
	carre (nf)			bedroom
	carreau(x)			wall tile, tiled floor, window-pane, checked (adj)
	carrefour			crossroads
	carrelage (nf)			tiled floor, tiling, tiles

	carrement		downright, completely, clearly, straight out, in no uncertain terms
	carres		squared (n₂)
	carrick		(Fig) reject, knackered old man
	carriere	de sable	sandpit
	carriere		course of life, career
	carriole		light cart
	carrosse		(horse-drawn) coach
	carte		menu, meal, (playing) card, map
	cartesien -enne (nmf)		Cartesian (i.e. s.o who follows Descartes philosophy)
	carton (nm)		cardboard
	cartonner		to bind, get one over
	cartouchiere		cartridge belt
	cas		instance, case, matter
	cascade		stunt, spate, cascade
	cascade (nf)		waterfall, stunt, series (of), cascade (hair)
	case (nf)		hut, cabin, compartment, square/box
	casemate		blockhouse (a fortified place, improvised fort made of logs)
	caserne		barracks (Mil)
	casier (nm)		rack, pigeon-hole, pot
	casque		helmet (Mil), crash helmet, headphones
	casquette		peaked cap
	cassant(e)		brittle, abrupt, curt
	casse		breakage, damage
	casse-cou		a daredevil
se	casser		break, snap, give way
	cassure (nf)		break, split, rupture, fracture (Geol), crease
	castor		beaver
	castrato		castrato (singer, c in boyhood)
	catalan(e)		Catalan
	catalpa		catalpa (Bot.)
	catastrophe		disaster
	catins		whores
	cauchemar (nm)		nightmare
	causant		causing, talking about
pour	cause		because, for a reason
etre en	cause		to be at issue, to be involved
etre hors de	cause		to be in the clear
mise en	cause		implication
remise en	cause		reappraisal, rethink
aimer a	causer	de	like to talk about

	causer		to chat, talk, cause, bring about
	causerie (nf)		chat
	caustique		caustic
	cauteriser		to cauterise
	cavaler		to be a womaniser, chaser of men/women
faire	cavalier	seul	to go it alone
	cavalier		partner (dancing), horseman/woman
	cavalierement		off-handedly
	cavatine		short operatic melody, cavatina
	cave		cellar, hollow, sunken (adj)
	caverne		cave, cave
	ceci	ou cela	one thing or the other
	ceder		to give up, yield, surrender
	ceindre		to girdle, buckle, put on, gird, become mayor (Fig)
	ceinture, ceinturon		belt
qu'a	cela	ne tienne	never mind that...
	cela	tient a	it's down to, due to
Voyes-vous	cela		Did you ever hear such a thing?!
	cela	va-t-il	is this going to be the same
	cela	va de soi	needless to say
	cela/ceci	etant	that being so
	celer		(of speed) fast, swift, celerity
	celibitaire		unmarried, single, batchelor, spinster, celibate
	cellule		cartridge, cell
	cendre (nf)		cinders, ashes
	cendre(e) (adj)		ash (grey)
	cendree (nf)		dirt track, cinder track (racing), mustard seed
	cendreux -euse (adj)		ashen, ash-grey, ashy
	cendrier		ashtray, ash-pan
	cenobite		cenobite (member of religious Order)
etre	cense	faire qch	to be supposed to do/develop/become s.t
	censement		supposedly
	centaure		centaur (Myth)
	centrale		prison (>2yr sentence), power station
	cep(s)	de vine	vine stock; vines
	cependant		however, nevertheless
	cercle		circle, hoop

	cercler	(de)	to encircle, ring, hoop (barrel), rim (with)
	cercueil		coffin
	cerf		deer, stag
	cerf-volant (nm)		stag beetle, kite (toy)
	cernable		understandable
	cerne		ring (eyes)
	cerner		to determine, work out, surround
	certainement		most probably, certainly
	certes		admittedly, certainly
	certitude		certainty, conviction
	cerveau -elle		brain, mind, intellect
	cesser		to leave off, stop, cease, give up (biz)
	chagrin (nm)		grief, sorrow
	chagriner		to grieve, distress, upset
	chahuter		to heckle, play up, give a hard time
	chaine		chain, shackles, fetter, cable (Naut), channel (TV)
	chair		flesh, pulp (fruit)
	chaire (nf)		pulpit, throne
	chaise	de poste	post carriage (Hist)
	chaland (nm)		barge, lighter
	chale		shawl
	chaleur		heat, warmth
	chaleureux -euse (adj)		enthusiastic, friendly, warm, welcoming
	chaloupe		a long-boat, launch
	chaloupe(e)		swaying (tango), rolling (gait)
	chambardement		shake-up
	chambranle (nm)		frame (door), mantel, fire surround
sur-le-	champ		right away
	champ		scope, range, field (of action)
	champetre		village, rural
	champignon		mushroom, fungus, edible fungus
	chance		(good) luck, chance, likelihood, fortune
pas de	chance		hard luck!
	chanceler		to stagger, totter, wobble
	chanceux – euse		lucky
	chandail		sweater
sans	changement		unaltered, unchanged
	changement		alteration, change, changing
se	changer	les idees	to take one's mind off things
se	changer		to get changed, change/turn into
	chanoiness		canoness

	chansonette		little song, light-hearted song
	chant		singing, ode, canto, edge (Tech), song (of bird)
qu'est ce qu'il nous	chant		what's he on about?
	chantant(e) (adj)		lilting, tuneful, singsong
	chanter		to sing of, sing, celebrate
	chantier		construction/building site, shambles, builder's yard, mess
	chantonner		to hum (s.t) to oneself
	chapelet	(de bombes)	rosary, (stick of bombs)
	chapelle		chapel, clique, choir, coterie
	chaperon (nm)		coping (stone), hood
	chapiteau		capital of column (arch)
	chapka		fur hat
	char		chariot, waggon, tank (Mil), car
	charabia (nm)		gobbledee-gook, gibberish
	charavari		row, racket, hullabaloo
	charbon		coal, carbon
	charbonnage		colliery
	charbonnier		coalman, collier
	chardon		thistle
	charge		load, burden, responsibility, trust, charge (Mil, legal)
	chargement (nm)		loading, lading, load, freight, cargo
	charger	de	to load, weigh down
se	charger	de	to take responsibility for
se	charger	de faire qch	to undertake to do s.t
	charger	qn de faire	to make s.o responsible for doing
	chariot		waggon, cart, truck, trolley, dolly (Cine.)
	charme		charm, captivation, "spell"
	charmes (nmpl)		physical attributes (fig)
	charnel -elle (adj)		carnal, physical
	charnier (nm)		mass grave
	charniere (adj)		pivotal, transitional
	charniere (nf)		hinge, bridge, joint
	charpente		frame(work), framing
	charroi		cartridge belt
	charrue		plough
	charvette (nf)		cart
	chas (nm)		eye (of needle)
	chasse		hunting, chase, shoot(ing), flush (toilet)
tirer la	chasse		to pull the chain
	chasse-croise (nm)		continual coming and going
	chasser		to hunt, expel, chase, go hunting, chase/drive s.o out/away, drive in (nail)

	chasseur -euse		hunter, huntsman
il n'y a pas un	chat		there isn't a soul (there)
	chataigne		blow, clout, (sweet) chestnut
	chataignier (nm)		(sweet) chestnut tree
	chatain(e)		brown-haired
	chateau		castle
	chateau	de cartes	house of cards
	chateau-la-pompe		tap-water
	chatiment		punishment
	chatouiller		to tickle
	chatouilleux -euse		touchy
	chatoyer		to shimmer, glow
	chatrer		to castrate, geld (stallion), neuter (cat)
	chaud(e)		warm, hot, sensitive, heated, turbulent
	chaudiere		boiler
	chaudron		cauldron, pressure-cooker (Fig)
	chauffe-eau (nm)		water-heater
se	chauffer		to warm oneself
	chauffer		to overheat, warm (up), get hot
	chauffeur		stoker, fire-man, driver
	chaume		thatch, stubble
	chausser		to put (s.t) on, wear, fit (s.t) with tyres
	chaussettes (nfpl)		socks
	chaussure (nf)		shoe, boot
	chauve		bald, bare-headed
	chauve-souri		bat
	chaux		lime
	chavirer		to overwhelm
	chef	de service	section, department, head, clinical director
	chef-d'oeuvre		masterpiece
	chef-lieu		administrative centre
	chemin	faisant	on the way
	cheminee		fireplace, chimney(stack)
	cheminot (nm)		railway worker
	chenal (aux)		channel, fairway, flume
	chene	(vert)	oak, (holm-oak)
en	chene	vermoulu	worm-eaten oak
	chenille/cheneau		caterpillar, tracked vehicle (e.g armoured car, tank)
	chenu(e) (adj)		hoary, leafless

	chercheur -euse		researcher
	chetif -ive		weak, puny, wretched, sickly
	cheval, chevaux		horse(s)
	chevalier	gambette	common redshank (Zool)
	chevalier		greenshank (Zool), knight
	chevaliere (nf)		signet ring
	chevauchement	de croupes	rump overlap
	chevaucher		to overlap, ride on horseback
	chevelure		hair, tail of comet
	chevet		bed-head, bedside table
avoir un	cheveu	sur la langue	to lisp
	cheveu(x)		hair
avoir les	cheveux	en brosse	to have a crew cut
	cheville		peg, pin, plug, ankle
	chevreuil		roe deer, venison (cul)
	chevronne		experienced, seasoned
	chevrotant(e) (adj)		quavering (voice), tremulous
	chez		in, among, at, at (s.o's) place, from
	chicane (nf)		legal quibbling, delaying tactics, bickering, double-bend, chicane
	chicaner		to quibble, haggle, wrangle with (s.o)
	chiche	que je le fais!	bet you I can do it!
	chiche (adj)		mean, stingy
	chichi (nm)		fuss
	chien, chienne (adj)		nasty, bloody-minded, wretched
	chiendent (nm)		couchgrass (Bot)
	chiffon		a rag, piece of cloth, scrap of paper, duster
	chiffonner		to crumple (paper), crease (dress), bother
	chiffre		figure, number, numeral, digit, cipher, total
	chiffrer		to assess, cost, encode, number (pp), put a figure on
	chignon		bun (hair)
	chimere		dream, fancy, chimera
	chimie		chemistry
	chiminee		fireplace
	chimiquement		chemically
	chipeau (nm)		gadwall (Zool)
	chipoter		to quibble, haggle, pick at one's food
	chirant(e) (adj)		really boring, bl**dy (Expl)
	chirurgien		surgeon
	chit		onomatopaeic exclamation
	choc		shock, bump, impact

	choeur		chorus, choir, chancel (arch.)
	choir		to fall
	choisi(e)		selected, choice
de	choix	courant	of standard quality
	choix		choice
	chomer		to be out of work, idle, unemployed, be at a standstill, not to work on
	chomeur -euse		an unemployed person
	chope		tankard, mugful, pint
(se)	choquer		to knock s.t against s.t, (se) to be shocked, offended
tout de	chou		sweet little thing
	chou		dear, darling, choux bun, cabbage
	chou (adj)		sweet
	choucroute		sauerkraut
	chouette! (Excl)		great! Brilliant! Neat!
	chouia		tiny bit, smidgen
	chouit!		shwee (i.e woosh)
	chronique		column/page (in press), chronicle
	chuchoter		to whisper
	chuintement		hissing
	chuinter		to hiss
	chute		fall, collapse (of ministry), off-cut, clipping
	chuter		to fall down/over, fall, drop
	ci-joint		enclosed
	cible		target, butt
	cibler		to target
	cicatrice		scar
	cicatricer		to heal (wound)
	cicerone		cicerone (after Cicero), guide
	cigogne		stork (Zool)
	cigue		hemlock
	cil (nm)		eyelash
	cime		peak, summit, top
	ciment (nm)		cement
	cineaste (nmf)		film director
	cinglant		scathing, stinging, driving
	cingle(e)		mad, crazy
	cinoque, sinoque		crazy
	cintre		hanger (clothes), curve

	circonscrire			to limit, surround, bound, circumscribe
	circonspection			caution, circumspection
	circonvallation			rampart, circumvallation
	circonvenir			to get round, circumvent
	circulation (nf)			traffic, circulation
	circuler			to circulate, flow, move about
	cire (nf)			wax
	ciseau(x)			chisel, scissors, shears
	ciseler			to chisel, polish, snip (plants)
	citadin(e) (adj)			city
	citadin(e) (nmf)			City-dweller
	citation			quotation, summons (Jur), commendation (Mil)
	citronnier			lemon tree
	civiere			litter (carry)
	clabauder			to clap
	clairieres			clearings, glades
	clairseme			scattered, sparse, thin
	clairvoyance			perceptiveness
	clairvoyant			perceptive, clear-sighted
	clamer			to proclaim
	clameur			outcry, clamour, roar
	clampin			lazybones (coll)
	clapotement			lapping
	claquement			slamming, banging, cracking
	claquer			to slam, bang, click, slap
	clarine			clarinet
a la	clarte	de		by the light of
	clarte			clearness, clarity, light
	classe (nf)			form, lesson, class
	classement (nm)			classification, filing, grading, ranking, closing (Jur)
	classer			to classify, size (s.o) up, file (s.t) away, rank, class
	classeur (nm)			ring-binder, file, filing cabinet
	claustrer			to confine
	clavecin			harpsicord
	clavette			key

	clavier		keyboard
	cle clef		key, (in the key of), spanner
	cliché		snapshot, negative (photog), cliché
	clignant	l'oeil	blinking the eye
	cligner		to blink
	clignon		bun
	cliquet		catch, pawl
	cliqueter		to jingle, rattle, click, go clickety-click, clank
	cloaque (nf)		cesspit (Fig)
	clochard		tramp, down-and-out
	cloche		bell
	clocher		bell tower, belfry, steeple
	cloison		bulkhead (Naut.), partition, division
	cloitrer		to shut away, put (s.o) into a convent
	clope		a fag, ciggy, cigarette
	clore		to close up, shut up
	clos		concluded, closed, shut
	clos (nm)		enclosure
	cloture (nf)		fence, hedge, railings, chain-link fence, wire-mesh fence, surrounding wall, enclosure
	clou		boil, nail, star turn (Fig)
	clouer		to nail down
	cloute(e)		studded
	cluistrerie (nf)		priggishness, oafishness
	coasser		to croak
	cocasse (adj)		comical
	cocher		coachman
porte	cochere		carriage entrance
	cochon -onne		dirty/blue (Fig), smutty, pig, slob, sex-maniac, explicit
	coco (nm)		coconut, darling, pet, guy, customer, head (Anat)
	cocon		cocoon (Fig)
secouer le	cocotier		to clear out the dead wood
	cocotier (nm)		coconut palm
	cocotte		a loose woman (coll)
	coequipier -ere		team-mate
aller droit au	coeur	de qn	to cut s.o to the quick, touch s.o deeply
un	coeur	fidele	a faithful friend
avoir un coup de	coeur	pour qn	to fall in love with s.o
un	coeur	simple	a simple soul
si le	coeur	t'en dit	if you feel like it
(c'est) de bon	coeur		willingly, (you're) welcome
	coeur (nm)		heart, courage, mood, core

	coffre		bin, chest, deposit box, coffer, trunk (of car)
	coffrer		to put (s.o) in prison/inside
	coffret		coffer, trunk (of car)
	cogner		to knock (against), bang (against), hit (out), pound (heart)
	coherence (nf)		consistency, cohesion, coherence
	cohue		crowd, throng, crush, scramble
se tenir/ rester	coi/coite		to keep quiet
se	coiffer	de qch	to put s.t on
se	coiffer		to do one's hair, comb one's hair
	coiffer		to control, make hats for, do (s.o's) hair
	coin		corner
	coin-coin (nm)		quack-quack
	coincer		to wedge s.t open/shut, trap, catch, nick (police)
se	coincer		to get stuck/jammed/caught
	coincer		to wedge (s.t) open, wedge (s.t) shut, trap (s.o), jam, wedge, corner (s.o), catch (s.o) out, nick (Police), cause problems
	coite, coi		quiet
	col		col (geog), collar
	colifichet		trinket, nick-nack
	collaborateur -trice		colleague, assistant, contributor, collaborator
	collectif -ive (adj)		shared, group, mass, collective
	collectivisation		collectivisation
	college		secondary school (11-15)
	coller		to paste, stick, glue, cling, adhere (closely)
	colleret(te)		frill, ruffle
au	collet		at the collar
	collier		necklace
	colline		hill
	collodion		collodion (a solution of gun-cotton in ether)
	colmater		to plug, seal off, seal
	colombe		dove
	colorer		to tinge, tint, colour
	colporteur		peddlar, hawker
	colvert		mallard (Zool)
	colza		rape (Agric)
hors de	combat		out of action, disabled
	combat		fight, battle, action, combat, conflict, struggle
	combativite		fighting spirit
	combattant		fighting, combat
	combattant-varie		ruff

	combattre			to fight against, combat, strive, struggle
	combature (nf)			ache; (adj) stiff
O	combien			Isn't it just?! Isn't he/that just?! Isn't that right?
	combinaison (nf)			overalls, slip, combination, combining, jumpsuit
il est	combinard(e) (adj)			He's a schemer/wheeler-dealer
	combine (nf)			trick, scam, fiddle, wangle, slip (clothing)
	combine (nm)			hand-set, receiver ('phone), pantie-corselette
	combiner			to arrange (ideas), contrive, combine
au	comble		le soir	at the end of the evening
	comble			limited, filled
	combler			to make good, overwhelm, fulfil
	comedie			palaver, play-acting, comedy
	cominge			gathering?, co-mingling?
le	comique		c'est que	The funny thing is that...
	comitat			committee
	commander			to order, command, operate, control
	commando			commando unit
	commensal			commensal (Zool), mess-mate (one who eats at the same table as others)
	commentaires			comments, remarks
	commerage			gossip
	commetre			to carry out, perpetrate, commit, appoint
	comminatoire(s)			threatening(s)
	comminautaire			Community
	commis			clerk, shop assistant
	commis (adj)			committed
	commis du fisc			tax clerk
	commiseration			commiseration
	commissaire-priseur			auctioneer
	commissariat		(de police)	commission; police station
	commission			errand, message, commission
	commissure			corner
	commode			convenient, handy, easy; chest of drawers (n)
en	commun			together
	commun			general, usual, universal, common
si peu	commune			so unusual
	communiant			communicant (Rel)
	communier			to commune, receive Communion (Eccl), share in
	compagne			(fem)companion, partner (life), mate (animal)
	compagnon (nm)			mate, companion, partner, journeyman
	comparaitre		devant	to appear before
	comparer		a	to compare with/to

	comparse (nf)		extra (Theatre), sidekick
	compasse(e)		prim, affected, stuffy
	compatir		to have compassion, be sympathetic
	compenser		to compensate for, offset, make up for
	complaisamment		obligingly, complacently, with satisfaction
	complaisance		obligingness, being so kind as to
	complaisant		obliging, self-satisfied, complacent, indulgent
	complice		accessory, accomplice, 'partner in crime'
	complicite		bond, complicity
les	compliments		greetings, compliments
	complot		plot
	comportement		behaviour, manner, attitude, performance (sport)
	comporter		to compose, include (s.t), to call for, require (s.t), allow (of)
se	comporter		to behave, perform
	composante (nf)		element, constituent part, component
	compose		compound
	composer		to make up, compose, write, select, put (s.t) together, typeset
	compote (nf)		stewed fruit, compote
	compras		(a pair of) compasses
air	comprime		compressed air
	comprime		tablet (Med)
	comptable		accountant, book-keeper
argent	comptant		face value, cash
	compte	rendue	report, review
ne tenir aucun	compte	de qch	to ignore s.t, disregard s.t
en fin de	compte		at the end of the day (Fig)
tout	compte	fait	all things considered
au bout du	compte		in the end
	compte (nm)		count, amount, number, account, notice
	compte-rendu		report, review
	compte-tours		rev-counter
payer	comptent		to pay in cash
	compter	faire qch	to intend to do s.t, reckon on doing s.t

	compter		to count (on), reckon (up)
	compteur (nm)		meter (water, gas etc)
	comptine (nf)		rhyme
	comptoir (nm)		bar, counter, trading post
	comte		county
	comte (nm)		earl, count
	comtesse		countess
faire le	con		to mess up/about
	con (nm)		c*?! (Expl)
	con, conne, connement		stupid, bl**dy (Expl), f*?!ing (Expl), dead easy
	concasser		to crush, mix (Mus)
se	concentrer		to be concentrated, gather one's thoughts, concentrate
	concert		agreement, entente, concert
de	concert		together
	concessionair		licensee, franchisee, distributor, dealer
	concevoir		to conceive, imagine, understand
	concierge (nmf)		caretaker, concierge
	conciliabule		consultation, discussion, secret meeting
	concitoyen -enne		Fellow-citizen
	conclure		to conclude
(se)	concocter		to concoct, devise
	concordance (nf)		compatability, concordance, conformability
	concordant(e) (adj)		corroborating, conformable
	concorde		harmony
	concourir		to concur, unite, combine, compete
	concours		co-operation, help, coincidence, competition
	concret(e)		tangible, concrete
ainsi	concu		(letter) worded as follows
	concu(e)		designed, conceived, imagined
	concurrence		competition
	concurrent		competitor, candidate
	condamne(e)		sentenced, condemned
	condescendance (nf)		condescension
a	condition	de	on condition that
	condition		state, stipulation, condition
	conditionne		conditioned, packaged
se	conduire		to behave
	conduite		behaviour/conduct
la	confection		preparation, making, ready-to-wear clothing industry
	confectionner		to make (clothes etc), prepare (meals)

		conference		lecture, conference
		conferer	a	to confer, give (s.t) to
		confidence (nf)		secret, confidence
	se	confier	a	to confide in
		confier		to entrust, confide (s.t) to s.o
		configuration (nf)		the lie of the land, shape, configuration
		confiner	a	to border on (Fig), verge on
	les	confins		the limits (of science), borders (of country), confines
		confire	qch dans	to preserve/pickle s.t in...
	se	confondre		to blend, intermingle, confuse
		confondre		to confuse, mistake, confound, astound
		conformation		truth, consistency, conformation, compliance
		confort		cozy, comfort
		confrere		colleague, fellow-member, fellow-
		confrerie		brotherhood
		confus		mixed, indistinct, chaotic, confused
	prendre	conge	de qn	to take one's leave of (s.o)
		congedier		to dismiss s.o
		congeneres		persons of the same nature; congeners
		congere (nf)		snowdrift
		conjoint		united, joint, married
		conjugaison		combination
		conjuger		to combine, unite, conjugate
		conjure	les sorts	makes up spells
		conjurer		to ward off (danger), exorcise (demons), entreat s.o to do s.t
	avoir	connaissance	de	be aware of
	la/les	connaissance(s)		knowledge, understanding, consciousness, experience
	Il n'y	connait	rien	He knows nothing about it
		connaitre		to experience, enjoy, know
	se	connaitre		to know oneself, know each other, know about
		connard		stupid bas?*!d (Expl)
		connement		see con, conne
		connivence		tacit agreement, connivance
		conquerant		triumphant, conquering
	faire la	conquete		to conquer (country), win the heart
		consacrer		to establish, devote (one's time/life), consecrate, sanction
		conscience		awareness, consciousness, conscience
		conseil		advice
		consentement (nm)		consent)

	consequence		outcome, result, consequence
	consequent		consistent, consequent, important
	conservation (nf)		preservation, conservation
	conserve		canned/tinned food, preserve (Cul)
	conserver		to preserve, keep, retain
	considerable		eminent, significant, considerable
se	considerer	comme	to gaze at each other, to consider oneself (to be), to regard each other as being
	consigne		order (instruction)
	consigner		to write (s.t) down, record, confine (Mil), consign
	consister		to consist in/of
	consoeur (nf)		female colleague, counterpart
	console (n)		console (projection like a bracket)
	consommateurs		customers, consumers
	consommation		drink, consumption, consummatiojn
	consommer		to consume, drink, consummate
	constance		patience, constancy, steadfastness
	constant(e)		firm, unshaken
	constat		assessment, acknowledgment, certified report
	constater		to establish, record, state, note (a fact)
	contact (nm)		touch, contact, connection
	contagion (nf)		infectiousness (Fig), contagion
	conte		story, tale
	contempteur -trice		denigrator
	contenance (nf)		a capacity
se	contenir		to control one's emotions, contain oneself
avoir son	content	de	to have one's fill of
	content (adj)		happy, pleased, satisfied with, content
	contenter		to satisfy s.o, content, gratify (curiosity)
	contenu		contents, restrained, suppressed
	conteste		disputed, controversial
se	contester		to dispute, contest
	contigu(e)		contiguous (adjacent, touching, near, neighbouring)
	contiguite		close proximity
	continence		continence (self-restraint)
les	contingences (nfpl)		trivial circumstances
	contour (nm)		outline, line, contour
	contourne		skirted, bypassed
	contourner		to skirt, go round, bypass, trace
	contours (nmpl)		twists and turns
	contractant(e)		contracting party
	contracte		tense (muscles), contracted
se	contracter		to tense up, tighten, shrink, contract
	contraction (nf)		tenseness, shrinking, drop, contraction

		contradicteur		opponent
		contraindre		to compel, force, constrain, restrain s.o
		contraint(e)		strained, forced, duress
		contrarier		to thwart, opposed (plans), bother
	par	contre		on the other hand
		contre (nm)		counter-attack, double
		contre-jour		against the light
		contrebas		below, lower down
		contrecarrer		to counteract, foil, thwart
		contrecoeur (nm)		guard-rail, fire back
		contrecoup (nm)		consequence, repercussion
	sans	contredit		unquestionably, indisputably
		contree		place, region
		contrefaire		to imitate, feign
		contrefaisant		disgusting, irritating
		contrefait(e)		disguised, feigned, counterfeit
		contrefort	ajoures	openwork buttresses
		contremaitre (nm)		the foreman
		contreplaque (nm)		plywood
		contrer		to counter, double (cards)
		contrescarpe (nf)		the outer slope of the ditch/counterscarp
		contresens		misinterpration, wrong way
		contretemps		mishap, hitch
		contrister		to pity
		contrition		remorse, contrition (deep regret for sin)
		controle (nf)		test, monitoring, control, audit
		controler		to monitor, control, test, inspect, verify, audit
		controleur		inspector
		contusion (nm)		bruise, contusion
		convaincre		to convince
		convalescent(e) (adj)		on-the-mend, convalescent
		convenable		fitting, appropriate, suitable, decent, proper
		convenance (s)		appropriateness, suitability, fitness (etiquette - plural)
		convenir		to suit, agree, fit
		convention (nf)		agreement, covenant, convention, article, clause
	il	convient	de s'entendre	you have to agree
		convient	a	suitable for
	ce qu'il	convient	de faire	the right thing to do
		convier	a	to invite (to)
	les	convives		guests (at table)
		convoi		convoy, train (of vehicles, people)

	convoquer			to convene
	cooperer			to work together, co-operate
	copain, copine			friend, mate, crony
	coq			cockerel, cook (ship's)
	coque (nf)			shell, husk, hull (ship), chrysallis(?)
	coquelicot (nm)			poppy
	coquette (adj)			flirtatious, smart, stylish
	coquette (nf)			flirt
	coquetterie (nf)			vanity, affectation, interest in one's appearance
	coquillage			shellfish, (empty) shell
	coquille			shell, guard, spinal jacket (Med), misprint
	coquin(e) (adj)			naughty
les	coquins			rogues, naughty ones
	cor			horn
	corbeau			crow
	corbeille		a papier	waste paper bin, waste paper basket
	corbin			little crow
	corde			rope, cord, line, string
du	cordeau			line
	cordeliers			Cordeliers
	cordier			ropemaker
	cordon			chord, string
	cordon (nm)		de la sonnette	the bellpull
	coriace			tough, hard-headed
	cornac			mahout, elephant driver
	corne			horn, antennae (beetle)
	corneille			crow
	corner			to turn down the corner (of a page)
	cornet			cornet, horn (mus.), cone, paper cone, square-topped academic hat, cone-shapped holder
	cornichon			gerkhin (pickled); nitwit (slang)
passer sur le	corps		de qn	to trample s.o under foot
	corps			substance, body, corpse, main part, bodice
	correctionnelle (nf)			magistrates court
	correspondance			mail, correspondence, agreement, dealings
(se)	correspondre			to suit, match, correspond (match)
	corriger			to give (s.o) a thrashing, correct/mark (papers), proof-read, cure (habit), rectify (mistake)

	corrompre		to corrupt, debase, deprave, bribe (s.o)
	corruscations		flashes of light
	corsage		bodice
	corse(e)		strong, full-bodied, spicy, racy
	cortege (nm)		train, procession
	corvee		chore, fatigue (duty)
	coryphee (nm)		ballet-dancer
	coryza (nm)		head-cold
	cosse		pod, husk
	cossu		well-off, fancy (house)
	costaud		strong, sturdy
chambre	cote	rue	room overlooking the street
a	cote		nearby, close by, close, by comparison
d'un (autre)	cote		on the one (other) hand, in one respect, in one way
de	cote		on one side, on the one hand
de tout	cote		on all sides
	cote		side, way, direction
	cote	travail	as far as work is concerned
tout a	cote		very close
	coterie		clique, circle
aux	cotes	de	beside, alongside s.o or s.t
On lui compte les	cotes		He's all skin and bones
	cotillons		party favours
	cotoyer		to keep close to, coast along
	cotte		dungarees, overalls, tunic coat
	cottonade		blend, cotton fabric
	cottonier (nm)		cotton plant, cotton (industry)
au	cou		on the neck
	couchant (nm)		sunset
etre	couche	en chien de fusil	to be curled up
fausse	couche		miscarriage (med)
	couche		bed, layer, strata, coat (of paint)
	coucher	de soleil	sunset
	coucher		to put (s.o) to bed, sleep
	coucher (nm)		bedtime
	couchette (nf)		berth, sleeper (car), Pulman
	coucou (nm)		cuckoo clock, cuckoo, cowslip (Bot), coo-ee (greeting)
pousser de	coude		to nudge

	coude		bend (in road), elbow
avoir les	coudees	franches	to have elbow room, have a free hand
se tenir les	coudes		to stick together
se	coudoir		sew, mingle
(se)	coudoyer		to rub shoulders with s.o
	coudre		to sew, stitch, sew up (wound)
	couenne		pork rind, skin, fool (Coll)
	couille		testicle, ball (Coll), cock-up (Coll)
	couisse		squeal
Ca c'est	coule	de source	it's obvious
	coule(e)		fluid, moving, sunken (Naut)
	coulee (nf)		flow(ing) of liquid, running, casting (Met)
	couler	des jours heureux	to live a happy life
	couler		to flow, run, cast (metal), pour, sink, have a cr*p, make (s.o) fail, leak, go under (Comm)
	couleuvrine (nf)		a colour window
	coulisse		groove, runner, wings (theatre)
	couloir		passage, corridor
d'un	coup	d'aile	with a flap of its wings
un	coup	d'arret	a halt
	coup	d'oeil	glance, view
a	coup	des Euros	by forking out Euros
donner un	coup	sur le table	to dust the table
a tout/ chaque	coup		each time, every time
rendre un	coup		to hit back
apres	coup		in retrospect, afterwards
d'un seul	coup		just like that
du	coup		as a result
un bon	coup		a good lay (coll), good f*?! (Vulgar)
	coup	d'essai	trial shot
donner un	coup	de collier	to put one's back into
	coup	fourre	dirty trick
a	coup	sur	definitely
	coup	bas	punch below the belt
tenir le	coup		to make it, hold on, cope
	coup (nm)		knock, blow, bang, stroke, rap, flick, poke, prod, chop, thump, thud, shot, punch, kick, trick, racket (Fig)
	coupable		guilty, culpable, culprit (nm)
	coupe		section, cut, bowl, glass, haircut, boundary, cup

	coupe (nm)		coupe (vehicle)
les jambes	coupees		legs not functionning
	couper		to cut, cross, stop, interrupt
	couperose(e)		with broken veins, affected by roseacea
	couple (nm)		relationship, couple, pair
	couplets		verses (of song)
	coupole (nf)		dome, cupola (Arch)
etre aux cent	coups		to be in a state, be worried sick
faire les quatre cents	coups		to be up to no good
	coupure	de presse, journal	newspaper cutting/clipping
	coupure (nf)		break, cut
faire la	cour		to court (romance)
etre bien en	cour		to be in favour
	cour (nf)		court(yard), forecourt
	cour-jardin		courtyard, courtyard garden
etre se	courable		to be a good Samaritan
	courant	Janvier	sometime in January
etre tres au	courant		to know all about s.t
	courant		running, current, stream, trend, common, everyday, usual, ordinary
en	courant		hastily, in a ruh
	courante		running, current(trend)
	courbe		curve
se	courber		bow, bend, stoop
	courbure (nf)		curvature
	coureur		runner, racer
	courir	les boutiques	to go round the shops
	courir	qn	to get on s.o's nerves
	courir	un danger	to be in danger
faire	courir	un risque a qn	to put s.o at risk
	courir		to run (in), ride (in), drive (in), roam, search, race, rush
	courrament		running
	courrier		mail, post

	courriere (nf)		courier
	courroie		strap, belt
	courronne		crowned
	cours		path, course, circulation, lesson, textbook
	course (nf)		run, running, race, excursion, hike, outing, journey, path, course, movement (mech)
	course-poursuite (nf)		chase, race (Fig)
faire des	courses		to go shopping
a la	court		at court
etre a	court		to be at a loss (words/s.t to do)
	court		short
	court-metrage		short (film)
	courtepointes		quilts
	courtine (nf)		curtain (geog)
	courtisan (nm)		sycophant, courtier
	courtiser		to woo
	couru		popular
	couscous		couscous
air de	cousinage	entre	similarity between
	cousinage (nMo		distant relationship, cousinhood
	cousu(s)		sewn
	coute	que coute	at all costs
Ca	coute	dans les 20 Euros	It costs around 20 Euros
	couteau		knife
	couterait		would cost
	couteux -euse		costly
	coutumier -ere (adj)		customary, usual
	couture (nf)		sewing, needlework, dress-making
aux	coutures		at the seams
	couturier -ere		fashion designer, dressmaker
	couvant		monastery, convent
	couvee		brood
	couvercle		lid, cover
	couvert		place setting at a table, cover(ing), shelter
	couverture	cartonnee	case-cover
	couvreur		roofer
se	couvrir		to cover oneself (with glory, shame), put on one's hat, protect oneself
	crabier (nm)		crab-eater (Zool – bird)
	crac		rip, bang!, crack
	crachat (nm)		spit
	cracher		to spit (out), hurl abuse at (s.o), despise (s.o), spit

	crainte		fear
	cramoisi(e)		crimson
se	cramponner	a qch	to hold on to s.t, cling to s.t, clutch s.t
	cran		notch, cog (of wheel), hole (in belt)
	crane (nm)		skull, head
	cranerie (nf)		gallantry, swaggering
	crapahutage		trudge
	crapaud		little monkey
	crapulerie		dirty trick, villainy
	crapuleux		sordid, loathesome, villainous
	craquement		creaking sound, creak, crack
	craquer		to spit, burst, strike, crack
	crasseux -euse (adj)		filthy, grimy
	cravate (nf)		tie, ribbon
	crayeux -euse		chalky, chalky-white
	crayon (nm)		pencil
	creance (nf)		belief, credence, debt, claim (Jur)
	creancier (nm)		creditor
	crecelle		rattle, rasping
se	creer		to create, build up
changer de	cremerie		to take one's business elsewhere
	creneaux		slots
	crenellee		crenellated
	creole		Creole (Spanish American or West Indies with European parentage)
	crepe		pancake
	crepir		to render (e.g a wall)
	crepiter		to crackle, sputter, patter
	crepu(s)		frizzy
	crepuscle		twilight, dusk
une	crete	rocheuse	a rocky ridge
	creusement		digging
se	creuser		to dig out, to become hollow, deepen, widen, be whipped up, come across (people)
	creuser		to dig, erode, cut, sink, plough, hollow (out), rrill a hole in, eat into, deepen, increase, research, go into (s.t) in depth, burrow through
	creuseux		hollow
	creusois(e) (adj)		from Creuse (region in France)
	creux		hollow, trough (of wave), pit (of stomache)
	crever		to burst, split
	crevette	(rose)	shrimp (prawn)

	criaillement (nm)			squeal, screech, honk
	criard			shrill
	cribler			to sift, screen, riddle (with bullets)
sans	crier		gare	without any warning
pousser des	cries			to scream
	criniere			mane (of hair)
a	crins		rougatre	reddish-haired
	cris		qui dechiraient	heart-rending cries
	crise (nf)			emergency, crisis, fit or attack (med),
	crispation			tension, clenching, tensing, state of tension
	crisper		qn	to get tense, get on s.o's nerves, irritate s.o
se	crisper			to clench, tense (up), get nervous, freeze
	crissement (nm)			squeak, crunch, scratching
	crisser			to squeak, crunch, screech, scratch
	crochet			hook
	crochu			hooked (nose)
a en	croire		divers	to believe various
	croire			to believe, think
Tu y	crois			Do you believe it?
	croisee (nf)			junction, crossing, (casement) window
	croisement			crossroads, junction, crossing
	croiser			to cross, intersect, cruise, fold over, meet
	croisiere (nf)			cruise
	croissant			crescent (moon)
	croitre			to grow, swell, increase
	croquer			to crunch, munch, give a thumbs-nail sketch of, squander
	croquinole			a light blow on the nose
	croquis			sketch
	crosse			butt (of gun)
	crotte			muddy
	crotter			to dirty, cover in mud
	croupe			brow (of hill), rump (horse)
	croupir			to stagnate, rot
gagner sa	croute			earn one's crust (bread n butter)
	croute			crust, rind, pastry, daub, scab (Med)
	croyances			beliefs
	cruche (adj)			stupid
	crument			crudely
	cubique			cubic
	cueillette			harvest, crop, picking, gathering, together

	cueillir		to pick, gather, pick up, win
	cuillere, cuiller (nf)		spoon, spoonful, safety catch, ladle
	cuirasse (nf)		armour (of warship, tank), cuirass
	cuisant		bitter (disappointment), stinging, burning (pain), biting (cold), caustic (remark)
	cuisine (nf)		kitchen (furniture), galley, (French) cooking, jiggery-pokery (coll)
	cuisinier -ere (nmf)		chef, cook
	cuisses		thighs
	cuistot (nm)		cook
tenir/ prendre une	cuite		to get plastered/p**!?d (Coll),
	cuivre		copper (rouge); brass (jaune)
faire	cul	sec	to down it in one
	cul	sec	bottoms-up
histoire de	cul		dirty joke/story
	cul		bum, backside, bottom, arse, rump (Zool)
	cul (adj)		simple, twee
	cul-de-sac		cul-de-sac, dead-end
	culasse		breech (of gun), cylinder-head
	culbuter		to topple (over), knock over s.t, overwhelm (enemy), somersault]
	cullotte(e) (adj)		cheeky
	culminant(e) (adj)		peak, highest
	culmination (nf)		high point
	culot (nm)		base/head (of cartridge/shell), cheek/nerve (coll)
	culotte (nf)		shorts, panties, trousers
	culte		worship, form of worship, cult, religion
	cultivateur		farmer
	culture		(farm)land
	cunette		wedge, wedge-shaped (cuneat is Latin for wedge)
	cupidite (nf)		greed
	cure		parish priest
	cure (nf)		therapy, course of treatment, cure
	cursif -ive (adj)		cursory, cursive
	cuver		to ferment, sleep it off (Fig)
	cuvette (nf)		basin, bowl
	cyclopeen		Herculean, cyclopean
	cygne		swan
	cylindre (nm)		roller, cylinder
	D		

	dactylo(graphe)		typist (abbrev)
	dactylographier		to type (out)
	daigner		to deign
	daim		(fallow) deer, buck
	dallage		paving, flagging
	dalle		slab, flagstone, paving stone
Que	dalle		damn all! Nothing at all
	damer	le pion a	to outsmart s.o
jeu de	dames		checkers, (game of) draughts
en	damier		checkerboard
	damne(e) (adj)		cursed, damned
	dans	cette optique	from this perspective
	dans	l'immediat	for the time being
etre	dans	un train	to be on a train
	dans		in, on, into, onto
	danseur -euse		partner, dancer
	dard (nm)		sting, spear (Mil)
	datcha (nf)		country house/cottage (in Russia)
	date	limite de vente	sell-by date
prendre	date		to set a date
	date-butoir		deadline
a	dater	de ce jour	from today, from this day
boeuf en	daube		beef casserole
	davantage		more
	deambuler		to wander (about)
	debarquer		to land, disembark, turn up, unload (cargo)
Bon	debarras		Good riddance!
	debarras (nm)		junk room, clearance
(se)	debarrasser	de	to get rid of, clear out
se	debattre		to struggle, put up a struggle
	debaucher		to entice s.o away, to lead astray
le	debit		flow (of alcohol), rate of flow, output, debit, turnover
	debitee(s)		debited
	debiter		to retail, sell, discharge, debit, cut up (meat), yield
	deboires		disappointments, setbacks, trials, difficulties
	debordant(e)	(de)	overactive, overflowing (with), brimming with
	debordement (nm)		flood, excess, overflow(ing)
	deborder		to go beyond, jut out from, overwhelm
	deborder	de	to be overflowing with, bursting with

		deboucher	to emerge, come out
		debouler	to charge down, bolt, sprint
		deboussoler	to confuse, throw
		debout	standing, upright (thing), on end
		debraille	untidy, sloppy, rude, slovenly
		debris (nm)	fragment (piece of wreckage), debris, ruins, rubbish, remains, scraps
	se	debrouiller	to manage, extricate oneself from
		debusquer	to flush (out), bring (s.t) to light
	des le	debut	from the outset/start/very beginning
		debutant	novice, beginner
		debuter	to start (out), begin
		deca	here
		decacheter	to unseal (post)
		decalage	interval, time-lag, gap, discrepancy, shift
	etre en	decalage	to be out of step
		decalcomanie (nf)	transfer, decal (US)
		decale(e) (adj)	out of sorts
		decaler	to put (s.t) back, bring (s.t) forward, move/shift (s.t) forward or back
		decamper	to clear off (scarper)
		decapotable (nf)	convertible (car)
		decapote	with its (car) top down
		deceler	to detect, reveal, indicate, divulge
		decerner	to award (prize), issue summons (jud)
		decevoir	to disappoint, be disappointing, fail to fulfil
		dechainement	outburst of fury/passion, breaking loose
	se	dechainer	to break out
		dechainer	to unchain, let loose, unleash (passion/anger), provoke (laughter)
		decharne(e)	bony, emaciated
		dechausser	to remove s.o's shoes, take s.o's shoes off
		decheance	decline, degeneration
		dechiffrer	to decode, decipher, fathom out
		dechiquiter	to cut/slash/tear into strips, shreds
		dechirant(e) (adj)	heart-rending, agonising, divisive
		dechirer	to tear, rip open, tear up
		dechirure (nf)	tear, rift
		dechoir	to strip (s.o) of, wane, demean oneself, lower oneself
		dechu(e)	deposed, fallen

	decide(e) (adj)		resolute, confident (person), determined, settled (matter)
	decidement		really
	decider	de	to decide on, arrange, set
se	decider		to make up one's mind, be set/decided on
double	decimetre (nm)		double ruler, 20cm ruler
	declamateur		spouter, ranter
	declamer		to spout (speech), declaim
	declencher		to start, initiate, launch, cause, prompt, produce, lead to
	declencheur (nm)		shutter release (camera), trigger, shutter
	declic (nm)		trigger, turning point, click
	decliner		to turn down, decline, state/give (name), fade, wane
	declivite		slope, incline
	decocher		to shoot, fire (arrow)
	decolorer		to bleach (hair), cause (s.t) to fade
	decombres		ruins, debris, rubbish
(se)	decommander		to call off, cry off
	decomposer		to contort, distort (features), split (light), decompose
	decompte (nm)		detailed account, breakdown, deduction
	deconneur -euse		wacky, wild
	deconsiderer		to discredit
	decontenancer		to disconcert
	decontraction		casual attitude, ease, relaxation
	décor		decoration, décor, setting, set, scenery
	decorer		to trim, decorate (with), decorate (Mil honour)
	decortiquer		to shell, peel, husk, dissect
	decouler	de	to follow from, result from
	decoupe(e)		serrated, carved, cut out
se	decouper		to stand out, show up
	decoupure		cutting
	decousse		disconnected, disjointed, unseen
	decouvert		bare
	decouvrir		to uncover, expose, disclose, perceive, discover, discern
	decrepitude		degeneration
	decrier		to disparage, run s.t down
	decrire		to describe

	decrocher		to get, win, uncouple, clinch, land, kick the habit, disengage (Mil)
etre en	decroissance		to decrease
	decroissant(e) (adj)		declining, fading, decreasing, falling, lessening
	decu (decevoir)		disappointed, thwarted
	deculpabiliser		to justify, free (s.o) of guilt
se	deculpabiliser		to stop feeling guilty
	decupler		to increase tenfold
	dedaigner		to scorn, disdain
	dedain		scorn, disdain
	dedale (nm)		maze, labyrinth
	dedaleen		maze-like
en	dedans	de	within, inside, in
	dedicace		dedication, consecration
	dedire		to retract (statement)
	dedommager		to compensate (s.o) for
	dedoubler		to split in two, separate (s.t) into strands
	deesse (nf)		goddess
	defaillance		lapse, failing, failure (to do s.t)
	defaillir		to lose strength, faint, flinch
se	defaire	de qch	to come undone/apart, get rid of s.t
	defaire		to undo (knot), unpack, strip (bed), dismantle, defeat
	defait(e) (adj)		drawn (features), disshevelled (hair)
	defaut		absence, fault, lack, flaw
a	defaut	de	for lack of
	defection (nf)		desertion, defection
se	defendre		to defend oneself
	defenestration		defenestration
	deferer		to refer (a course to court), hand s.o over
	deferler	(sur)	to pour out, flood in, sweep through
	defi		challenge, defiance
	defiance		mistrust, distrust, defiance
	defiant(e) (adj)		distrustful, wary
	defier		to challenge, defy, brave (danger)
	defile (nm)		parade, the defile
	defiler		to march, parade, line the streets with (e.g trees)
	definir		to characterize, specify, define
Je	defirais	d'apprendre	I would like to understand
	deflagration		combustion, explosion
	defoncer		to stave in, smash in, knock down
	deformer		to distort (image), deform, put s.t out of shape
se	defouler		to let one's hair down, let off steam
	defrayer	de qn	to pay s.o's expenses
	defrayer	la chronique	to dominate the news

	defrayer	la conversation	to dominate the conversation
	defunt(e) (nmf)		the deceased
	Degage		Get lost! Clear off!
	degagee		cleared, free and easy (manner)
	degagement		release, redemption (of pledge), clearing (of road), clearance, escape/release (steam, gas), emission (of heat, smell)
se	degager		to free oneself, get free, get clear of
	degager		to free, free (s.o) of responsibility, emit, emanate from, clear
	degaine (nf)		odd walk, odd appearance
	degainer		to draw (weapon), strip (cable)
les	degats		damage
	degeler		to thaw, warm up, unfreeze (assets)
	degenuille		ragged, tattered
	degommer		to dismiss, fire, sack, put (s.o) down, lay into (s.o)
	degouliner		to trick, drip
	degourdi		smart, bright (person)
se	degourdir		to restore circulation, to smarten up
	degout		disgust, distaste
	degouter		to put s.o off s.t, to disgust
	degrade (nm)		fading, gradation
	degrader		to damage, degrade
	degrafer		to undo, unfasten
	degraisser		to streamline, trim the fat off
	degre		degree, level, grade, step
premier	degre		first meaning
	degringoler		to tumble down, rush down, collapse (biz)
se	degriser		to sober up, come to one's senses
	degrossir		to knock a few corners off (s.o) (Fig), break the back of
	deguerpi		cleared out, decamped
en	dehors	de	outside
	dejete		discarded
	dejeuner		to have lunch
	dejouer		to foil (plan), thwart
au	dela	de	beyond
	delabre		delapidated
	delabrement		poor state, impairment, dilapidation
	delais		delays
	delaisse(e)		abandoned
	delaisser		to forsake, abandon, desert
se	delasser		to relax

	delateur (nm)		informer
	delave(e)		faded, washed-out, waterlogged
	delectation (nf)		delight, ecstasy, rapture
	delester	(de)	to relieve (of), interrupt the power supply to
	deletere		noxious, toxic
	delicat		gentle, refined, discerning, sensitive
	delicatesse (nf)		fineness, kindness and consideration, delicacy
	delice (nm)		delight
	delicieux -euse (adj)		delightful, sweet, delicious
	delie		slender, fine, nimble, agile
	delimiter		to set out, define, circumscribe
	delinquant		delinquent, offender
	deliquance		crime
	deliquescence		declining, failing
	delirer		to be delirious, rave
	delit		offence
	delivrance (nf)		relief, award, delivery
	delivrer		to rescue, release, deliver, get rid of s.o
se	demander		to wonder
	demaquiller		to remove make-up from
faire une	demarche	aupres de	to approach (s.o.)
	demarche		step, gait, walk
	demarrage		starting up, spurt
	demarrer		to start (up), get (s.t) off the ground, drive off
	demasquer		to expose, unmask
	demele		contention
	demeler		to sort out, unravel, disentangle
	demenager		to leave, push off, move (out), clear, relocate, lose one's reason
	demence (nf)		madness, insanity
se	demener		to exert oneself, struggle, thrash about, make a great effort
	dement (adj)		mad, insane, terrific, fantastic, amazing, outrageous
	dement(e) (n)		mentally ill person
	dementir		to deny, give the lie to, refute, belie, contradict
	demesurees		disproportionate
	demesurement(e) (adj)		excessively, inordinately
	demeure (nf)		abode
	demeure(e) (nmf)		half-wit
	demeure(e) (adj)		retarded, half-witted
	demeure(e) (nmf)		simpleton
	demeurer		to stay (in place), live, remain

au	demeurrant		for all that, after all
	demi-lieue		half-league (c2km)
	demi-ligne (nf)		half a line
j'ai compris a	demi-mot		I took the hint
	demi-solde (nf)		half-pay
	demission		resignation
se	demoder		to go out of fashion
	demonter		to take apart/down, dismantle, throw off (rider)
	demontrer		to demonstrate, prove s.t, indicate/show s.t
	demordre	de	to budge from
	demuni(e) (adj)		impoverished, helpless, penniless
	demuni(e) (adj)		helpless, penniless, impoverished
	demunir		to divest
	denaturer		to change, distort, misrepresent
	denegation (nf)		denial (Jur)
	deni (nm)		denial
	deniaiser		to make (s.o) worldly wise; to wisen (s.o) up
	denicher		to dig out, track down, flush out, discover
	denier		to deny
le	denier	de la veuve	the widow's mite (Bibl)
	denivellations		unevenness
	denombrer		to count
	denommer		to name, call, designate
	denoncer		to reveal (injustice etc), denounce s.o
	denouement		result, outcome
	denouer		to unknot, untie, undo, unravel, disentangle, resolve
	denree		commodity, produce, foodstuff (?)
	dense (adj)		concentrated, heavy, dense
avoir la	dent	dure	to be scathing
en	dentelles		in lace (wear)
etre sur les	dents		to be worn out, be overworked
un coup de	dents		a bite
	denude		bare
	denuder		to strip, reveal, bare

		depailler		to strip the rush off (chair)
		deparer		to mar, spoil
		depart		start, starting off, exodus, departure, resignation
		departager		to decide between
		departemental(e)		local, regional, secondary (B-road)
		depassement		overtaking, overrun(ning), excess
	se	depasser	la mesure	to overstep the mark
		depasser		to pass, go beyond
		depayser		to provide (s.o) with a pleasant change of scenery, to disorient
		depecer		to cut up, carve (meat)
	se	depecher		to hurry, be quick
		depecher		to despatch
	les	depeches (nfpl)		despatches
		dependre	de	to depend on, be subordinate to
		depense		spent, extended (energy)
		depensier		extravagant
		deperdition		waste, loss (of heat, energy)
		deperir		to wither, waste away
	se	depetrer		to extricate oneself
	se	depiter		to vex, spite (s.o)
		depiter		to vex, despite
	etre en	deplacement		to be away, out on business
		deplacement (nm)		trip, moving, movement, change, transfer, displacement (Psych)
	se	deplacer		to move around, travel, walk
		deplacer		shift, move, dislodge, dislocate, change, distract, call (s.o) out (e.g plumber, doctor), displace, change the place (of s.t.)
	se	deplaire		to be dissatisfied, displeased
		deplaire		to displease, dislike
		deplier		to unfold, open out, display
		deployer		to display, open out, unfurl, spread, deploy (Mil)
		deposee		set, laid, put down
		deposer		to set/put/lay down, deposit, dump, drop off, give (s.o) a lift
		depositaire (nm)		trustee, custodian, depository
		depot		warehouse, outlet, store, deposit, sediment, depositing
		depouille (adj)		stripped off, cast aside
		depouille (nf)	(mortelle)	skin, hide, husk; (mortal remains)
		depouiller		to skin, strip, deprive, plunder
		depouilles (nfpl)		spoils (I.e of war)
	etre pris au	depourvu		to be caught off one's guard
		depourvu		devoid

se	deprecier		to put oneself down
	depuration		purification
	depute		delegate, deputy (pol.), representative
	deraciner		to eradicate, uproot
	derailler		to be derailed, go wrong, talk drivel
	deraisonner		to talk nonsense
	derangements		disturbances
	deranger		to disturb, upset, turn s.t upside down
se	deranger		to move, disturb, trouble
	deraper		to slip, get out of control
	derechef		again
	derider		to cheer (s.o) up
	derisoire		pathetic, trivial, derisory
	derivatif -ive		distraction, derivative
se	derober		to escape, give way, slip away
	derober		to steal, slip away, make away with s.t, conceal, hide
se	derouler		to uncoil, unwind, unroll
	deroute		crushing defeat
en	deroute		in disarray
	derriere		behind, at the back, under
	des	lors	from that time on, from then on, henceforth, therefore
	des	que	as soon as
	des		since, from, as early as, as soon as
	des	lors que	since, once, from the moment that
	des (n)		rye
	desabuse(e) (adj)		cynical, disillusioned
	desabuser		to disenchant
	desaccorde		out of tune
	desagreable		unpleasant
	desagrement (nm)		inconvenience, annoyance
se	desalter		to quench one's thirst
	desaltere		lop-sided
	desamorcer		to defuse, drain
	desarconner		to take (s.o) aback, throw (Fig)
	desarmer		to disarm, invalidate, abate, diffuse, allay
	desarroi		distress, confusion, disarray
se	desder		to be upset
	desembuer		to demist, defog
	desemparer		to throw (s.o) into confusion, be at a loss, be thrown
	desennuye		bored
	desennuyer		to not bore/annoy

	desesperant		discouraging, hopeless
	desesperee		desperate
	desesperer		to lose hope, despair
	deshonorer		to bring disgrace on, bring (s.t) into disrepute, disfigure, dishonour
	designant		designating
	designer		to designate, indicate, show, appoint
	desintegrer		to break up, disintegrate
	desinteresse		disinterested
	desinteresser		to pay off (creditor)
	desinvolte		casual, off-hand
	desinvolture (nf)		casualness, off-handedness, off-hand manner
	desoeuvre(e) (adj)		at a loose end, at loose ends
	desoeuvrement (nm)		lack of anything to do
	desolant(e) (adj)		distressing, upsetting, depressing
	desole(e) (adj)		sorry, desolate
se	desoler		to be upset
	desordone(e) (adj)		messy, disordered, disorganised, untidy, unco-ordinated
	desordre (nm)		mess, chaos, disorder (Mil)
	desormais		from now on
	desosse		lithe, boned (Cul)
	dessecher		to dry out, wither, harden
a	dessein		deliberately, by design
	desserrer		to release (brake), loosen, slacken, unclench (fist), relax, work loose
	desservir		to serve, stop at (bus stop etc), lead into (a room)
	dessine(e)(s)		drawn
se	dessiner		to stand out, take form
aux	dessous		underneath, beneath
en	dessous		below
la	dessous		under that, underneath, under there
par en	dessous		underneath
en	dessus		above, over, on
	dessus		upper, top, on top of (it)
la-	dessus		on that, on it, about that
	destinataire		addressee, consignee
	destination (nf)		purpose, destination
	destiner	qch a qn	to intend/mean s.t for s.o
	desuet(e) (adj)		obsolete, out-moded, quaint, old-world
	desunir		to divide, break up
il ne se	detache	point	it doesn't come off

	detachement (nm)		indifference, detachment
se	detacher	(de)	to separate, break off, flake off, stand out (from)
	detacher		to loose, untie, separate, break off, detach
	detailler		to scrutinise, detail
	deteindre		to fade, run (colour)
	deteler		to unharness, ease off (coll)
se	detendre		to slacken, relax, calm, release, lose shape
	detenir		to keep, hold, possess, detain
	detente (nf)		trigger (of gun), relaxation, detente, slackening, easing (of situation)
	detenteur -trice		guardian, possessor, holder
	detenu(e)		prisoner
se	determiner	a	to resolve (to do s.t)
	determiner		to cause, give rise to, determine
avoir une tete de	deterre (nmf)		to look like death warmed up
	deterrer		to dig up
se	detester		to hate o.s, hate each other
se	detirer		to pull away
	detoner		to go off, detonate
	detonner		to sing out of tune, be out of place
	detour		curve, bend, deviation, turn
	detourner		to divert, distract
se	detourner		to look away, neglect, turn away from
	detremper		to saturate, dilute, waterlog, soak
	detroit		strait (geol)
	detromper		to put s.o. Right
	detrousser		scavenger
	detruire		to demolish (building), destroy, dash s.o's hopes, ruin
	dette		debt
	deuil (nm)		mourning, sorrow, bereavement, period of mourning, funeral procession
Cela	devait (see devoir)	arriver	It was bound to happen
Ce qui	devait (see devoir)	arriver arriva	The inevitable happened
ne	devait (see devoir)	rien	owed nothing
	devaler		to descend, slope down
	devancer	l'appel	to enlist for military service before call-up
	devancer		to be ahead of, anticipate
	devant		before, in front
	devastateur -trice (adj)		devastating

		deveine		(run of) bad luck
	se	developper		to spread out, expand
		developper		to evolve (theory), develop (muscles)
		devenir		to become, grow into
		devenir (nm)		the future
	(se)	devergonder		to lead a debauched life
		deverser		to pour (water), tip, dump (rubbish)
		devier		to divert, deflect, deviate, diverge, veer off course
		devin		soothsayer, seer, psychic
		deviner		to guess, predict, solve (mystery)
		devis (nm)		estimate
		devisager		to stare at (s.o)
		devise		motto
		devisser		to unscrew, undo
		devoiler		to reveal, disclose (secret)
		devoir	(Je dois...)	should, ought, to owe (I ought to...)
		devoir (nm)		duty, obligation
		devolu(e)		devolved, reserved
		devore	d'ambition	consumed with ambition
		devorer	(qn des yeux)	to devour, consume, gaze intently on s.o
		devot		religious, devout, bigot
		devouement		devotion, dedication
	se	devouer		to devote oneself to a cause
		diagnostique		diagnostic
		dialoguer	avec	to have talks with, enter into dialogue with
		dialoguer		to write in dialogue form
		diamant	a l'etat brut	diamond in-the-rough
		diapason		pitch, tuning fork
		dicible (from dire)		sayable
		dicte		dictation
		dicter		to dictate, impose one's will
		dicton		diction, saying, adage
		didactique		educational, technical, specialist, didactic
		diese (nm)		sharp (i.e. # Mus)
		diffamateur		slanderer
		differer		to defer, put off, postpone, be different
		diffus(e) (adj)		vague, loose, difficult
		diffusion (nf)		distribution (of books), broadcasting, diffusion
		digerer		to digest, swallow, stomach
		digne	de	worthy of
		digue (nf)		sea wall, harbour wall, dyke, barrier
		dilatation		expansion, dilation
	se	dilater		to expand, dilate
		dilettantisme		amateurism

	diligence (nf)			stagecoach, haste
	dime			tithe
	diminuer			to decrease
	diminutif -ive			diminutive; pet-name
	dingue (nmf)			nutcase, loony, freak
	diplomer			to award a degree/diploma to
au	dire	de		according to
autant	dire	que		you might as well say that, in other words
c'est peu de	dire			that's an understatement
a vrai	dire			actually
se	dire			to claim to be, to say one is, to tell oneself
au	dire (nm)	de		according to
en	direct			live (broadcast)
	direct			immediate, direct
Vous m'en	direz	tant!		You don't say!
	dirigeant (nm)			leader (national govt), manager, director
se	diriger			to make for, head for
	diriger			to be in charge of, run, manage, direct, supervise
	disconvenir			to disagree, deny
	discours			talk, speech, discourse
	discretement			quietly, soberly, unassumingly, discreetly
	discuter			to discuss, debate, examine
	disert (adj)			eloquent, talkative
	disette (nf)			scarcity, dearth, shortage
	disgrace			disfavour, disgrace
le	dishonore (nm)			the disgraced/dishonoured
	disjoint			separate, unrelated, uneven
se	disloquer			to break up, contort oneself
	disparition (nf)			disappearance, extinction
	disparu(e) (adj)			missing, lost, extinct
	dispenser	de		to exempt s.o from s.t, dispense, go without
	disperser			to scatter, spread, disperse, break up
	dispersion			scattering, dispersal, wandering
	disponible			available
se	disposer	a faire qch		to get ready to do s.t
	disposer			to arrange, dispose
	disposition			arrangement, layout, the disposal (beck and call)
	dispute (adj)			disputed, contested
	dispute (nf)			quarrel, argument

se	disputer		to quarrel, argue, fight over s.t
	disque		record, disc (Mus), discus
	dissequer		to dissect
se	dissimuler		to hide
	dissimuler		to conceal (feelings), hide, dissemble
	dissipation		squandering (£), wasting time, misbehaving, dissipation
	dissiper		to disperse (clouds), clear up (misunderstanding), waste (time), squander money, distract s.o
	dissocier	(de)	to separate from, break down (substance)
	dissolu		dissolute
	dissoudre		to dissolve, break up, melt
de	distance	en distance	at intervals
prendre de la	distance		to gain distance, distance onself
	distingue(e) (adj)		refined, distinguished
	distraire		to divert, amuse, distract s.o
soi	dit	en passant	incidentally
	dithyrambe		dithyramb (a speech or piece of writing bursting with enthusiasm/passion)
	diurne		daily, diurnal
	divagations		ravings, ramblings
	divaguer		to rave, ramble, stray, talk nonsense
	divan		couch, divan
	divers		various, diverse, several, miscellaneous
	diversement		in various ways
se	diversifier		to change, vary
	divertir		to entertain, amuse, misappropriate (£)
	diviniser		to deify
	division (nf)		partition, discord, disagreement, division
	divulger		to disclose, reveal, divulge
	dizaine		10, about 10
	docilement		obediently, meekly
	doctement		learnedly, eruditely
	doguin (nm)		young mastif dog
	doigt (nm)		finger
Tu	dois (see devoir)	avoir le faim	You must be hungry
Combien vous	dois-je		How much do I owe you?
Il me	doit	des excuses	He owes me an apology
il	doit	tout a sa femme	He owes it all to his wife
	doleance		complaint
	domaine		field, scope, sphere, domain, estate, property

	dome (nm)		dome
	domestique (nm)		servant
	domicile		home, registered address, domicile, place of residence
	dominer		to tower over, dominate
	dominical(e) (aux)		Sunday (adj)
	dommage		injury, damage
	dompter		to tame, master, crush, put down, bring s.o to heel
	donjon		the keep (of a castle)
Je lui	donne	40 ans	I'd say he/she was 40
je vous le	donne	en cent	you'll never guess
c'est	donne		it's dirt cheap
	donnees		facts, data
	donner	a boire a qn	to give s.o s.t to drink
	donner	a croire que	to suggest that
	donner	dans	to tend towards, fall into (e.g. trap)
	donner	du cor	to sound the horn (Hunt)
	donner	froid/faim a qn	to make s.o feel cold/hungry
	donner		to give, produce, yield, show
	donner	la tete contre qch	to hit one's head against s.t
	donneur -euse		donor, informer, dealer
	dore(e)		golden, gilded
	dorenavant		from now on, from then on, henceforth
	dorloter		to pamper
	dormir	a poings fermes	to be fast asleep
J'ai bon	dos		It's always me
voir qn de	dos		to see s.o from behind
Je l'ai dans le	dos		I'm stuck
	dos (nm)		back, spine, blunt edge
en tenir une bonne	dose		to be thick as two short planks
en avoir sa	dose		to have one's fill (Fig)
	dose (nf)		amount, dose, measure
	dossier(s)		back (of chair), document(s), file(s), record(s)
	dot		dowry
	dotation (nf)		endowment, salary, annuity
	douairiere		dowager
	douaniers		customs officers

	double	de	lined with, dubbed (Cine)
	double (adj)		double, two-ply, twice, dual
	double (nm)		double, twice, copy
	double-creme		cream-cheese
	doublement		in two ways
	douceur		softness, sweetness, mildness, mellowness
	doue		gifted, endowed
	douille (nf)		case (of cartridge), (lamp/plug) socket
	douillet -ette (adj)		cozy, snug, comfortable, oversensitive to pain
	douleur		pain, ache, sorrow, grief
	douloureux -euse (adj)		painful, distressing, aching
je m'en	doute		I can well believe it
sans nul	doute		without any doubt
se (s'en)	douter		to well believe, suspect s.t, think as much
	douve		moat
	doux, douce (adj)		soft, sweet, gentle, mild
	draguer		to chat up, come on to, drag (net)
	dramaturge (nmf)		playwright
	drame		tragedy, drama (cine), play
tourner au	drame		to end in tragedy
	drap (nm)		sheet
	drapeau		flag
se	dresser		to stand up, rise, straighten up
	dresser		to pitch (tent), erect, set (trap), draw up (plan, report, list), prepare
avoir	droit	a	to be entitled to, eligible for, have the right to
a bon	droit		with good reason
	droit (nm)		charge, fee, right, law
	droit(e)		straight, upright
de	droite	et de gauche	from all sides, by everybody
	droiture (nf)		uprightness
	drole		funny, odd
	drole (nm)		old rascal
	drolement		oddly, really
	dru(e) (adj)		thick, heavy, dense
Il a	du (pp devoir)	accepter	He had to accept
	du, due(s)		owing, due
	dubitatif -ive		sceptical
	ductile		malleable, tractable (Fig), ductile

	dunette (nf)		where the officers stay when on ship, or late-paying passengers, 'poop'-deck?
	duper		to dupe, deceive
	duquel (lequel)		which, whom
	dur(e) (adj)		hard, tough
	durant		for, during
sa vie	durant		his whole life
	duree		lasting quality, wear, duration
	durer		to last, continue
	durete		harshness, severity, callousness, hardness, toughness
	dusse-je (see devoir)	en mourir	even if I die for it
	duvet		down (chick), sleeping bag

E

	ebahir		to dumbfound, astonish
	ebaucher		to sketch out, outline
	eblouir		to dazzle, glare
	eblouissant		dazzling, glaring
	eblouissement		dazzle, dazzling experience, dizzy spell
	eboulement		crumbling, collapsing
	ebouli		scree
	ebouriffer		to ruffle (hair), startle
	ebouriffes		ruffled (hair)
	ebranlement		shock
s'	ebranler		to start (moving)
	ebranler		to shake, loosen, rock, to move off
	ebrecher		to chip, damage, make a hole in, tarnish
	ebriete		drunkenness, inebriation, intoxication
s'	ebrouer		to shake o.s, flap one's wings, snort
	ebullition (nf)		boiling
	ecaille		tortoiseshell, shell, scale
	ecailler		to cause (s.t) to flake, chip (s.t) off, de-scale (fish)
	ecarquiller		to open one's eyes wide, widen (eyes)
mettre qn a l'	ecart		to ostracise s.o, push s.o aside
a l'	ecart		isolated
l'	ecart		distance, gap, deviation, separation, digression (speech)
s'	ecarter		to move aside/apart, deviate, stray
	ecarter		to separate, spread (apart), open, part, move s.t further apart, move/brush/push s.t aside
	echafaudage (nm)		stack, edifice, scaffolding, construction, building up
	echafauder		to put (s.t) together, build up (s.t)
	echantillon		sample, specimen
	echantillonnage		selection, sampling
	echappement		exhaust (pipe)
	echapper		(to manage) to escape
	echardes		thorn, splinter
	echarpe		scarf
	echasses		stilts
	echauffer		to overheat, stir (up), warm (up)
	echaugette		watchtower
	echeance		date of payment, expiry date (bill of exch)
	echec		failure, set-back, defeat (sport)
jouer aux	echecs		to play chess
	echelle		ladder, helping-hand, scale

		echelonnement		staggering
		echelonner	(sur)	to be spread out (over)
		echeval (aux)		tangle, skein
		echevelee(s)		disshevelled
		echevin		municipal magistrate
		echine		spine, backbone
		echiner		to slog (at s.t)
		echiquier (nm)		chess-board, chequered patter
	en	echo		in response
	avoir un	echo		to get a response
		echo (nm)		piece of gossip, echo
		echotier		local news-reporter, gossip-columnist
		echouer		to fail, run aground (naut)
		eclabousser		to splash, splatter, tarnish (name)
		eclair		flash of lightning
		eclairage		lighting, illumination
		eclaircir		to clear (up), brighten, light up, be clearer, throw light on, solve
		eclaircissement		clarification, explanation
		eclaire (adj)		well-informed, enlightened, lit
		eclairer		to be lit, become clearer
		eclairie		enlightenment
		eclat		burst, flash, splinter, split
		eclatante		sparkling
		eclater		to shatter, burst, split, explode, burst out
		eclore (eclos is pp)		to dawn, hatch (out), open, bloom
		ecluse		lock (canal)
		ecoeurant(e) (adj)		sickly, over-rich, nauseating, revolting, sickening
		ecoeurement		nausea
		ecolier		novice, (primary) schoolboy/girl
		econduire		to reject, dismiss
		economiser		to save (on), economise
		ecorce		bark (tree), rind, peel, the earth's crust
		ecorche(e)		Hyper-sensitive
		ecorcher		flay, rip off (£), skin, graze, chafe, mispronounce (words)
	payer son	ecot		to pay one's share
		ecouant	la tete	shaking the head
		ecouerer		to nauseate, disgust, dishearten, make s.o feel sick
		ecoulement		drainage, dispersal (crowd), flow (traffic), discharge (med)
		ecouler		to flow out, pass, slip away, elapse

	ecouter		to listen, pay attention to
	ecouvillon		pull-through (gun cleaner), bottle brush
	ecran		screen
s'	ecraser		to collapse, crumple up
	ecraser		to crush, squash, swat (fly)
s'	ecrier		to exclaim, cry out
	ecrin (nm)		a jewel case, setting (Enviro)
l'	ecriture		writing, script, handwriting
	ecrivaillon (nm)		hack (Journ), scribbler
	ecrivain		author, writer
s'	ecrouler		to collapse, founder, crumble
	ecru		unbleached, natural-coloured
	ecu		crown (French currency)
	ecueil (nm)		pitfall, reef (Naut)
	ecuelle		bowl
chausseur	ecule(e) (adj)		shoe with a worn-down heel
l'	ecume		dross, foam, froth
	ecumer		to foam, froth, skim, scour
	ecureuil (nm)		squirrel
sentir l'	ecurie		to know one is nearly there
	ecurie (nf)		stable, pig-sty
	ecusssonnes	aux armes	coat of arms
	ecuyer -ere (nmf)		horseman, horsewoman
	edifier		to enlighten, instruct s.o, build, erect, edify
	editeur		publisher, chief editor
	edition		publication, issue, edition, release (of film, CD)
	editique		electronic publishing
	edredon (nm)		eiderdown
	effacement		self-effacement, obliteration (of word), wiping (of tape)
s'	effacer		to fade (away), erase, disappear, stay in the background
	effacer		to deface, obliterate, delete
	effarer		to frighten, scare, dismay, bewilder
	effaroucher		to startle, scare away
	effectivement		indeed, really, actually
	effectuer		to carry out
sous l'	effet	de la colere	in a rage
	effet (nm)		result, effect, operation, action, working, impact, impression
en	effet		actually, indeed
cet	effet		for that purpose

	efficacite		efficiency, effectiveness, efficacy
	effile		tapered, frayed, slender (figure)
	effleurer		to touch lightly, graze, skim
	effluve (nm)		unpleasant smell, fragrance, aroma
	effondre(e)		collapsed
	effondrement		breaking down, collapse, slump (in £)
s'	effondrer		to collapse, crumble, flounder, fall drastically
s'	efforcer	de (faire)	to try hard to (do s.t)
s'	efforcer		to try hard, endeavour
	effraction (nf)		break-in, burglary
	effrayant(e)		terrifying
s'	effrayer		to get/be frightened, take fright
	effrenee		unbridled, frantic
s'	effriter		to crumble (away)
	effriter		to crumble, break up
s'	effriter		to collapse, decline, crumble, dwindle (away)
	effroi		dread
	effronte		shameless, cheeky, impudent
	effroyable		dreadful, appalling
	effusion	de sang	outpouring (bloodshed)
(s')	egailler		to disperse
	egalement		also, equally
	egaler		to match, equal
a l'	egard	de qn	towards s.o
a cet	egard		in this respect
	egard		consideration, respect
	egare (adj)		lost, distraught, remote, wild, missing, disturbed
s'	egarer		to lose one's way, go astray
	egarer		to mislead, misguide, lose one's way, go astray
s'	egayer		to be amused
	egocentrisme (nm)		self-centredness, egocentricity
	egorgement		throat-cutting, blood-letting
	egorger		to cut the throat of (animal, s.o)
s'	egosiller		to bawl
	egout (nm)		sewer
	egratignures		scratches
	egregner		to chime out, drone out, remove the seeds from, smooth (s.t) off
	elaborer		to work out (plan), elaborate
	elaguer		to lop (tree), prune
	elan		momentum, impetus, outburst

	elance(e) (adj)		slender
s'	elancer		to rush forward
	elancer		to throb, shoot (with pain)
	elargir		to set (prisoner) free, widen (road)
	elegance		grace, neatness, elegance
	element (nm)		component, ingredient, element, factor, unit, fact, cell
les	elements		rudiments, first principles
	elevation		vertical section, erection, elevation, lifting, rise (in price)
	eleve		student
s'	elever		to rise up, raise, lift up, elevate (the mind), rear (child), grow (plants) set up (machines, statues)
	elire		to elect
	elivait		would elect
	eloge		praise, eulogy
	eloignement		removal, absence, distance, postponement
s'	eloigner	de	to go away from
	eloigner		to (re)move, get s.t out of the way
	eluder		to evade, elude, dodge (question)
les	elus		the elect, chosen
	emailler		to enamel, punctuate
	emaner	de	to emanate from
	emballage (nf)		packaging, wrapping, packing
	emballement		bolting (horse), outburst of anger, driving
	emballer		to pack, wrap, race (vehicle)
s'	emballer		to get carried away, bolt, race, get worked up
	embarcation		a boat, small craft
s'	embarquer	dans une entreprise	to embark on an u/t
	embarquer		to load, pick up, take on board, carry, board, put (folks) on a train/bus, ship (goods), nick, embark
s'	embarrasser		to feel embarrassed, burden s.o with, trouble s.o (about s.t)
	embarrasser		to encumber, obstruct, trouble, bother, embarrass, perplex
	embastiller		to imprison
	embaucher		to take on, hire, engage, recruit
	embaumer		to fill, smell of, embalm, be fragrant
	embellir		to make (s.t) more attractive, embellish
(d')	emblee		from the outset, at first sight, straight away
s'	emboiter		to encase
	embonpoint		stoutness
mal	embouche(e)		coarse, in a foul mood
	embouchure		mouth (of river), mouthpiece (Mus)
	embouteillage		traffic jam, tailback, bottle-neck
	emboutissage		stamping, denting
	embrasser		to contain, include, cover, take in, hug, embrace

	embrasure			window, door, recess, doorway
s'	embrouiller			to get muddled, confused
	embuche			trap, pitfall
	embuer			to mist (up), fog up
etre	emeche(e)			to be tipsy
	emerillon			merlin (Zool), swivel
	emerite (adj)			outstanding
	emersion			emersion (the re-appearance of a heavenly body from behind another after an eclipse)
	emerveille (adj)			amazed
	emerveiller		qn	to fill (s.o) with wonder
	emettre			to express, put forward, raise, produce, give off, emit, issue
	emeute (nf)			riot
	eminence (nf)			hillock, protuberance (Anat)
	emission			programme (radio/TV), emission
	emmagasiner			to store, warehouse, accumulate (energy)
	emmancher			to fit (in hand)
	emmenager			to move in
	emmener			to take (s.o) out, take, take away, lead
	emmerder			to annoy/bug s.o stiff
	emmitouffler			to wrap (s.o/s.t) up warmly
en	emoi			in turmoil, in a state of confusion
	emoler			to take flight, fly away
	emonder			to dump
	emotivite (nf)			emotion (charged)
	emousser			to blunt, dull, deaden
s'	emousser			to become dulled, become blunt
	emoustiller			to exhilirate, titillate
	emoute (nf)			riot
	emouvant			touching, moving
s'	emouvoir			to get excited, be touched/moved
	emouvoir			to move, touch
	empanachaient			plied
s'	emparer		de	to seize, take hold of s.t
	empater			to fur up, make puffy, thicken out
s'	empecher		de	to refrain from (e.g pity, laughing)
	empecher			to prevent, impede
	empeser			to starch (linen)
	empester			to reek, stink, stink s.t out
	empetrer		dans	to get mixed up in
	emphase			grandiloquence (pomposity of speech), emphasis
	empierrement			stonework
	empiler			to stack, pile up
	empiraient			worsened

	empire		dominion, sway
	emplacement		site, location
	emplatre		medicated plaster, patch
(s')	emplir		to fill up
	empoigner		to grab (hold of), seize
	empoisonner		to poison (s.o), be poisonous (plants), bore s.o stiff, poison (food)
	empoissoner	la vie de qn	to make s.o's life a misery
	emporte-piece		pastry-cutter, punch
	emportement		(fit of) anger
s'	emporter		to lose one's temper
	emporter		to carry, take away, tear, take off
	empourprer		to turn (s.t) crimson
	empreindre		to mark with, tinge with, imbue with
	empreinte (nf)		footprint, track, imprint, impression, stamp, mark
	empressement		eagerness, readiness
s'	empresser	de faire	to hasten to do
	emprise (nf)		hold, influence
nom d'	emprunt		pseudonym
faire un	emprunt	a qn	to borrow (£) from s.o
	emprunt		loan, loan word
	emprunter		to borrow, take (route, road)
	emprunteur		borrower
	emu(e) (pp emouvoir)		stirred, overcome, moved, touched
	emulation		competitiveness, emulation
	en		in, as, to, into, by
	en-cas		snack
	encadrement		frame, framework, supervision, control
	encadrer		to surround, frame
	encadrer		to supervise, train, frame, restrict (credit)
	encaisse		deeply embanked (river)
	encaisser		to take it, clear, take
s'	encanailler		to slam, slaughter oneself
	encapuchonne(e) (adj)		hood pulled up
	encarter		to insert
	encasernement		going into the barracks (Mil)
	encastrer		to embed, fit, build in
	encaussement		cashing in
	encaustiquer		to wax, polish
	enceinte		fence, enclosure, a surrounding wall, pregnant
	enchainement		chain, series, train (of ideas, events)
	enchainer		to chain up (dog), connect, link up
	enchanter		to delight, put a spell on
	enchasser		to set, insert, encase

	enchevetree		tangled
	enclaircies		breaks (in clouds), clearings
	enclencher		to set, engage, launch, set s.t in motion
	enclin		inclined
	enclume		anvil
	encoignure		corner (room)
	encombrer		to clutter (up), obstruct
a l'	encontre		against
	encourager		to cheer s.o on, encourage (s.o) to do
	encourir		to incur
	encre		ink
	encrier (nm)		inkpot, inkwell, ink-stand
	endetter		to put (s.o) into debt
	endiguer		to dam up (river), hold back, contain (invasion)
	endolorir		to make (s.o/s.t) ache
	endormi (adj)		sleeping, sleepy, sluggish, lethargic
s'	endormir		to fall asleep
	endormir		to send s.o to sleep, bore s.o, anaesthetise
	endosser		to put on (clothes)
	endroit		place, spot
par	endroits		in places
	enduire	de	to coat with
	enduit (nm)		coating, filler
	energumene		fanatic, ranter
	enerve		irritated, nervous, edgy
	enfant	ne du premier lit	child of the first marriage
	enfanter		to give birth to
	enfantillage (nm)		childishness
	enfantin		simple, easy, childish, child-like
feu d'	enfer		hellfire
	enfermement (nm)		imprisonment, detention
s'	enfermer		to lock oneself in
	enfermer		to shut, hem in, enclose, shut (s.o) in
(s')	enferrer		to tie oneself up in knots, impale oneself
	enfievre		fevered, fiery, feverish
	enfiler		to thread (needle), put on (clothes)
	enfin	(de)	well, oh well (sigh), finally

s'	enflammer			to catch fire, be stirred up, get excited, become inflamed (wound)
	enfle			swollen, idiot (colloq)
	enfler			to swell, puff out (cheeks)
	enflure			swelling (Med), bas!*rd (expl)
s'	enfoncer			penetrate, go deep into
	enfoncer			to get the better of s.o, to drive (in), break open/down (door), push in, knock in, sink (in sand)
	enfoui(e)			buried
l'	enfourchure			the furnace, straddle
s'	enfourner	dans		to dive into
	enfourner	dans		to put (s.t) in the oven/kiln, stuff s.t into
	enfreindre			to infringe
(s')	enfuir			to run away, escape, fly (away)
	enfumer			to fill (place) with smoke
	engagement			commitment, involvement, undertaking, engagement
s'	engager	a faire qch		to undertake, commit o.s to doing s.t
	engager			to catch, entangle, begin, start
s'	engager			to go into, begin, promise, get involved, embark on
	engaine			sheathed cutlasse, knife
	engendrer			to engender, generate
	engin			device, vehicle, missile, piece of equipment
	englober			to include, take in
	engloutier			to swallow, gulp
s'	engluer	dans qch		to become bogged down in s.t
	engorger			to block (up), clog (up), congest (Med)
s'	engouffrer			to rush (in/under), rush to take advantage of
	engourdir			to numb, dull the mind, make sleepy
	engourdissement			numbness, dullness, sluggishness
	engraisser			to fatten, get fat, put on weight
	engranger			to gather in, store (up), garner
	enhardir			to embolden
	enivrer			to intoxicate, inebriate, get drunk
	enjambe			stride
	enjamber			to step over, span (bridge)
	enjoleur			bewitching
	enjoliver			to embellish
	enjouement			cheerfulness
s'	enkyster			to form cysts
	enlacer			to intertwine, hug
s'	enlancer			to embrace, intertwine
	enlever			to take off (clothes), remove, take (away), carry off, kidnap
	enliser	dans		to get (s.t) stuck in
s'	enliser			to get stuck, get bogged down, drag on

		enneige(e) (adj)		snowy
l'		ennui		worry, problem, boredom
		ennuyer		to bother, bore, annoy
	s'	ennuyer		to be bored
		ennuyeux -euse		boring, tedious, worrysome
		enoncer		to express (ideas)
	s'	enorgueillir	de qch	to pride o.s on doing s.t, take pride, pride o.s
		enorgueillir		to make s.o proud
		enormement		a great deal, a tremendous amount
	s'	enquerir	de	to enquire about s.t
		enquete		enquiry, investigation, inquest, survey
		enracinement (nm)		taking root, rooting, setting
		enrager		to fume, be furious
		enregistrer		to record, note, make a record of, take, check in (luggage), register
		enregistreur – euse		recorder (i.e. like a cassette/tape)
		enrheumer		to give (s.o) a cold
	s'	enrheumer		to catch a cold
		enricher		to enhance, bring wealth to, enrich, make s.o rich,
		enrouer		to make hoarse
	s'	enrouler	autour de	to be wound round
		enrubanne(es)		wrapped
	s'	ensabler		to silt up
		ensaignement		bathe
		ensaigner		to teach
		ensanglanterent		bloodied
l'		enseign		the sign
		enseigne (nf)		sign, ensign (Mil)
		enseignement		teaching
		enseigner		to teach
		ensemble		the whole, entirety, together
		ensevelir		to bury
		ensoleille(e)		sunny
		ensommeille(e)		sleepy, drowsy
il s'		ensuit	que	it follows that
		ensuite		afterwards, next, then, after (that)
		ensuivre		to follow, ensue, result
		entamer		to open (bottle), cut into (loaf), eat into, damage (reputation), begin (chat), start, enter into
		entasser		to amass, pile up, heap, pack, crowd
	s'	enteler		to entangle
Il agit comme il l'		entend		He does as he likes

	entendement		understood, meant, intended, understanding
	entendre	la Messe	to attend Mass (RCC)
faire	entendre	un cri	to give a cry
s'	entendre		to agree, understand one another, get on/along, be heard
se faire	entendre		to be heard
	entendre		to intend, mean, understand, hear
reussir a se faire	entendre		to manage to make oneself heard
Elle ne veut rien	entendre		She won't listen
Ils s'	entends	tres bien	They get along really well
C'est une affaire	entendu		It's settled
Bien	entendu		Of course
J'ai mal	entendu		I didn't hear that properly
Tu as	entendu ?		Did you hear that?
	entente (nf)		harmony, understanding, arrangement
	enterrement (nm)		burial, funeral, death
	enterrer		to go and hole up
s'	enterrer		to bury, say goodbye to, shelve
	entetement		stubbornness
s'	enteter		to dig one's heels in, be stubborn, persist
s'	enteterer		to persist
	enticher		to infatuate
	entonner		to start singing, launch into (song)
	entonnoir		funnel
	entortillage		convoluted waffle
	entortiller		to wheedle, wind, twist, wrap s.t
	entourage (nm)		family circle, circle (of friends)
	entourer		to encircle (army), surround
	entournure (nf)		arm-hole (clothes)
	entourraient		surrounded
	entours		surroundings, around
	entr'ouvrir		to half-open
	entrailles		bowels (of earth), compassion
	entrain		drive, liveliness, high spirits
	entrainement		dragging, coaching, yearning
	entrainer		to entail, result in, involve, drag, carry along, seduce
	entrave		shackle, hindrance, fetter
	entraver		to hinder, impede, shackle, fetter
Il	entre	une part de chance dans tout	A certain amount of luck goes into everything

d'	entre			from among
Il	entre		dans la quarantaine	He's "pushing" 40
Ça n'	entre		dans la valise	It doesn't fit in the suitcase
s'	entre-dechirer			to tear each other apart/to pieces
	entre-deux (nm)			insert, intervening period
	entrechat (nm)			skip
	entrecoupe(e)			faltering (voice), occasional (replies)
	entrecouper			to punctuate, intersperse with
	entree			entrance, way in, slip-road, hall, admission (to org), ticket, starter (Cul)
	entrefacon (nf)			infringement, forging, counterfeiting, forgery, pirated copy
	entrefaites			just then, at that moment
	entregent (nm)			Savoir-faire
	entrelacement			network (of branches), intertwining
s'	entrelacer			to intertwine, interlace
	entrelacs (nm)			tracery
	entremelent		de	intermingled with
	entremise			mediation
	entreouvert			half-open
	entrepot			warehouse, store
	entreprendre		de faire	to undertake to do, set about doing
	entreprendre			to start, set out on, embark on, undertake, engage s.o in conversation
	entrer		dans la vie de qn	to come into s.o's life
	entrer		dans le capital de…	to take a stake in…(Comm)
	entrer		en convalescence	to start to convalesce
	entrer		en mouvement/ fusion	to begin to move/melt
	entrer			to bring (s.t) in, take (s.t) in, enter, get in, come in
	entresuivre			to follow
s'	entretenir			to talk, converse
	entretenir			to maintain, look after, support, cherish, feed, fuel, sustain, keep s.t up/going
	entretien			conversation, interview, upkeep, support
	entrevoir			to catch a glimpse (of), catch sight of, anticipate, forewarn
	entrevue			meeting, talks (Pol)
	entrevue			caught a glimpse of, caught sight of
s'	entrouvrir			to half-open

	envahir		to flood, invade, overrun, assail
	enveloppe		wrapping, sheath, cover, casing, envelope, pod
	envelopper		to wrap (s.o/s.t) up/in, surround, veil
	envergure		scope, scale, wing-span, proportion
nous	enverrons		we will send
a l'	envers		the wrong way
	envers (nm)		back, inside, reverse
Il vaut mieux faire	envie	que pitie	It's better to be envied than pitied (proverb)
	envie		desire, longing, envy
	envier		to envy, crave, desire, long for
	envisager		to foresee, consider, envisage
s'	envivrer		to get drunk, be intoxicated
	envol		flight, take-off, soaring, rise, escalation
s'	envoler		to fly away, take off
l'	envoye		messenger, envoy, correspondent (journal)
s'	envoyer		to get off with (Fig)
	envoyer		to send, throw (stone), despatch (goods)
	epais		thick, dense (foliage)
	epaisseur		thickness, depth
	epanchement (nm)		effusion, outpouring
	epancher		to pour out (liquid, one's secrets)
	epanouir		to light up, open (out), make (s.t) blossom
	epanouissement (nm)		opening out (flowers), brightening up (face)
	eparge		saving, economy
on ne s'y d'	epargne		you don't get used to it
s'	epargner		to save (energy/time/£), save up, put by
	epargner		to save, economise, put by
s'	eparpiller		to disperse, scatter
	eparpiller		to disperse, scatter
	epars(e) (adj)		scattered, straggly (hair)
	epatant		marvellous
au nez	epate		flat-nosed
	epate	de	amazed by
	epater		to impress, amaze
	epaulette		shoulder pad, shoulder strap
l'	epee		sword
	epeler		to spell
	eperdermique (adj)		skin-deep, extreme, epidermic, skin, epidermal
	eperdu(e) (adj)		frantic, desperate, overwhelming, overcome
	eperdument		madly, distractedly
	epervier		sparrowhawk (Zool)
	ephemere		may-fly
	ephemere (adj)		fleeting, short-lived, ephemeral
	epice (nf)		spice

	epicerie		grocers
	epicycle		epicycle (????)
	epier		to be on the look-out for, spy on
	epier		to spy on, be on the look-out for
	epigramme		epigram (neat, witty, sarcastic utterance)
	epinaies		thorns
	epine		thornbush
	epineux -euse (adj)		thorny, prickly
	epingle		pin
	epingler		to take (s.o) to task, single (s.o) out for criticism, pin, collar (coll)
	epis		ears (of corn)
	epistolaire		transacted by letter (epistolary)
	eploree		mourned
	eplucher		to peel, pick, go through (s.t) with a fine toothcomb (Fig)
	eplurer		to purify, purge
passer l'	eponge	sur qch	to forget all about s.t
	eponger		to mop up, absorb, soak up, pay off (debt)
	epopee (nf)		epic, saga
	epoque		epoch, era, age, date, period
	epoumoner		to talk oneself hoarse, shout
	epouser		to marry, espouse, wed, adopt, follow (closely)
en	epoussant		by marrying
	epoustufler		to amaze, astound
	epouvant(e)		appalling, dread
	epoux (nm)		spouse, husband
	eprendre		to have a passion for
a toute	epreuve		unfailing
	epreuve		proof, test, trial, event, ordeal, crisis
	epris(e)	de	smitten with, in love with
	eprouvee		tested, tried, experienced
	eprouver		to feel, experience, try, test, suffer (a loss)
	epuisant(e)		wearing, exhausting
	epuise		exhausted, out of print (publ), out of stock
	epuisement		exhaustion
s'	epuiser		to become exhausted, run dry, tire oneself out
	epuiser		to exhaust, use up, consume, drain
une	epure		a working drawing (tech), diagram
	epurer		to purify, purge, clean up, refine
l'	equerre		square
	equilibre		balance, stability

	equipage		crew, retinue, pack of hounds, equipage, ship's company
l'	equipe		team, bunch (part of the 'shift')
	equitation		(horse-)riding
	equivaloir	a	to amount to, be equivalent to, be tantamount to
	equivoque		questionable, ambiguous, dubious, misunderstanding
	erables		maples
	ereinter		to exhaust, slate, slam, pull (s.o) to pieces
	erethisme		erethism (med: abnormal excitement)
	ergots		spurs (of cock)
	eriger		to erect, set up, establish
	errant(e) (adj)		wandering
	errements (nmpl)		transgressions
	errent	a travers	wander through
	erudit		scholarly, erudite scholar
s'	esbaudir		to scoff
	esbroufe		show, ostentation
	escabeaux		(wooden) stools, stepladders
	escadrille (nf)		squadron
	escalader		to scale, climb
s'	escamoter		to retract, fold away
	escamoteur		conjurer
l'	escarbille (nf)		a speck of soot
	escarpe(e) (adj)		steep, craggy
	escarpin		pumps, court shoes
s'	esclaffer		to burst out laughing
	esclandre		scene, public outburst
	escompte		discount (biz)
	escouade		squad, gang
	escrime (nf)		fencing
s'	escrimer	a faire qch	to try hard to do s.t
l'	escroc		crook, swindler
l'	espace		space, interval, area, gap
	esperance		hope
	espieglerie		prank, mischievousness
	espingole		blunderbuss (Mil)
	esplanade		esplanade
	espoir		hope
	esprit		mind, wit, spirit, ghost
	esquisse (nf)		hint, outline, suggestion
	esquisser		to sketch, outline
	esquisser	un geste	to make a vague gesture
l'	esquive		dodging, evasion, dodge
	esquiver		avoid, evade, dodge

	essai		trial, test
	essaim		swarm (of bees etc)
	essarter		to wipe out
	essence		petrol, essence, extract, gasoline, species (of tree)
	essentiel -elle		main (thing), basic, essential
	essor		development, soaring (bird), increasing popularity
	essoufflement (nm)		breathlessness, loss of impetus (Fig)
s'	essouffler		to get out of breath
	essouffler		to leave (s.o) breathless
	essuyer		to wipe (s.t) clean, suffer, endure (insult)
	est		east, eastern
	estacade		boom (naut), breakwater, landing stage
	esthetique		aesthetics (love of beauty in nature and the fine arts), aesthetic (quality), grace
s'	estimer		to consider, think, esteem oneself
	estimer		to value, appraise, estimate, consider
	estival(e) (adj)		summer(y)
etre	estomaque		to be flabbergasted, astounded
	estomper		to shade off, blur
s'	estomper		to become blurred, fade
	estrade		stage, platform
	estropier		to cripple, maim, mutilate (text)
	etage		Level, stage, tier, age, floor (e.g. first, second)
a l'	etage		upstairs
	etain		tin, pewter
	etalage		display, spread
	etalagiste		tanker
	etaler		to display (goods), spread out, roll (s.t) out, scatter, parade
	etalon		standard, yardstick, stallion
	etamine		stamen (bot)
	etanche		water-tight, waterproof (watch)
	etancher		to quench, staunch, make (s.t) watertight, stop up
	etandard		flag, standard
	etang		pool, pond
	etant		being
	etape		stopping place, stop
	etat		condition, state, report, return (tax), profession, trade, (form of) government
	etat-major		headquarters, staff
	etau		a vice (grip)
	etaye(s)	de	propped up

	ete		summer	
	eteindre		to extinguish, subdue, put out, turn off, switch off	
	eteint(e) (adj)		lifeless, dull, faded, extinct, dead, put out, extinguished	
s'	etendre		to stretch out, extend, lie down, expand	
	etendre		to spread, stretch, extend	
l'	etendue (nf)		expanse, scope, extent, size, scale, stretch (of water), range, dimensions	
	eternel(le)		endless, inevitable, eternal	
	ethylisme (nm)		alcoholism	
	etinceler		to throw out sparks	
	etincelle (nf)		spark	
	etiquette		label, etiquette	
s'	etirer		to stretch	
	etoffes		fabrics	
	etoile (nf)		star	
s'	etonner		to be surprised, astonished	
on ne s'	etonnera	pas	it won't go away	
	etouffe		steamed, braised (meat)	
	etouffement		choking sensation, suffocation	
	etouffer	qch dans l'oeuf	to nip s.t in the bud	
	etouffer		to suffocate, smother (s.o, fire), muffle (sound), choke	
	etourdi(e)		thoughtless, foolish, scatterbrained	
	etourdir		to stun, daze, make (s.o) dizzy, ease/deaden pain	
	etourdissante		stunning, deafening (noise), staggering, astounding	
a l'	etranger		abroad	
acheter a l'	etranger		to buy foreign goods	
	etranger -ere (adj)		unrelated to, foreign, with no bearing on, unfamiliar	
plus d'	etrangers		more foreigners	
	etrangete (nf)		strangeness	
s'	etrangler		to choke with, strangle o.s	
	etre		to be (this is often used with other verbs)	
	etreindre		to embrace, hug, clasp (in one's arms)	
	etreinte (nf)		embrace, hug, grasp, grip, clutch	
	etreinte (nf)		grip, embrace	
	etresillon		strut	
	etrier		stirrup	
	etrique(e) (adj)		cramped, restricted, skimpy	
	etroit		narrow, tight, confined (space)	

	etude		office (of solicitor), chambers, study, research, survey, (lawyer's) practice
	etui (nm)		case, box
	eu (from avoir)		had
	euphonie		euphony (pleasant/smoothness of sound), assonance
s'	evader	de	to escape from, get away from
	evaflure (nf)		scratch, graze
	evanouir		to die away, fade, faint, disappear, vanish
l'	evanouissement		faint, black-out, fainting fit, vanishing, disappearance
s'	evaser		to widen, open out
	evasion		escape
	eveche		diocese, bishop's palace
	eveil		awakening, warming, alarm
	eveiller		to wake up, awaken
s'	eveiller		to awake
	eveneaux		battlements
l'	evenement		event, occasion
	event		blow-hole, vent
	eventail		fan, fan-shaped
	evente		flat, past its best, stale
	eventer		to air, fan (s.o), go stale/flat (beer)
	eventre(e) (adj)		disembowelled, burst, gutted, shattered, smashed up
l'	eveque		bishop
s'	evertuer		to try one's best, strive
	evident(e)		obvious, marked, clear
	evier		sink
	evincer		to oust, evict (Jur)
	eviter		to avoid, shun, dodge
	evocation		mention, reminiscence, recalling of
	evoluer		to develop, evolve, change, advance, glide, manoeuvre
	evolution (nf)		change, variation, development, advancement, evolution
	evoquer		to recall, mention, bring back, be reminiscent of, conjure up, evoke
	exagerer		to exaggerate, exceed
	exaltation		extolling, elating, exalting, over-excitement (Med.)
	exalte(e)		elated, impassioned, heightened
	exalter		to elate, thrill, glorify (s.o), heighten
l'	exam		examination
	excedent		excess, surplus
	exceder		to tire s.o out, exasperate s.o, to exceed

		excepte		besides, except(ing), but
		excepter		to exclude, except (from)
		excitation		excitement, incitement, excitation
		exciter		to arouse, incite, stimulate, excite
	s'	excuser		to apologise
		executant(e)		performer
	s'	executer		to comply
		executer		to perform, fulfil, carry out, execute
		exemplaire	en velin	copy printed on vellum
		exemplaire (adj)		exemplary, textbook, model
		exemplaire (n)		model, copy, example
	s'	exercer		to practise, do exercises, drill, produce, perform
		exhausser		to raise
		exigeant		demanding
		exiger		to demand, require, necessitate
		exigu(e)		confined, cramped, narrow, tight, restricted
		expectative (nf)		expectancy, expectation
	l'	expedient		device, expedient
		expedier		to despatch, get rid of, hurry along, ship (goods)
		expeditif -ive		brisk, efficient, hasty
		expedition (nf)		despatching, sending, shipping, authenticated copy (Jur)
		expirer		to exhale, breathe out, fade, expire
	je m'	explique		this is what I mean
	s'	expliquer		to explain oneself
	s'	expliquer	avec qn	to have it out with s.o
		exploit		writ, feat, achievement, exploit
		exploitation	agricole	farm
		exploitation		mining, working, operation, running, exploitation
		exploser		to burst forth, soar, boom, explode
		exposer		to exhibit, put (s.t) on display, show, lay open, expose, explain, expound, introduce, set out, list
		expres		deliberately, on purpose
		express		express train, espresso (coffee)
		expression		voicing, phrase, show (feelings), expression
		exprimer	(de)	to express, squeeze (s.t) from
		exquis		exquisite
		exsangue		bloodless
	s'	extasier		to go into extasies
		extension (nf)		stretching, extension, expansion, spread

etre	extenue		to be tired out
	exterieur(e) (adj)		outside, outer, external, outlying, from outside, outward, foreign
	extirper	de	to pull out, root out, drag (s.o) out of/from, eradicate
	extorquer	a qn	to extort from s.o
	extra (adj)		fabulous, great, extra
	extraire		to extract, remove, mine, quarry
	extumescence		extumescence (a swelling or rising) (Med)

F

	fable (nf)		invention, story, fable
	fabrication (nf)		making, fabrication
	fabrique (nf)		factory
	fabuliste		fabulist (composer of fables e.g Aesop), story-teller
	facade (nf)		front, facade
faire	face	a	to face (up to things), cope with
en	face	de	opposite, compared with
de	face		head-on, full-face, full-frontal
a la	face	de	in someone's face
	facetieux -euse		mischievous
	fache		annoyed, angry, sorry
se	facher		to make upset/angry
	facherie		annoyance
	facheux -euse		tiresome, annoying, troublesome
	facies		facies (Med), face
	facon		style, manner, way, mode
de toute	facon		anyway
	faconde		way of
	faconneur		maker, shaper
	factice		immitation, feigned
en	faction		on duty, on guard
	faculte (nf)		option, ability, right
	fadaise		(piece of) nonsense
les	fades		bland ones
	fadeur		dullness, tastelessness, insipidity
	fagot		bundle of firewood, faggot
	fagoter		to rig (s.o) out
	faiblesse		weakness, faintness, dimness
	faiblir		to get weaker, weaken, wane, decline, fail, fade, grow faint/dim
	faille		break, flaw (in argument)
	faillir		to fail
	faillite		bankrupt
	faineant		idler, lazybones
	faire	de l'essence	to get petrol
	faire	les quatre cents coups	to be up to no good

	faire	part	to share, apportion
venir de	faire	qch	to have only just done s.t.
J'ai du	faire	tout la ville	I had to go all round town
ils auront beau	faire		no matter how much they do
se	faire		to become, make oneself (e.g tea, dinner), happen, mature, to adapt oneself, put up with, worry
Pour quoi	faire		What for?
s'en	faire		to worry
	faire	du bois dans le foret	to gather wood in the forest
	faire	du violon	to study/play the violin
	faire	le malade	to pretend to be ill
	faire		to do, make, shape, produce, cause s.t, pretend, seem, endure (lasting)
	faire	jeune	to look young
	faire	sien qch	to make s.t one's own
se	faire	un cafe/ des amis	to make oneself coffee/friends
Je n'en ai rien a	faire		It's nothing to do with me
	faire-part (nm)		announcement
Je ne m'y	fais	pas	I can't get used to it
	faisceau (nm)		beam, searchlight, bundle (of sticks), body, array, fasciculus
	faiseur		maker
au	fait		by the way
de	fait		de facto, indeed, effectively
en	fait	de	as regards
On ne me la	fait	pas	Nothing doing! / I wasn't born yesterday
Il ne s'en	fait	pas!	He's not the sort to worry about things!
Je suis ainsi	fait		That's how I am
Qu'est-ce que cela	fait		what does that matter?
au	fait(e)	de	made of
	faitage (nm)		the ridge
	faite		ridge (roof), pinnacle
les	faits		acts, deeds, feats
	falaise (nf)		cliff
	falloir		to need, be necessary, must, should
	falot		lantern

	familial(e) (adj)	family
	familier	known face, familiar, domestic
	fanal	lamp, lantern
se	faner	to wilt, fade, wither, toss (hay)
	fanfaron (nm)	boaster
	fanfarronades	boastings, braggings
	fange (nf)	mud, mire
	fantaisie	imagination, fancy, desire, whim, fantasy
	fantaisiste (nmf)	mildly eccentric person
	fantasme (nm)	fantasy
	fantassin	infantryman, foot-soldier
	fantoche	puppet
	farce	joke, farce, stuffing (cul.)
	farceur -euse	practical joker, joker
	farcir	to cram, stuff
sans	fard (nm)	natural, simple, openly
	fardeau (nm)	burden, load
	farder	to disguise, put make up on
	fardmineux -euse	colossal, staggering, incredible
	farfadet (nm)	elf
	farine	flour, meal (also: farinaceous plant)
	farouche	fierce, timid, unsociable, shy, staunch, wild
	fasciner	to entrance, bewitch
	faste (nm)	ostentation, display, splendour, pomp
	fastoche (adj)	dead easy
	fatal(e) (adj)	inevitable, fatal, fateful
	fatalite	misfortune, fate, mischance, fatality
	fatigue	wear and tear, tiredness, fatigue
	fatras (nm)	jumble
	fatuite	self-conceit
	faubourg	suburb
	faubourienne	working-class (Parisian)
	faucher	to scythe, mow, cut, pinch, flatten, mow down
	faucheuse -eur	reaper, mower
	faucille	sickle
	faucon	falcon, hawk
	faudrait	should
se	faufiler	to squeeze in/through, worm one's way
	faufille	tacked, threaded
	faune	animal life, fauna, faun (myth)
	faussaire (nm)	forger
	faussement	wrongly, wrongfully, deceptively
	fausser	to distort, alter, falsify

		faute	de	through/for lack of, for want of
		faute (nf)		a mistake, error
		fauteuil		easychair, armchair
		fautif -ive (adj)		guilty, at fault, in the wrong, culpable
		fauve (adj)		tawny, fawn-coloured
		fauve (nm)		faun
		fauvette	a tete noire	blackcap (Zool)
		faux (nf)		scythe
		favorisee		favoured, patronised
		fayotage		crawling, zealous to be well-perceived (fayotage)
		febrile		feverish, nervous
		feconder		to fertilise, inseminate, impregnate, make (s.t) fruitful, pollinate, enrich
		fecondite		fruitfulness, fertility
		federer		to federate (states), bring together (states)
		fee		fairy
		feerie		enchantment
		feindre		to feign, simulate, sham
		feler		to crack, damage
		felicite		bliss(fulness)
		feliciter		to congratulate
		felin		feline (cat)
		felure (nf)		crack
		femelle		female
		feminin		female
		femme-enfant (nf)		a little-girlish woman
		fendre		to split, crack, lunge
		fenil (nm)		hayloft
		fente (nf)		slit, groove, split, crack, crevasse, vulva (Biol)
		feodal		feudal
		fer (nm)		sword, iron
		fer-blanc		tin
		ferme		firm, steady, firmly
	se	fermer		to close, shut, heal (wound), release
		fermete (nf)		firmness, steadiness
		fermier -ere		farmer, farmer's wife
		fermoirs	d'argent	silver clasps
		feroce		savage, fierce, ferocious
	etre	ferr	sur un sujet	to be well up on a subject
		ferrailleur		scrap(metal) dealer, swashbuckler
	(voie)	ferre		Iron-shod (railway track/line)
		ferrer		to fit/mount s.t with iron, shoe (horse),
		ferroriaire (adj)		rail, railway
		ferrure (nf)		the fitting (window)
		ferrurerie		ironwork

etre	feru	de qch	to be very keen on s.t
	fesser		to spank
les	fesses		buttocks, backside
faire la	fete		to live it up
faire une	fete		to have a party
	fete		party, celebration, festival, feast, fete, fair, entertainment, public holiday
	feter		to celebrate, fete
	fetiche (adj)		lucky
faire long	feu		to hang fire
	feu	de bois	bush-fire, forest-fire
	feu	rouge	red traffic light
	feu	d'artifice	firework, firework display
	feu	de joie	bonfire
	feu (adj)		flame-coloured
	feu(e) (adj)		late (i.e. recently deceased)
	feuillages		leaves
les	feuilles		leaves (plant), sheeves (paper), rags (colloq journal)
	feuilleter		to leaf through, turn and roll (Cul), laminate
	feuillistes		those who leaf through (critics? Editors? censors?)
	feutre		felt, felt-tip pen, felt hat
	feve		bean (veg)
faire	fi	de qn	to treat s.o with disdain
	Fi!		Pooh!
	fiacre		hackney carriage
	fiasco		failure, failing, sexual failure, fiasco
	ficelle (nf)		string, twine
en	fiche		wasteland, uncultivated
	fiche (nf)		peg, pin, plug, voucher, slip (of paper), (index) card, memorandum
se	ficher	de qn	to make fun of s.o
	ficher		to put s.t on file, open a file on (s.o), do, drive in (nail)
	ficher	la paix a qn	to leave s.o alone
se	ficher	par terre	to fall
	fichu		small shawl, headscarf
	fictif		imaginary, fictitious
	fieffe		Fiefed (held on condition of military service)
	fiel		bitterness, malice, gall
	fier -iere (adj)		proud, haughty, stuck up
	fierte (nf)		self-respect, pride, haughtiness
	fievre		excitement, restlessness, fever

	fige		fixed (attitude), fossilized, deadlocked, set
	figer		to thicken, clot, be frozen to/with
	figuier (nm)		fig tree
	figurant(e)		extra (Theatre), bit part player
au	figure		figuratively
	figure		(geometrical) figure, shape, figure, face
se	figurer	qch	to imagine s.t
	figurer		to represent, figure, appear
	figurez-	vous que	as it so happens
	fil	rouge	red string
au bout de	fil		on the 'phone
	fil		thread, cotton, yarn, wire, line, tape
au	fil	des ans/annees	over the years
	filamenteux – euse		fibrous
	filao		filao (Bot)
	filasse (nf)		tow
	file		queue, line, lane
	filer		to spin (out), prolong, flow smoothly, slip by, shadow, trail
	filet (nm)		fine thread, thin trickle
allez	filez		buzz off! Scram!
	filiale (nf)		subsidiary
	filiation		filiation
	filiere (nf)		course of study, field, chain, official channels (pl)
	filigraine (nm)		watermark, filigree (work)
lire en	filigrane		to read between the lines
	fillette (nf)		little girl, half bottle
	filou (nm)		pickpocket, thief, swindler, trickster
	filtrer		to filter (through), leak out
en	fin	de comte	at the end of the count
a seule	fin	de	for the sole purpose of
	fin (nf)		end, close, ending, aim, purpose
	finage		ending
	finement		finely, smartly, subtly
	finition (nf)		finishing, finish
	fioles		vials
	fisc (nm)		tax office
	fissure		rift, crack

Il se	fit (from faire)	que	It (so) happened that
au beau	fixe		looking good
	fixer		to fix, set, regulate, establish, be attached to
se	fixer		to be attached to, settle, settle down, set oneself
	flacon (nm)		bottle, flask
	flageoler		to shake, tremble
	flagornerie (nf)		sycophantic behaviour, toadying
	flagrant		obvious, glaring, blatant
	flairer		to nose (out) game, scent, smell, sniff (at)
	flamant		flamingo
	flambaison		blazing
les	flambeaux		torches, candlesticks
	flambeur -euse		big spender, big-time gambler
	flanc		side, flank
	flaner		to stroll, loaf around
	flaneur -euse		stroller, idler
	flanquer		to flank, give, be flanked by
	flaque (nf)	(d'eau)	puddle
	flatter		to flatter, delight, stroke/caress (animal)
	flatteur		flattering
	fleche		arrow, direction, sign, spire (eccl)
	flechir		to move (s.o to pity), bend, flex, give way, sway, weaken, sag, flag, falter, waver, fall, fall off, come down, yield, relent
	flechissant		weakening, bending, giving way, sagging
	flechissant(e)		weakening, bending, sagging
	flegme		composure, phlegm
	flemingite (nf)		bone idleness
	flemingite (nf)		bone idleness
	fletrir		to brand (criminal), condemn (injustice), cast a slur on (s.o's name)
	fletrissure (nf)		blot, stain
faire une	fleur	a qn	to do s.o a favour
	fleurir		to bloom, blossom, flourish, decorate with flowers
	fleuve (nm)		river
	flic (nm)		cop, policeman
	flinguer		to blow (s.o) away, shoot
	flocon		flake, speck, wisp
	flopee (nf)	de gamins	a load of kids
	flots		floods (tears), waves, streams (of abuse), crowds (of people)
	flotte (nf)		fleet (ships), water, rain, float (of net)

	flotter		to waver, hesitate, hang loose, float
	flou		blurred, soft, hazy, vague, woolly, loose
	flouer		to cheat
	flute		flute (Mus), flute (Champagne glass), leg; damn! (Expl)
	flux		flow, flux, influx
	fluxion	(de poitrine)	inflammation (pneumonia)
il est de bonne	foi		he is completely sincere
	foi		faith
	foie		liver
crise de	foie		indigestion
	foin		hay
	foire (nf)		funfair, fair
a la	fois		at one and the same time
	fois (nf)		occasion, time
	foisonnement		proliferation, profusion, expansion
	foisonner	(de)	to abound, teem with
	fol folle fou		crazy, mad
	folatre		playful, frisky
	folie		madness
	follet		wisp
	fomenter		to stir up, foment
	fonce		deep(ened), dark(ened)
	foncierement		fundamentally
	fonctionnaire		civil servant, govt official
	fonctionner		to work, run on, operate
de	fond	en comble	from top-to-bottom
a	fond		fully thorough, totally, deeply
dans le	fond		basically, fundamentally
	fond (nm)		back, far end, content (Lit), drop (drink), background, bottom, seat, shallow
	fonde		justified, grounded
	fonde (nf)		sling, (toy) catapult
	fondement (nm)		foundation
	fonder		to found (biz), start up (biz), base/build (one's hopes on)
	fondeur - euse		foundry owner/worker
	fondre	en larmes	to burst into tears
se	fondre		to merge, amalgamate (biz)

	fondre			to smelt (ore), melt (snow, wax), dissolve, melt down
les	fonds			stocks, funds
	fonds (nm)			business
	fondu	(pp fondre)		mad, crazy, molten, dissolved, melted
	fonte (nf)			cast iron, cast, casting, founding, melting, thawing, smelting, saddle holster, saddle-bag
dans mon	for	interieur		in my heart of hearts, deep down
	forage (nm)			drilling, boring, borehole, drill hole
	forains			fairground
	forcat (nm)			convict, (galley) slave
a	force	de		by means of, by dint of
etre a bout de	force			to be exhausted
dans la	force	de l'age		in the prime of life
avec	force			firmly, strongly
	force (nf)			strength, force, dint
	forcene (nmf)			madman, madwoman, maniac
	forcene(e)			insane, furious, crazed
	forcer			to compel, force, strain, overdo s.t
	forer			to drink, bore, sink (a well)
	forfait (nm)			fixed price, flat rate, heinous crime
	forfait (nm)			fixed rate (Comm), pass (access), forfeit, package, hideous crime
	forfaitaire (adj)			all-inclusive price, contract price
	forfaiture (nf)			felony (Hist), malfeasance (Jur)
	forfanteries			boastings
	forger			to forge (iron), fabricate (story), make up (excuse)
	forgeron (nm)			blacksmith
se	formaliser			to take offence
	formation			training, education, formation (of Govt)
	forme (nf)			shape, form, figure, method of procedure, build
	formel			express, categorical, precise, formal, strict, absolute (veto)
se	former			to take shape (plan), form, develop
	formol (adj)			formalin, disinfectant, from formaldahyde
	formule (nf)			expression, formula, option (comm)
	formuler			to express, put into words, state
avoir des	fort	a faire		to have a lot to do
	fort			strong
	fortuit			chance, accidental, fortuitous

de	fortune		makeshift
	fortune(e)		wealthy, well-off, fortunate
	fosse		ditch, trench, pit, hole
	fosse (nf)		pit, grave, sandpit, diving pool, trench, pitfall
	fosse (nm)		ditch, moat, gap, rift
	fossette		dimple
Qu'est-ce qu'il	fou		What the hell is he doing?
J'en suis	fou		I'm crazy about (her/him/it)
	fou fol folle		crazy, mad
	fou (nmf)		madman,, court jester, bishop (chess), fool
	foudre		thunderbolt, unexpected event
	foudroyant(e)		crushing (news), withering (look), lightning (speed), staggering (success)
	foudroyer		to blast, crush (one's opponent), strike (down)(by lightning)
de plein	fouet		full force
	fouet (nm)		whip, whisk
	fouetter		to whip, flog, whisk
	fougue		spirit, ardour, fire
	fougueux – euse		fiery, spirited, ardent
	fouille (nf))		excavation, search, pocket
	fouille(e)		detailed, elaborate
	fouiller		to search, dig, rummage through, frisk
	fouillis		clutter, jumble, mess
	foulard		scarf, headscarf
	foule (nf)		crowd, mob, mass
	fouler		to trample, press, crush (grapes)
se	fouler		to twist, sprain
	foulque		coot (Zool)
	foultitude (nf)		multitude
	four		oven, furnace, kiln
	fourbe		deceitful, cheating
	fourche (nf)		the fork
	fourguer		to flog (slang)
	fourmi (nm)		an ant
	fourmiliere (nf)		hive of activity (Fig), ant-hill
	fourmiller	de	to teem (with), swarm
	fourneau		furnace, boiler
	fournee (nf)		batch
	fourni(e) (adj)		thick (hair), well-stocked
	fournisseur (nm)		supplier
	fourniture		supply equipment
	fourrage (nm)		fodder, forage
	fourre (nm)		thicket (adj) fur-lined, lined
	fourrer		to stick, line, cover/line with fur, to stuff

	fourrer (nf)		sticking it, stuffing it
en tenu de	fourrnee		in camping gear
	fourrure		fur
	fourvoyer		to go astray, lose one's way
je m'en	fous		I don't give a damn/s*!t
	fous-moi	le camp	get out (of here)! Get lost!
se	foutre	de ma gueule	to take the p*!! out of me
se	foutre	de/du monde	to not give a s*?t about(expletive), to have a hell of a nerve
se	foutre	en colere	to fly off the handle (Fig)
ne rien	foutre		to do f*!? all (expletive)
se	foutre		to not give a s*?t/f?*! (expletive)
	foutre	le camp	to be off, split (Coll), fall apart
faire	foutre		to go to hell (Expl)
	foutre (nm)		sperm
	foutu (adj)		bl!*dy (Expl) awful/stupid, damn
	foyer		fireplace, hearth, centre (of learning), home, source (of heat), foyer
	fracas		din, crash
	frai (nm)		spawning, fertilisation
	fraiche, frais (adj)		cold, cool, fresh
	fraicheur (nf)		freshness, coolness, coldness
	fraichir		to get cooler, chillier
faire les	frais	de	to bear the cost of s.t
les	frais		expenses, cost
	fraise	des bois	wild strawberry
	franc		free, real, true, franklly, candidly, openly, quite, really
	francais(e)		French, Frenchman/woman
	franchement		frankly
	franchir		break through, cross, jump over
	franchise		frankness, openness
	francite		Frenchness
	franger		to fringe
	frapper	(de)	to strike, hit
	fraternel -elle (adj)		fraternal, brotherly
	fraternite (nm)		brotherhood, fraternity
se	frayer		to clear a way
	fredonner		to hum (tune)
	frein (nm)		brake, horse's bit, restraint
	freiner		to curb, restrain, impede, slow down
	frele		weak

	fremir		to tremble, shudder, vibrate
	fremissement		rustling (leaves), quivering, trembling
	frenesie (nf)		agitation, frenzy
	frenetique		wild, frenzied, frenetic
	frequenter		to associate with, frequent, visit
	fresque		panorama (fig), fresco
	fretillement		wriggling, wagging, quivering
	fretiller		to wriggle, quiver
	fretter		to fret (guitar etc)
	friandise(s)		delicacy, sweets, candy (US)
	fricassee		fricassee (ie minced game with rich gravy)
	friche		waste land, fallow land
	frileux -euse (adj)		sensitive to the cold, cautious
	fringant		dashing, spirited
	friper		to crumple
	fripon -onne		rogue, rascal
	frique(e)		very rich, loaded (Coll)
	frise		curly
	friser		curl, wave, border on (rudeness), be on the brink of
	frissonnement		shiver, shudder
	frissonner		to shiver, shudder, be thrilled
	friture		fried food, frying, oil, fat
	fritz		Jerry or Kraut (German – Coll)
	froisser		to crease, crumple, offend (s.o)
	froler		to skim, brush, touch lightly, graze, scrape, come close to
	fromager		cheese-maker, cheese-seller
	fromager – ere (adj)		cheese
	froment (nm)		wheat
	froncer		to frown
	frondaison		foliage
	frondeur -euse		rebellious, anti-authoritarian
	front (nm)		forehead, face, brow
	frontiere (nf)		border
	frottement (nm)		rubbing, friction
	frotter		to rub
	frousse		fright
faire	frout	a qn/qch	to stand up to s.o/s.t
	fruit	confit	candied/glace fruit

	frustrer		to defraud, frustrate, thwart (s.o), cheat (s.o) out of s.t
	fugace		fleeting, elusive
	fugacite		fleetingness, elusiveness, transience
	fugitive		fleeting, transitory
	fugueur -euse		runaway child
	fuir		to flee, run away
	fuite		flight, running away, passage (of time), escape, leap
	fulgurances		lightnings, dazzles, sparkles
	fulgurant		lightning, searing(pain)
	fulminant		furious, detonating, fulminating
	fulminer		to detonate, hurl (insults)
	fume-cigarette		cigarette-holder
une	fumee		smoke
	fumier		dung, manure, b*!!rd (slang)
	fumisterie		joke
	fumoir (nm)		the smoking room, smoke-house
	funambule		tightrope walker
	funeste		deadly, fatal, catastrophic
au	fur	et a mesure	progressively, proportionately
	fureter		to pry, ferret, nose about
	fureur (nf)		passion, fury, rage, wrath
	furneau		furnace
	fusant		bursting
	fuseau(x)		spindle, lace bobbin
	fusee		rocket
	fusele(e) (adj)		streamlined
	fuser		to crackle, fuse, melt, spread (colours), run, stream in (light)
	fusible (nm)		a fuse
	fusiilier (nm)	marin	marine
	fusil (nm)		gun
	fusillade (nf)		gunfire, shooting, shoot-out
faire	fusiller	qn	to have s.o shot
	fusion		fusion, melting, merging of companies
se	fusionner		merge
ne	fut (from faire)	ce que	it was only
il s'en	fut (from faire)		he left, went away
les	futaies		the woods, forests
	futs		stocks(rifles), boles(tree), casks, barrels
	fuyant(e) (adj)		slippery, elusive, fickle, shifty, receding
	fuyard(e) (nmf)		runaway, deserter

G

	gacher		to throw away, ruin, waste, spoil
faire du	gachis		to be wasteful, create havoc
	gachis		mess, waste
	gager		to bet, wager
les	gages		wages, pay
Il	gagne	bien sa vie	he makes a good living
Il a	gagne	de l'assurance	he has grown in self-confidence
Tu y as	gagne		You got the best deal
C'est	gagne!		We've done it! Well done (irony)
	gagner	au change	to gain on the deal
	gagner	du terrain	to gain ground
	gagner		to earn, gain, profit, win, reach, arrive at (place)
y	gagner		to come off better
	gagner	tout juste de quoi vivre	to earn just enough to live on
	gagneur -euse		winner
	gagnoter		to win
	gai (adj)		happy, gay
	gaillard (adj)		strong, rigorous, spicy (story)
	gaillarde (nm)		strapping fellow
	gain (nm)		earnings, gain, saving
	gaine		sheath, girdle, casing
	gainer		to sheathe
diner de	gala		gala dinner
	gale		mange, scabies
	galerne		gallery
	galimatias		gibberish
	galonne(e)		braided
	galopade		galloping, gallop, rush
	gambade (nf)		skip
	gambader		to wander, flit, gambol
	gamelle (nf)		mess tin
	gamin(e)		lively, mischievous, kid (coll)
	gamme		range
	ganter		to put gloves on
les	gants		gloves
	garant		guarantor, surety, bail, authority, guarantee
	garantir		to warrant, guarantee, shelter, protect
	garce (nf)		bitch, cow
	garde	des Sceaux	French Minister of Justice

mise en	garde		warning
	garde (nf)		guardianship, custody, protection, guard
	garde (nf)		nurse, guard
	garde-fou (nm)		railing, handrail, parapet, safeguard
	garde-robe (nf)		wardrobe
se	garder	de faire	to be careful not to do
se	garder	de recontrer	to beware of meeting
	garder		to keep, retain, protect, keep watch (over), respect, observe
	garder		to keep
	gardien		caretaker, security guard, keeper, guard, guardian
	gare (excl)		Watch!!
	gare (nf)		railway station
	garer		to park, store
se	garer		to park, move out of the way, pull over, avoid
	gargote		cheap eaterie, "greasy spoon"
	gargousse		cartridge
	garnir	(de)	to fill, stock, stuff (with), cover (with), garnish, line (with)
	garnison		garrison
	garniture		fittings, trimming(s), set, packing, stuffing
	garroter		to tie up (prisoner)
en	gars	amiable	as a friendly guy
	gater		to spoil, damage
	gauche		awkward, clumsy, crooked, left
	gaufrure (nf)		embossing
se	gaussser	(de)	to mock, laught (at)
	gaver	de	to stuff, cram
	gavotte		gavotte (music for an old dance)
	gavroche		street urchin (n); cheeky (adj)
	gaze (nf)		gauze
	gaze(e) (nmf)		gas victim
	gazon		grass, turf, lawn
	geant(e)		giant(ess) huge, enormous, giant, jumbo
	geindre		to moan, groan, whimper, whine, wail, creak
	geler		to freeze
	gemir		to groan, moan, wail
	gemissant		moan
	gemissement (nm)		moan, groan, moaning, groaning
	gemissent		groaning, wailing

	genant		cumbersome, embarrassing, awkward, discomforted
	gendre		son-in-law
	gene		embarrassed, ill-at-ease, hard-up (colloq)
	gene (nf)		embarrassment, discomfort, inconvenience, poverty
	gene (nm)		gene
se	gener		to put oneself out
	gener		to hinder, obstruct, cramp, inconvenience
	generale (nf)		a dress-rehearsal
	genial(e)		brilliant, great, fantastic
	genie		genius, engineering, military engineering, genie, (guiding evil/good) spirit
J'ai les	genoux	en compte	My knees are killing me (Fig)
ce n'est pas mon	genre		it's not the sort of thing I like, it's just not me, he/she's not my type
	genre		sort, type, kind, genus, style, manner(s), taste
les	gens		folk, people
C'est y pas	gentil		How nice!
	gentillesse		kindness
	gentiment		quietly, kindly
	geolier -iere (nmf)		jailer
	gerbes		sheafs, bouquets, showers (of sparks)
se	gercer		to crack (lips), chap (hands)
	gerer		to manage, run, handle
	germain(e)	cousin	first cousin
	gesir (git pp)		to be lying (about/around), lie (be set)
	gesir (gisait)		to be lying (was lying)
	geste		gesture, motion, movement
	gestionnaire		administrator
	gibbeux		gibbous (humped, convex, protuberant)
	gibeciere (nf)		game bag, shoulder bag
	gibier (nm)		game (ie hunted)
	gicler		to spurt, squirt, split, to p*!! off
	gifle (nm)		a slap in the face
	gigogne (adj)		hideaway, hidden away
	gilet (nm)		waistcoat, cardigan
	gimblette (nf)		wink???
	girouette		weathercock, vane
	gisements		deposits

	giter		to list (Naut.)
	givre (nm)		frost, ice
	glabre		smooth-skinned, glabrous
	glacage (nm)		glazing, icing
papier	glace		gloss(y) paper
	glace (nf)		plate-glass, ice, mirror
	glacer		to freeze, make (s.o) blood run cold, chill to the bone
	glaner		to glean, laze around
	glapir		to yelp, yap, bark
	glas		knell
	glauque (adj)		murky, squalid, grim
	glissade (nf)		slide, slip, skid
	glissement		shift (Pol), swing (Pol), sliding
	glisser		to slide, slip, be slippery, skid, glide, creep into
	global(e) (adj)		total, overall, comprehensive, global
	globe		globe, earth, glass case
	glorieux -euse (adj)		self-satisfied, glorious
	glousser		to chuckle, cluck
	glycine (nf)		wysteria
	gnole		hooch, spirits (pl)
tout de	go		straight out
	goeland		gull (Zool)
	goguenard(e)		quietly ironic
	golfe (nm)		gulf, bay
	gomina (nf)		hair cream
	gommer		to erase, rub out
	gommeux		gummy, sticky
	gommeux (n)		dandy
	gondoler		to crinkle, warp, buckle
	gond		hinge
	gonfle		swollen, inflated
	gonflement		distension (of belly), inflating, swelling
	gonfler		to inflate, pump up, puff out, tense, flex, saturate, make (s.t) bulge, make (s.t) swollen, exaggerate
	goret		piglet, little pig
	gorge (nf)		bosom, bust, throat, gorge (geo)
	gosier		throat
	gosse (nmf)		kid, child
	gouailleur -euse		cheeky
	goudron		tar, tarmac
	gouffre (nf)		chasm, abyss
	goufler		to blow up, pump up, tense, flex, swell, inflate, exaggerate
	goujaterie (nf)		boorishness
	goulet (nm)		gulley, narrows (naut)

boire au	goulot			to drink from the bottle (neck)
	gourde			flask
	gourmand (nm)			glutton, sucker (hortic)
	gourmand(e) (adj)			fond of sweet things/good food, greedy
	gourmandise			weakness (for sweet things), gluttony
	gourme (nf)			a stranglehold
	gousset			waistcoat, pocket, fob
	gout			flavour, taste, liking, preference, manner, style
	goutte			spot, splash, fleck, drop, gout
	gouttelette			droplet
	gouverner			to rule, steer (Naut), control, govern
	grabat			pallet, litter of straw (aka bed)
en	grace			as a favour
	grace			grace, charm, favour, elegance, mercy, pardon, thanks
avec mille	graces			very graciously
	gracier			to pardon, reprieve
	gracieusement			free of charge, gracefully, graciously
recours	gracieux			application for Review (Jur)
	Gracieux – euse (adj)			graceful, kind, gracious
	gracile (adj)			slender
	grain (nm)			gust (of wind), squall, grain, atom, particle, speck (of dust), bead
	graine (nf)			seed
	graisse			fat, blubber
en	grand			on a large scale, full size
	grand-chose			much (a great deal)
	grand-gravelot (nm)			ringed plover (Zool)
	Grand-livre (nm)	de la dette publique		National debt register
	Grand-livre (nm)			ledger
	grandiose			spectacular, imposing, grandiose
se	grandir			to make o.s (look) taller, magnify, grow
	grandit			grew up
	grange (nm)			a barn
	grappe			bunch (of grapes, people etc)
	grappiller			to pick up (fruit), glean
	gras (adj)			oily, sticky, fat, slimy, crude, coarse, plump, bold (type)
	gras (nm)			the fleshy part, fat
	grasseyement			guttural pronunciation, uvular trill
	gratification (nf)			bonus, tip, gratuity
	gratifier			to give s.o s.t
	gratte-ciel (nm)			skyscraper

	gratte-cul (nm)		rosehip
	gratter		to scrape, scratch
	gravats (nmpl)		rubble
	grave		serious(ly), solemn, grave
	graver		to engrave, carve, cut (a record)
	graveur		engraver, wood-cutter
	gravier		pebble (Geol), gravel
	gravir	le croupe	climb the rump (mountain)
	gravures		engravings, carvings
de	gre	en gre	by mutual agreement
de bon	gre		willingly
	gre		liking, taste
savoir	gre	a qn de	to be grateful to (s.o) for (s.t)
bon	gre	mal gre	whether he/we like(d) it or not, willing or otherwise
	greffe (nm)		office of the Clerk of the Court
se	greffer	sur qch	to come along on top of s.t
	greffer		to graft, transplant
	gregois		Greek
	grele (adj)		pock-marked
	grele (adj)		slender, skinny, thin (legs), high pitched (noise), hail
	greler		to hail
	grelot		small (spherical) bell
	grenade (nf)		pomegranate, grenade (Mil)
	grenadier		infantryman, guardsman
	grenier (nm)		attic, storehouse, loft, granary
	grenouille (nf)		frog
	gres		sandstone
	gresiller		to crackle
	greve		(sandy) beach, (sea)shore, (sand)bank, strike, walk-out
faire	grief	a	to blame
coup de	griffe		scratch
	griffe		claw, talon
	griffonage		scribble, scrawl, doodle
	griffoner		to scrawl, scribble, rough sketch
	grignoter		to nibble, gnaw, encroach on, fritter away
	gril (nm)		grill
	grillade (nf)		grill, grilled meat
	grillager		to put chicken wire/wire netting around, fit a screen to
	grille		iron bars, iron gate
	griller		to burn out, grill, roast, smoke, give the game away about s.o
faire la	grimace		to make a face

	grimacer		to make faces, grimace
	grimper		to climb up
	grincer		to grate, grind
	grincheux -euse (adj)		grumpy, grouchy
	gris-gris		an amulet/charm of African origin
	gris-pommele		dapple-grey
	grisant(e) (adj)		exhilarating, intoxicating
	grisatre		greyish
se	griser		to get drunk, tipsy
	griserle (nf)		exhilaration
	grisonnant(s)		greying
	grisonner		to be going grey (hair)
ras et	grissonants		short and greasy (hair)
	grive		thrush (Zool)
	grivoiserie		suggestive remark, suggestiveness
	grognement		grunt, growl, snort
	grognon(ne)		grumpy, grouchy, fretful, fractious
	grommeler		to mutter, murmur
	grondant		growling
	gronder		to growl, snarl, tell s.o off, roar, be brewing
en	gros		roughly, broadly, wholesale trade
	gros grosse		big, bulky, large, loud, stout, fat, heavy, deep, coarse, rude
	grossesse (nf)		pregnancy
	grosseur (nf)		bulk, size, volume, weight, swelling (med), growth (med)
	grossier		rough, coarse
	grossierement		roughly, coarsely, crudely, rudely
	grossierete		rudeness, coarseness, crudeness, bad word
	grossir		to swell, magnify, enlarge, increase
	grossoyer		to engross (Jur)
	grotesque		ridiculous, preposterous, grotesque
	grotte (nf)		cave
	grouiller	de recontrer	to swarm about/with, mill about
	grouper		to arrange (in groups), group
	grue		crane (bird), prostitute, tart (colloq), crane (Mech.)
se	guarantir		to protect oneself
	gue (nm)		ford (ie water)
	guenille (nf)		rag
	guenon (nf)		monkey
	guepard (nm)		cheetah
	guepe (nf)		wasp
	guepier (nm)		wasp's nest
ne	guere		hardly

	gueridon		pedestal table
se	guerir		to get better, be cured
	guerir		to be cured, heal, cure
	guerison		recovery, cure, healing (wound)
	guerite		cabin, shelter
entrer en	guerre		to go to war
	guerre (nf)		strife, warfare, feud, war
	guerre (nm)		warrior
	guet (nm)		look-out, watch (Mil)
	guetre		gaiter
	guetter		to line in wait for, watch for s.o
	guetteur -euse		look-out, watchman (Mil)
coup de	gueule		outburst (verbal)
	gueule (nf)		mouth, look, muzzle (of gun), mouth (of tunnel), face
	gueuler		to yell, bawl (out), kick up a real fuss (Coll), blare out
	gueux		beggar, tramp, rogue, scoundrel
	guichet		ticket office, box office, counter, window, portico (Arch)
	guichtier -iere (nmf)		ticket clerk
	guillemets (nmpl)		quote marks ("), inverted commas
	guilleret -ette		perky, jaunty
	guilloche		guilloche (an ornamental pattern made of interlacing curved lines)
	guinde		stiff, stilted
	guingois		askew, gangly, lop-sided
la	guirlande		wreath, garland, festoon
	guise		manner, way, fashion
en	guise	de	by way of, as a
	gutta-percha		the hardened juice of a Malayan percha tree

	H		
	habile		skilful, clever
	habilete		ability, skill, cleverness, smartness
	habiller		to dress
	habit		clothes, dress, costume
	habitabilite (nf)		fitness (for habitation), capacity
	habiter		to live, reside, inhabit
	habituel -elle		usual, regular, customary, habitual
s'	habituer		to get used to, get accustomed to
	habitues		customers, frequenters
	hableur -euse		boastful; boaster (n)
	hachurer		to hatch
	haie (nf)	vive	hedge
les	haillons (nm)		rags
	haine		hatred
se	hair		to hate each other
	hair		to detest, loathe, hate
	haissable		detestable, hateful
	haleine		breath
	haler		to tan
	haletantes		pantings, breathless
	hallebardier		halberdier (soldier with an halbend ie spear and axe)
	halles (nfpl)		covered market
	hallier (nm)		thicket, copse, brake
	hallucine		wild, suffering from hallucinations
	halte (nf)		stop, end
	hameau – euse		hamlet
	hampe (nf)		pole, shaft, flank, scape (Bot)
	hanches		hips
	hanneton		June-bug/cockchafer (Zool)
	hanted		haunted
	hantise		dread
	happer		to catch, seize, grab
	haquebute		haquebute (Mil) (an antiquated small canon)
	harceler		to harrass, pester
	hardi		bold, daring, fearless, rash, impudent
	hardiesse (nf)		boldness, daring
	hardiment		boldly, brazenly, rashly, daringly, impudently

		hargne		aggression
		hargneux -euse		bad-tempered, aggressive
	s'	harmoniser		to go together, be in harmony with
		harnacher		to harness, rig out
		harnais (nm)		harness
		harre		story
		hasard	a voulut que	as luck would have it
		hasard (nm)		luck, chance, accident
	se	hasarder		to take risks, venture, hazzard (a guess)
	a la	hate		hastily
		hater		to hasten, hurry (s.t) on, accelerate (proceedings)
		hatif, hative		hurried, hasty
		hausser	(les epaules)	to shrug (one's shoulders), praise
		hausser		to raise, increase, shrug
	de la-	haut		from the top, up above
	en	haut		upstairs, up above, at the top
		haut		high, long, tall, senior, high-ranking
		haut (nm)		top part, top half, top
		haut-le-coeur (nm)		retching, gagging, heaving
		haut-parleur (nm)		loud-speaker
		hautebois		oboe
		hauteur		pitch (Mus), altitude, height
		have		haggard, gaunt, sunken
		havre		haven, small port
		he!		well! Hey!
		hebdomadaire		weekly
		heberger		to put s.o up, accommodate
		hebetement		stupefaction (dazed)
	s'	hebeter		to stupefy, daze
		hebetude (nf)		stupour
		hein?		eh?
		helas		alas, sadly
		hematome		hematoma, bruise
		hennissement (nm)		whinnying, neighing
		herbe		aromatic herb, herb, marijuana, grass
		herbes		plants, herbs
	un pauvre	here (nm)		a poor wretch
		herisse(e)		bristling, standing on end, spiky, bristly, prickly
		herisser	(qn)	to bristle (up), ruffle (feathers), make s.t bristle, get s.o's back up, cover with spikes
		herisson (nm)		hedgehog
		heritier - iere(s)		heir(s)

	hermetique		airtight, watertight, closed, sealed off, impenetrable, solid
	heros		hero
	heteroclite		Ill-assorted (collection)
	heterodite		heteregenous, ill-assorted
	hetre		beech tree
a l'	heure	actuelle	at present
a la bonne	heure		well done! Fine!
de bonne	heure		early
tout a l'	heure		just now, presently, soon
pendant les	heures	de creuse	during slack periods
aux	heures	de pointe	during rush hour
a ses	heures		in his/her spare time
	heureux -euse		happy, pleasant, pleasing, felicitous, "lucky"
	heurter		to bump into, knock
se	heurter	a	to come up against (probs)
	hexogene		hexogenous (six-types, all kinds?)
	hibou (nm)		owl
	hidalgo		a nobleman with an hereditary title
	hieratique		priestly, hieratic
etre	hilare		to be laughing
	hirondelle		swallow (bird)
	hirondelle		swallow
	hisser		to hoist
se	hisser		to pull oneself up
	hiverner		to winter, spend the winter
	hochant		nodding
	hockeyeur -euse		Hockey-player
	homard (nm)		lobster
	hommage		homage, respect, tribute
	homme	d'affaires	businessman
	honneur		honour
	honte		(sense of) shame
	honteur		shame-faced person
	hoquet		hiccup
	hoqueter		to hiccup, sputter
l'	horaire		timetable, schedule
avoir	horreur	du vide	to abhor a vacuum
c'est vraiment l'	horreur		it's the pits!
Ca me fait	horreur		It horrifies me, it disgusts me
	horreur (nf)		awful thing, horror, loathing

	horrible (adj)		dreadful, filthy, horrible, horrid, horrific, terrible, hideous
	horripilant		exasperating, maddening
	hors	du commun	exceptional
	hors		except
	hospice		home, hospice
	hospitalier -ere		hospitable
	hostile		hostile
	hote (nf)		guest, occupant
	hote (nm)		host, inhabitant, occupant
	hotelier -ere (nmf)		hotel-keeper
des	houees		boos, jeering, jeers
	houille(r)		coal
	houle (nf)		swell
sous la	houlette (nf)	de	under the leadership of
	houleux		stormy
	houppe		pompon, tuft (of hair), tassle, powder puff
	houppelande		greatcoat
	housses		covers
	hublot (nm)		porthole, scuttle
	huee (nf)		booing, jeers, jeering
	huelotte		tawny
	huer		to boo (actor), hoot (owl)
	huiler		to oil, slick (hair)
a le	huis	clos	in camera (Jur)
	huis		door
	huissier		bailiff, usher
	huissler (nm)		porter, usher
	huitaine (nf)		week (also: about 8)
	huitre		oyster
	huitrier		oystercatcher (Zool)
	huitrier-pie		pied oystercatcher (Zool)
	humecter		to dampen, moisten
	humer		to sniff, smell
	humide		damp, humid, rainy (season)
	huppe(e)		upper-crust, crested
	hure	de lion	lion's head
	hurlements		howlings, yellings
	hurler		to yell, holler, howl, roar, blare out (radio/TV)
	hutte (nf)		shed, shanty, hut

	hydropique		dropsical (abnormal collection of fluid in body tissues)
	hydroscope		hydroscope (a kind of water-clock used by the ancients)
	hyperbole		exaggeration, hyperbole
	hypetrophier		to hypertrophy, over-develop (Med)
	hypogee		underground chamber or passage, hypogeum
	hypotheque		mortgage
	hypothese		hypothesis, speculation (in the event of)
	hypothetique (adj)		hypothetical

		I		
		icelle		here
		iconoclaste		iconoclast (breaker of images, exposing/destroying sham)
		idealiser		to idealise
		idee		notion, fancy, whim, idea, imagination, view, opinion, mind
		idiotie (nf)		stupid thing, rubbish, garbage, stupidity, idiocy (Med)
		idiotismes		idioms
		idolatrer		to idolise
	l'	idylle		love affair
		igname (nf)		yam
		ignare (nf)		ignoramus; ignorant (adj)
		ignorer		not to know, not to have heard of, to be unaware of, ignore, not to feel
		illetre(e)		illiterate
		illumine(e)		visionary, crank (Fig)
	s'	illusionner		to delude oneself, have illusions of
		illusoire (adj)		illusory
		illustre		illustrious, famous, renowned
		ilot		islet, block, have
		image		picture, image, reflection
		image(e) (adj)		colourful
		imaginer		to picture, conceive, invent, imagine
		imbecile		idiotic
		imbriquer		to overlap, interlock
		imitation		forgery, copy, imitation
		imiter		to copy, do the same, imitate, forge
		immacule(e) (adj)		immaculate
		immanquablement		inevitably
	dans l'	immediat		for the time being
		immerger		to immerse, plunge, dip, submerge, bury s.o at sea, lay cable underwater
		immeuble (nm)		building, real property/estate, block (flats)
		immobile		still
		immobiliere (nm)		property
	s'	immobiliser		to stop, come to a halt/standstill
		immobilisme (nm)		opposition to change
		immobilite		motionless, immobility
		immodere		excessive, immoderate
		immuable		unchanging, perpetual, immutable
		impair		odd, odd-numbered
		impalpable (adj)		very fine to the touch, impalpable
		imparable		irrefutable, unanswerable, unstoppable
		impartagable		indivisible

faire une	impasse		to review, skip one's revision (Educ)
	impassible		impassive (calm, unmoved, apathetic), impassible
	impatienter		to annoy (s.o), make s.o impatient
	impavide		unperturbed
	imper (nm)		mac, raincoat
	imperial		imperial (from one with supreme authority); emperor
	imperieusement		urgently
	impertinent		rude, impertinent
	impie		ungodly, impious
	impitoyablement		ruthlessly, mercilessly, pitilessly
	implacable		relentless, implacable
s'	impliquer	dans	to get involved in
	impliquer		to involve, implicate
	importable		too awkward to carry, unwearable
sans	importance		unimportant
qu'	importe		what does it matter?
	importer		to matter, be important
	importun		intruder, nuisance
	importuner		to inconvenience, trouble s.o
en	imposer	a qn	to command respect (from s.o), to impress s.o
	imposer		to oblige (s.o) to do (s.t), impose
	imposition		taxation, imposing (of conditions), imposition
	imposture		deception, fraud
	impracticable		impassable, impracticable
	impregner		to immerse in, impregnate
	imprenable		impregnable
	impresario		agent, impresario
	impression (nf)		printing, pattern (material), impression
	impressionant		impressive
	impressionner		to impress, act on, disturb
	imprevisible		unpredictable
	imprevu		unexpected
	imprimatur		official approval, licence to print a book, imprimatur
	imprimer		to stamp, print, imprint, publish (a book)
	imprimerie		printers, printing works, printing
	improbation		disapproval
a l'	improviste		unexpectedly
	imprudent		carelessly, unwisely, rashly
	imprudent(e) (nmf)		foolhardy person
	impubere (adj)		prepubescent
	impudiquement		shamelessly, brazenly

	impuissance		powerlessness, helplessness, impotence
	impulsion		impetus, boost, impulse, drive (Psych), pulse, instigation
	impunement		immune, securely
	inaccessible (adj)		unapproachable, inaccessible, unattainable
	inaccompli(e) (adj)		unfinished, unfulfilled
	inacheve(e) (adj)		unfinished
	inadequation (nf)		unsuitability, disparity
	inamical(e) (adj)		unfriendly
	inassouvi(e) (adj)		insatiable, unsatisfied, unfulfilled, unquenched
	inattentif -ive (adj)		distracted, inattentive
	inavomible (adj)		fixed for life, irremovable
	inavouable		shameful
	inavoue(e) (adj)		hidden, unconfessed, undisclosed, undeclared
	incamer		to embody, represent
	incapacite		inability, incompetence, disability, incapacity
	incarnation (nf)		embodiment, incarnation
	incarne(e) (adj)		incarnate, ingrowing, itself
	incertitude		uncertainty
	incidemment		by chance, in passing
	incommode		inconvenient
	incompris (nmf)		the misunderstood (person)
	incongruite (nf)		Faux-pas, incongruity
	inconnu		unknown, stranger
	inconscient		unaware, unconscious
	inconsequent		inconsistent, inconsequential, thoughtless, irresponsible
	inconstance		fickleness, inconsistency
	inconstant		fickle
	incontestablement		indisputably, unquestionably
l'	inconvenient		disadvantage, drawback, inconvenience
	incredulite		disbelief, indcredulity
	incruster	de	to inlay with, fur (s.t) up, scale (s.t) up
	inculture (nf)		lack of culture
	incursion		foray, incursion
	incurver		to curve, bend
	indecent(e) (adj)		improper, obscene, indecent
	indecises		indecisive
	indefictible		unfailing, enduring
	indefini		vague, undefined, indefinite, indeterminate
	indelebile (adj)		indelible
	indemne		unscathed, unharmed
	indice (nm)		indication, sign, mark, token
	indicible		unspeakable
	indifferent		unimportant, immaterial, indifferent

		indifferer		to not be of any concern to
		indigent		poor, destitute, pauper
		indigne		unworthy
	s'	indigner		to be indignant, be outraged
		indignite (nf)		disgraceful act, despicable act, despicableness
		indiscret(e) (nmf)		tactless person, indiscreet person
		indiscret(e) (adj)		inquisitive, indiscreet
		indiscutible		unquestionable, indisputable
		indissociable (adj)	de	inseparable from
		indivisible		not separable into parts, indivisible
		indocile		rebellious
		indument		unduly, unjustifiably
		inebranlable		unstoppable, unshakeable, unwavering
		inedit(e)		(previously) unpublished, unreleased, (totally) new
		ineffable		unutterable, ineffable
		inegalite		unevenness, disparity (irregular, uneven)
		ineluctable (adj)		inevitable
		inemploye(e) (adj)		unused, untapped
		inepuisable		inexhaustible
		inetendu		unexpected, unpredictable?
		inexplicable		inexplicable
		infaillible (adj)		infallible
		infame		infamous, disgusting (smell)
		infeodation		dependence, infeudation
		inferieur(e) (adj)		lower, bottom, shorter, smaller, inferior
		infime		tiny, minute
		infime		tiny, minute
		infiniment		immensely
		infirme (adj)		disabled, infirm
		infirmier -ere		male nurse, nurse
		inflecher		to bend, curve, inflect
	s'	inflechir		to soften, beg, sag, deflect, level off, inflect
		information		information, reporting news item, piece of information/news
reunion d'	information		briefing
		informe		informed
	s'	informer	de qch	to enquire about s.t, keep o.s informed
		infortune		Ill-fated, unfortunate, wretch
		infos (nfpl)		news (slang)
		infraction		infringement, offence
		infructueux -euse		fruitless
		infuser		to brew (tea), infuse
		ingambe (adj)		sprightly
	s'	ingenier	a	to contrive, make an effort

	ingenu		artless, ingenuous, naïve
	ingenuite		simplicity, naivety, artlessness
	ingrat(e)		ungrateful
	ingurgiter		to gulp down, swallow, learn
	inhabituel(le)		unusual
	inherent(e) (adj)		inherent
	inhumer		to inter, bury
	inimitie		enmity, hostility, ill-feeling
	initiatique (adj)		initiatory
	initie(e)		inmate, insider, inside trader (Fin)
s'	initier		to start to learn
	injure		insult, abuse
	inlassablement		tirelessly
	inne(e)		innate
	inoffensif -ive		harmless, innocuous, inoffensive
	inopine(e)		unexpected
	inopportun(e)		inappropriately, ill-timed
	inouie		extraordinary, unheard of, outrageous
	inoxydable		rustproof, stainless steel
	inqualifiable		unspeakable
	insane		rubbish
	insatisfaction		dissatisfaction
	inscription	de faux	plea of forgery (Jur)
	inscription (nf)		registration, enrolment, inscription
s'	inscrire	(en faux)	to put s.o's name down (biz), (to deny)
	inscrire		to write down, take down (note, details), enter s.o's name
	insense		mad, insane
	insensibilite		insensitivity
	insensiblement		imperceptibly
	inserer		to insert
	insigne		distinguished, notorious
s'	insinuer		to penetrate, to worm one's way into
	insipide		dull, flat, insipid, tasteless
	insistance		insistence
	insolent		cheeky, arrogant, insolent
	insolite		unusual
	insondable		unfathomable, immense
	insouciant(e) (adj)		carefree
	installer		to put in/up, set up/out, connect, install
s'	installer		to settle, become established
	instamment		insistently

	instant		moment, instant
	instauration (nf)		institution, establishment
	instituteur		primary school teacher
	instruire		to teach, educate, instruct
	instruit		educated, well-read
a mon	insu		without my knowledge
	insufficance		short-coming, poor standard, insufficiency, shortage
	insuffler		to instil, breathe (life) into
	insupportable		unbearable, intolerable
	intact		undamaged, untouched, in tact
	intarissable		inexhaustible
	intediction		prohibition, ban
	integrale		full, integral
	intemperies		the elements, bad weather
	intemporel -elle		timeless
l'	intendance		bursary
	intendant (nm)		steward, bursar, quartermaster (Mil)
a mon	intention		aimed at me, intended for me
	intention		intention
	intercaler		to insert (into/between)
s'	interdire		to give s.t up, to refrain from s.t
	interdire		forbid, prohibit
	interdit(e)		disconcerted, bewildered, taken aback
	interesse		concerned, interested
s'	interesser	a	to be interested in, take an interest in
l'	interet		advantage, benefit, (feeling of) interest, share
	interieure (adj)		inner, internal, interior, inside, domestic
	interieurement		inwardly
	interlocuteur		recognised spokesperson, representative
	interlope		shady, illegal
	interloquer		to take s.o aback
	interminable		never-ending, endless, intermediate
	interne		inner, interior
	interpellation		questioning
	interpeller		to challenge s.o, question s.o
l'	interprete		interpreter
	interrogation (nf)		questioning, question, test, query
s'	interroger	sur	to wonder
	interrompre		to intercept, interrupt, cut in, break in, stop
	interrupteur (nm)		a switch (elec)
dans l'	intervalle		distance, gap, space, interval

	intervenir		to step in, intervene, happen, occur, arise, interfere
	intervertir		to invert, reverse
	intestine		bowel, intestine(s)
	intime		private, in private, intimate; close friend (nf)
	intimiste		intimate
	intimite		intimacy, closeness of friendship
	intitule (nm)		heading, title
	intraduisable (adj)		inexpressible
	intraitable		uncompromising
	intrigant		scheming, a schemer
	intrigue		a love affair, plot, scheme, intrigue
	intriguer		to scheme, intrigue
	intrus		intruders
	intrusion (nf)		interference, intrusion
	inusite		unusual
	inutilite		uselessness
	invavoue(e) (adj)		unconfessed, hidden, undeclared, undisclosed
	invectiver		to hurl abuse at
	inventaire (nm)		list of contents, inventory, stocktaking
	inventer		to devise, dream up, invent
	inverse		opposite, reverse, inverted, inverse
	inverser		to reverse, invert
	invetere(e)		compulsive, deep-rooted, inveterate
	invite (nmf)		guest
	inviter	a faire	to invite to do, ask to do, induce (s.o), lead (s.o) to
	inviter	a la reflexion	to be thought-provoking
	involontaire (adj)		unintentional, unwitting, involuntary
	invraisemblable		incredible, unlikely, unbelievable
	invraisemblance		unlikeliness
	ironiser	sur	to be ironic about
	irradiations		spreadings, irradiations
s'	irrecusible		irrefutable
faire	irreductible		implacable, relentless, indomitable, tenacious
	irreel -elle		unreal
	irregulier -ere		irregular, illegal
	irremediable		irreparable, irretrievable, irremediable, irreversible

		irremplacable		irreplaceable
		irreparable (adj)		beyond repair, irreparable
		irreprehensible		blameless
		irrespectueux -euse		disrespectful
		irriter		to get angry, annoyed, become irritated
		irruption	dans une salle	to burst into a room
		isba		Russian log hut
		isolement (nm)		remoteness, loneliness, isolation, insulation, solitary confinement
		isoler		to soundproof, insulate, isolate, put (s.o) in solitary confinement, set (s.o) apart from
		issue		exit, way out, outcome
	l'	issue	a	solution to, way out to
		itineraire (nm)		career (Fig), route, itinerary
		ivre		drunk, intoxicated
		ivresse		ecstasy, rapture, intoxication, drunkenness
		ivrogne (nm)		drunkard

J

	jabot (nm)		frill, ruffle, crop (of bird)
	jadis		formerly, once
	jaillir		to spring, gush out, squirt out
	jais		jet, jet-black (eyes/hair)
(poser des)	jalon(s)		(range) pole (to pave the way, blaze a trail)
	jalouser		to be jealous of
	jaloux -euse (adj)		careful, jealous
Plus	jamais	ca!	Never again!
	jambes		legs
	jambon-beurre		(buttered) ham sandwich
	jambon-blanc		cooked ham
	jambonees		calves (Anat)
	janseniste		Jansenist (see English dictionary)
	japper		to yap
	jardiner		to do some gardening
	jarret		ham(in man), bend of knee
	jasement		chattering, gossiping
	jaser		to gossip, blab, chatter
	jaseur		chatterbox, gossip
	jauger		to gauge, measure, size up (a man), weigh up
	jaunatre		yellow(ish)
un	jean (nm)		a pair of jeans
	jet		flash, spurt (of blood etc), throw, cast, jet
se	jeter	(sur qn)	to take the plunge, throw oneself, fall (on s.o)
se	jeter	dans le vide	to leap into the unknown
	jeter	l'ancre (nf)	to cast anchor
	jeter		to fling, throw away, throw
	jeu	de cartes	set of cards
maison de	jeu		gambling house
	jeu	d'epreuves	set of proofs (photos)
cercle de	jeu		(sports) club
	jeu		play, (manner of) playing, acting, game
a	jeun		sober, on an empty stomach
	jeune		fast(ing)
	jeune		young (adj), young person (nmf)
	jeuner		to fast

se	joindre		to join, unite
	joindre		to reach, get hold of, enclose, link, join, put (s.t) together, combine, fit properly, shut properly
ci	joint		enclosed
	joint	au	attached to
	joli		pretty, good-looking
	joliment		nicely
	jonc (nm)		rush (Bot), plain bangle
	joncher		to cover, litter
	jongler		to juggle
	joucher		to litter, strew with
	joue (nf)		cheek
	jouer	dans la couleur	to follow suit (cards)
	jouer	dans la court des grandes	to take on the 'big boys'
	jouer		to play, perform, act, risk
	jouer	des coudes	to elbow one's way (through crowd)
	jouet		the toy
	joueur		performer, player, gambler
	joug		yoke, beam (gym)
	jouir		to enjoy, enjoy the use of
	jouissance		pleasure, enjoyment, possession
	jouissif -ive		really great
	joujou		toy (baby-talk)
	jour	encore	it was still daylight
un beau	jour		one fine day
voir les choses au	jour	le jour	to take each day as it comes
a	jour		up to date
d'un	jour		fleeting, passing, for a day
	journal		newspaper, paper, news bulletin, newspaper office, journal
	journaliere		daily task, daily labourer
	journee		day, daytime, day's work
	journellement		every day, all the time
quinze	jours		a fortnight
dans huit	jours		in a week's time
	jours-charnieres		pivotal days, momentous days, key days
bain de	jouvence (nf)		rejuvenating experience
	jouvenceau(x) – elle		youth, maiden
	jouxter		to adjoin

	joyau (nm)		jewel, gem
	jube		rood screen
	jubiler		to rejoice, be jubilant
	jucher		to roost
	judas (nm)		peep-hole, door viewer
	judiciaire (adj)		judicial
	jugement		judgment, verdict
	jugeote (nf)		common sense
	juger		to judge, think, believe, imagine
se	juger		to consider oneself, be heard
	juguler		to stamp out, curb
	julep		julep (sweet drink esp one in which meds are taken)
	jumeaux – elles		twins
	jumelle (nf)		binoculars
	jupe		skirt
	jupon		slip, underskirt, petticoat
	jurer		to curse, swear
	juridique (adj)		legal, of the Court
	jurisconsulte		legal adviser
	jurisprudence (nf)		case law, precedent (Jur)
	juron (nm)		swear-word
	jusque	au bout	all the way, right to the end
	jusque		til, until, up to
	juste		just, right, fair, righteous, legitimate, justifiable, valid, justice, true
	justesse		precision, exactness, accuracy
	juteux -euse (adj)		juicy, profitable
	K		
	kaoua		Moroccan cuisine
	kiosque (nm)		pavillion, kiosk
papier	kraft (nm)		brown paper
	kyrielle (nf)	(de qch)	a string (of s.t)

L

	la	haut	up there, upstairs
d'ici	la		in the meantime
est-ce qu'il est	la		is he in?
de	la		from this...
	La-dedans		in here, in there, in it
y en a	La-dedans		I'm (he's/she's etc) not just a pretty face!
	labo (nm)		lab (abbrev of laboratory)
	laborieux -euse		arduous, difficult, hard-won, laborious
	labourer		to plough, churn up
	lache		loose, cowardly, slovenly, despicable, slack, lax, coward
	lachement		cowardly
	lacher		to release, slacken, loosen (spring, string), let go, give up
	lachete (nf)		despicableness, cowardliness, cowardice, cowardly act
	lacis (nm)	de ruelles	maze of small streets
	laconisme		laconism (max meaning with min words), terse
	lacune		gap, deficiency, lacuna
	lacustres		lacustrine (rock deposits at bottom of lakes)
	ladite, ledit(s)		the aforementioned
	laid		ugly, plain, unattractive, disgusting
bas de	laine		savings, nest-egg
	laine (nf)		wool
se	laisser	faire	to give in
se	laisser		to let oneself be...
	laisser	sur les bras	to be left lumbered with
	laisser-aller (nm)		scruffiness, sloppiness
	laiterie (nf)		dairy (building)
	laiteux -euse (adj)		milky, creamy, milk-white
	laitier -iere (adj)		dairy, milk, milk-yielding
	laitiere (nf)		a milk cow
	laiton		brass
	lambeau(x)		scraps, shreds (of cloth, paper, flesh), tatters
	lambrisse		panelling
	lame (nf)		thin plate, strip (of metal), sword (Lit), wave
	lamelle		flake, sliver, small strip
	lamies		sirens?
	lampadaire		streetlight, lamp, floor-lamp (US)
	lampiste (nm)		lampman, subordinate (Fig)

		lance		spear, nozzle, lance
		lancement		launching
	se	lancer		to dash, rush, leap, jump, embark on, take up
		lancer		to throw, fling, shoot (arrow), hurl, throw out
		lancinant(e)		nagging, insistent
		lande		moor (land)
		langagier -iere		linguistic, language, speech
		langue (nf)		tongue, language
		langueur		listlessness, languour
	se	languire	de	to pine for
	se faire	lanlaire		to get lost (Coll), go away
		lapemer		to gulp down (soup, wine etc)
		lapidaire		pithy, lapidary (terse and forceful)
		lapin		rabbit, doe
		lapsus (nm)		slip
		laquais		lackeys
		laquer		to lacquer, paint (s.t) in gloss
		lard (nm)		fat streaky bacon
		lardon (nm)		bacon cube, kid (coll), brat (coll)
	prendre le	large		to make oneself scarce, sail (Naut)
		large (adj)		broad, wided, loose-fitting, loose, full, big, sweeping, substantial, long, generous, comfortable
		largement		broadly, widely
		largeur		width, breadth
		larguer	les amarres	to cast off, set off
		larguer		to drop, unfurl, release, chuck, leave, give up
		larmes		tears
		larmier (nm)		the drip
		larmoyant(e) (adj)		tearful, whining, full of tears
		las, lasse		weary, tired
		lassant		tedious, tiresome, tiring
	se	lasser	de (faire)	to get tired of s.o/s.t (of doing)
		lasser		to bore, weary
		lassitude		weariness, lassitude
		laureat		laureate
		laurier (nm)		laurel (bot)
		lavabo (nm)		wash basin
		laver		to wash, cleanse

se	lazarder		to crack wall, laze in the sun
	lazaret (nm)		lazaretto (leprosy hospital)
	lecher		to lick, polish
	lecon (nf)		lesson
	lecteur (nm)		reader
	lecture		reading, interpretation
	ledit		aforementioned
	legendaire (nf)		legendary
	legerete		frivolousness, lightness, slight (pain), faint (sound), mild, weak
	legiste (nm)		jurist
	legitime		justifiable (anger), legitimate (child, excuse), lawful
	legitimite		lawfulness, legitimacy
	leguer		to leave (s.t), bequeath, pass on, hand down
	lendemain (nm)		the following day, next day, the future, tomorrow
	lendemains (nmpl)		the outcome, consequences
	lenifier		to soothe
avec	lenteur		slowly
	lenticulaire		lenticular (resembling a double convex lens)
	lentille (nf)		lens, lentil
	lequel (duquel)		which, whom
	lese-tabac		crime against tobacco
	leser		to wrong s.o, injure s.o, endanger (s.o's interests)
	leste		light, nimble
	lester		to cram in (pocket), to ballast
	lettre (nf)	de change	a bill of exchange (Merc)
les	leurs		theirs, their own (family, friends)
	levain		leaven
	levant		rising
se	lever		to rise, stand up, get up, arise
	lever (nm)	du soleil	sunrise
	levier		lever, handle, crowbar
	lezarder		to crack
	liaison		joining, binding, liaising
	liane (nf)		liana (Bot), creeper

		liard (nm)		old coinage (value c farthing)
		liasse		wad, bundle
		libelle		lampoon
		libeller		to draw up a document, word
		liberateur -trice		liberator
	se	liberer		to free oneself (of/from), get rid of
		liberer		to free, release, relieve, liberate, give free reign to, allow (s.o) to go (empl)
		liberte (nf)		freedom, liberty
		libertinage		debauchery
		libraire (nm)		bookseller
	en	librairie		in bookshops
		libration		libration (an apparent oscillation of a heavenly body e.g. moon), quivering motion
		libre		free, unrestrained
		licence		permission, permit, licence, licentiousness
		liee (adj)		related
	cafe	liegoir		iced coffee with whipped cream
		lien		strap, connection, link, bond (Fig), lien (Jud)
	se	lier		to make friends
		lier		to bind, fasten, tie, link up
	au	lieu	de	instead of
	donnait	lieu	de la croire	gave reason to believe it
	au	lieu	que	whereas
	cela n'a pas	lieu	d'etre	it shouldn't be so
	au	lieu	que	rather than
	s'il y a	lieu		if necessary
		lieue		league (c4km)
		lieux (nmpl)		premises, parts, place
		lievre		hare
		ligne	droite	straight piece of road, straight line, straight
		ligne (nf)		line, cord
	se	liguer		to join forces
		lilas		lilac
		limicole		shorebird, wader (Zool)
		limitrophes		bordering, neighbouring
		limon		silt, shaft, lemon
		limoneux -euse		silly
		limpide		clear, limpid
		linge		linen

	linotte		linnet (Zool)	
	lionne (nf)		lionness	
se	liquefier		to turn to jelly (Fig), get all wobbly (Fig)	
	lis		lily	
	lisere		edging, piping	
	lisible (adj)		legible, readable	
	lisiere		edge, border (of woods), outskirts, verge	
	lisse		smooth, sleek, polished	
	lit		bed	
	literie		bedding	
	lititation (nf)		bidding	
	litteralement		verbatim, literally	
	litterateur		man of letters	
Tout cela n'est que	litterature		It's a load of waffle (coll)	
	littoral (n)		coast, coastal region	
	littoral(e)		coastal, inshore	
	livarde (nf)		spirit	
	livide		ghastly (pale), pallid, livid	
	livre (nm)		book, the book trade, pound (lb), sterling (£)	
	livree (nf)	(de la misere)	livery, badge (of poverty)	
se	livrer		to take to, give way to, indulge in, despair	
	livrer		surrender, left to itself, hand over, betray, deliver, pass s.t on	
	livresque (adj)		bookish, book-learning	
	livret (nm)		booklet, small book, record book	
	local (aux)		premises, offices, units	
	localier		local	
	location (nf)		hire, renting out, rented accomodation	
	locution		expression, phrase	
	log		box (theatre)	
	loge (nf)		dressing room (theatre), lodge	
	loger		to provide accomodation for, house, live	
	logis		home, dwelling	
	loi		law	
de	loin	en loin	every now and then, now and again	
au	loin		in the distance	
de	loin		from afar, from a distance	
	loin		far, a long way	

dans le	lointain		in the distance
	lointaine		far away
les	lombes		loins
de	long	en large	up and down
au	long		at length
le	long	de	alongside
	long (nm)		length, long
	long-courrier (nm)		ocean-going ship
	long, longue (adj)		long, long-standing, a lot, a long time, along
	longer		to border, pass
la	longeur		length
	longiligne		lanky, rangy
a la	longue		in the end, eventually
	longue-vue (nf)		telescope
	longuement		at length, for a long time
le	lopin		patch, plot
	loquace		talkative
	loque (nf)		pile of rags
	loquet		latch
	lorgner		to peer at (s.t), have one's eye on (££, inheritance)
	lorgnette		spyglass
	lorgnon (nm)		pince-nez (glasses), lorgnette
des	lors		since then
	lors	de	at the time of
	lorsque		at the moment/time, when
	lot		a part
	lotissement (nm)		housing estate, plot
	louable		praiseworthy
	louange (nf)		praise
	loucher		to squint
	louer		to rent, hire, let(out) commend, praise
	loufiat		waiter
	loup		wolf
	loupe (nf)		magnifying glass
	loupiete (nf)		small lamp
	loups-garous		werewolves
	lourd		ungainly, heavy
	loutre (nf)		otter, otter-skin

	louveteau			cub (scout), wolf-cub
se	lover			to coil/curl itself up
	loyer			to rent, hire
	lubie (nf)			whim
	lucarne			skylight
	ludion			cartesian devil, diver
	lueurs			gleams, glimmers
	luge (nf)			sled, toboggan
	lugubre			dismal, gloomy, lugubrious
	lui			him, he, her, it
	luire			to shine, glow, glisten
	luisant			shining, bright, glossy, glowing (embers)
	lumiere (nf)			light, aperture, touch-hole (firearm)
avoir des	lumieres		sur qch	to have sound knowledge about s.t
	lumineux -euse			radiant, luminous, brilliant
	lunaison			lunar month
	lunette (nf)			lunette (a watch glass with flattened centre, crescent-shaped opening in a vault to let in light)
les	lunettes			glasses, bezel
	lustre			chandelier, lustre, polish, gloss
	lustre(e)			shiny, glazed
	lutte (nf)			the struggle
	lutter			to wrestle, struggle, fight
	lutteur			wrestler, fighter
	luxe (nf)			wealth (of detail), abundance, luxury
	lycee			high school
	lyrique			lyrical

	M		
	macaque		ugly man
	macher		to chew, chew up
	machine	a ecrire	typewriter
faire	machine	arriere	to back-pedal (Fig), go astern (Naut)
	machine	sous	fruit/slot machine, one-armed bandit
	machine		machine, engine
	machiner		to scheme, plot
les	machoires		jaws
	machonner		to chew away (at s.t)
	machurer		to blotch, blur, dirty, get s.t dirty
	maconner		to build, line with stone/bricks
	maconnerie		stonework, brickwork, masonry
	maculer	de	to spatter with, smudge
	madrigal		madrigal (short love poem)
	maestria (nf)		brilliance, panache
	magasin		store, shop
	magie (nf)		magic
	magistere		magisterium
	magistral-aux		masterful (manner), authoritative, magisterial, masterly
	magistrat		judge, magistrate
	magnetophone		tape-/cassette-recorder
	magouille (nf)		a fiddle, fiddling
	magouiller		to scheme
	maigre		thin, skinny, lean
	maille (nf)		stitch, mesh (of net), link (of chain)
	mailles	de plomb	lead mesh
	maillot	de bain	swimsuit
	maillot		vest, singlet, undershirt
	main-d'oeuvre (nm)		manpower, labour
se	maintenir		to last, hold on, be maintained, continue
	maintien (nm)		a bearing, carriage, maintenance
	maints		many
	maire		mayor
non	mais	quel culot!	Really! What a nerve!
	mais (nm)		corn, maize
	maitre -esse		teacher, master, mistress

	maitrise		mastery, control, supremacy (Mil)
se	maitriser		to control oneself
	maizena (nf)		cornflour
	majorer		to increase
avoir du	mal	a faire	to find it difficult to do
en	mal	de	in need of
avoir	mal	partout	to ache all over
ce fait	mal		it hurts
faire	mal		to hurt
	mal		evil, wrong, harm, difficulty, pain
beaucoup de	mal		much/great trouble
	mal (adj)		wrong, badly, difficult
	maladif -ive (adj)		sickly, pathological
	maladresse		clumsiness, awkwardness, tactlessness
	maladroit(e) (adj)		unskilled, clumsy, awkward
	malaise		difficult
	malavise		Ill-advised
	malchance		misfortune, bad luck
	malefices		evil spells
	malencontreusement		unfortunately
	malencontreux		awkward, unfortunate, untoward (event)
	malentendu		misunderstanding
	malfaisant		harmful, evil, evil-minded
	malfaiteur		criminal, malefactor
	malformation		malformation
	malfrat (nm)		criminal
	malheur		misfortune
	malignite		malignancy
	malin		a smart (one)/ 'aleck', clever person
	malin, maligne (adj)		clever
	malingre		sickly, wasted
	malouin		native of St Malo
	malsain		unhealthy
	mamelle		breast, udder, teat
	manche		sleeve
	manchot -otte		one-armed/one-handed (person)
	mandarin		mandarin, any high-ranking official (Fig)
	mandat (nm)		money order, authorisation, order
	mander		to summon
	maniaque (adj)		fussy, cranky, particular, fanatical, obsessive
	manie		mania, craze, obsession

	manier		to handle, manage
	maniere		way, manner, style
de cette	maniere		this way, like this
de toute(s)	maniere(s)		in any case, anyway
	manierement	des armes	handling of arms, drill
	manifestation (nf)		demonstration, rally, event, appearance
	manifeste		manifesto, proclamation, (ship's) manifest
	manigances		schemes, plots
	manitou		big noise (i.e extremely important) (Fig), big wheel
	mannequin		model
	manoeuvre		scheme, manoeuvre, working (of machine), drill (Mil)
	manouche		gypsy
Il n'en	manque	pas une	You can rely on him to put his foot in it
	manque (nm)		gap, lack (of), defect, emptiness
	manquer	de	to be lacking, miss, be in short supply, to spoil, ruin, botch
	manquer	sa vie	to make a mess of one's life
se	manquer		to miss each other, bungle one's attempt at suicide
	mansarde		attic
	mansuetude (nf)		indulgence
	manteau		coat, cloak, blanket, mantle
	mantelet		mantle
	manuscrit		manuscript
	maquereau(x)		mackerel, pimp (coll)
	maquillage		make-up, making up, doctoring
	maquiller		to make s.t/s.o up, doctor (Fig)
	maquilleuse		make-up woman
	marais	insalubre	an unhealthy swamp
	marasme (nf)		stagnation, depression, doldrums, marasmus
	maraude		pilfering, thieving, marauding
en	maraude		cruising for fares, on the prowl
	marauder		to thieve, pilfer
	marbre		marble (statue)
	marchand (nm)		dealer, shopkeeper, merchant (adj) commercial, marketable
	marchandage (nm)		haggling, bargaining
	marchander		haggle

tout en	marchant		while walking, as she walked
bon	marche		cheap
faire son	marche		to do one's shopping at the market, market research
	marche (nf)		walk, walking
	marchepied (nm)		step, foot-plate
	marcher	a reculons	to walk backwards
	marcher		to tread, be brisk (in biz), go, walk, move, progress, travel, work, run
	marecage		marsh, bog, swamp, quagmire
	marechal	ferrant	blacksmith, farrier
	marechal (nm)		field-marshall (Mil), general (US mil)
	mares		ponds
	marge		horder, edge (of road), margin (book), time, scope
	margelle		coping, curbstone
	marginal(e) (aux)		marginal, fringe, drop-out
	mari		husband
	marier		to marry off, marry (a couple)
les	maries		the newly-weds
avoir le pied	marin		to have one's sea legs
	marin (adj)		offshore, marine, seaworthy
	marine (nf)		marine (plant-equipment, engine)
	marine (nm)		sailor, seaman
	mariner		to stew, marinate
	mariol(le)		wise-guy, smart-ass
	marmite (nf)		casserole, pot
	marmonner		to mutter, mumble
	marmotter		to mumble, mutter
	marouffle		rascal, slapstick
	marque		unmistakeable, distinct, pronounced
	marque (nf)		brand, make, mark, sign, score
	marquer	un temps d'arret	to pause
	marquer		to stand out, write, mark
	marquise		awning, glass porch, Marchioness
	marraine		godmother, sponsor
	marrant		funny, odd
en avoir	marre	de qch	to be fed up with s.t
	marre	basse/haute	tide (low/high)
y en a	marre		enough's enough
faire	marrer	qn	to make s.o laugh
se	marrer		to have a great time, have a good laugh
	marri(e) (adj)		saddened, grieved
	marron		brown (adj); bent, unqualified, unlicensed

	marteau		hammer, (door) knocker, crazy (colloq)
	marteler		to beat, pound, hammer
	martingale		half-belt (e.g around a coat)
	martyriser		to torment, batter, martyr
	mascaron		mascaron (grotesque face – usually on a door-knocker)
	masque		mask, look, expression, appearance
etre a la	masse		to be nuts (Coll), be mad (Fig)
	masse (nf)		mass, bulk, sledgehammer
	masser		to assemble, mass, massage
	massif		clump (of shrubs), mountain mass (geog.)
	mastoide		mastoid (linked to the female breast)
	masure (nf)		hovel
	mat (nm)		mast (ship)
	mat(e) (adj)		olive, mellow, dull
	matelas (nm)		mattress, bed
	matelasse		quilted, padded
	matelot		sailor
	mater		to bring into line/under control, take (s.t/s.o) in hand
	materiel		equipment, material
	materiel -elle		worldy, financial, tangible, material
	maternelle (adj)		maternal, motherly
	maternelle (adj)		maternal, motherly
	materner		to mollycoddle, mother
	materner		to mother, mollycoddle
	matiere (nm)		material, matter
a cette heure	matinale		at this early hour
	matine		crossed with, mixed, cross-bred
	matinee (nf)		morning, matinee
	matrice (nf)		womb
	maudit		(ac)cursed
	maugreer		to curse, fume, grumble
	maussade		sullen, sulky, disgruntled, surly
	mauvais		evil, wicked, ill, bad
	mauvais	aloi	bad faith
	maux		ailments
	maxillaire		jawbone, maxilla (upper jaw)
	meandrer		meanderings
	meandres (nmpl)		maze, rambling
	mec (nm)		bloke (Fig), guy

	mecanique		engineering, mechanics, mechanical, mechanism, piece of machinery
	mecano (nm)		mechanic
	mechamment		spitefully, maliciously, mischievously
	mechancete (nf)		wickedness, spitefulness, mischievousness
	mechant		wretched, dreadful, mediocre, nasty, mean, vicious, bad, terrific (storm)
	meche		lock (hair), streak, fuse, wick, packing (Med)
	mecher		to pack (Med), sulpharize (wine)
	mechette		small lock (hair)
	meconnaissable		unrecognisable
	meconnaitre		to fail to appreciate/recognise, misread, disregard (duty)
	meconnu		unappreciated, misunderstood
	mecontenter		to displease s.o, dissatisfy s.o, annoy s.o
	medailler		to award a medal to
	medaillon		locket, medallion
	medicin (nm)	juriste	forensic surgeon
	medisance		malicious gossip
	mediter		to muse, contemplate, meditate
	mefiant		mistrustful
	mefier		to distrust, mistrust
	megarde		inadvertently, accidentally
un	megot		cigarette butt/end, stub
	melanger		to blend, mix (up), combine
	melee (nf)		fray, melee
se	meler	a	to mingle or mix with, blend
	meleze (nm)		larch (tree)
	melo		slushy; TV soap-opera (n)
	melomane		music lover
	membre		limb, member
en	meme	temps	at the same time
c'est cela	meme		that's it exactly
quand	meme		even so, all the same, really, come on!
tout de	meme		really, all the same
	meme		same, even, very, itself
	mement		likewise
	memoire		recollection, remembrance, memory
	menacer		to threaten
faire le	menage		to do the cleaning (up)
faire bon	menage	avec	to get on well with, be compatible with

	menage		household, relationship, housework, couple
	menagement		caution, consideration
se	menager		to spare oneself, take care of oneself
	menager		to use sparingly, economise, save, contrive
	menagere		household
	mendiant(e)		beggar
	mendicite (nf)		begging
	mendier		to beg
	mener		to go ahead of, lead, manage, conduct
	meneur -euse	(de jeu)	leader, (moving spirit), agitator, ring-leader
les	menhirs		standing stones
avoir les	menottes	aux poignets	to be handcuffed
	mensonge (nm)		lie, fib
	mensuel - elle		monthly (mag)
	menthe (nf)	verte	spearmint, garden mint
	mentir		to lie
	menton (nm)		chin
	menu		small, slender, tiny, menu
	menuisier		joiner
	mephitique (adj)		foul, mephitic
se	meprendre		to be mistaken, make a mistake
	mepris		scorn, contempt
	meprisable		abject, despicable, contemptible
	mepriser		to scorn, despise
ce n'est pas la	mer	a boire	it's quite easy
	meridionale		southern
	merite (nm)		credit, merit
	merle (nm)	blanc	the one in a million (person)
	merle (nm)		blackbird
	merveilleux (adj)		marvellous, wonderful
	merveilleux (nm)		the supernatural
	mesquinement		meanly
	messager -ere (nmf)		messenger, envoy
	messe (nf)		Mass (RCC)
	messer		mister???
dans la	mesure	ou	in so far as
a	mesure	que	in proportion as
mis en	mesure		put in a position
	mesure		action, proportion, measure
	mesure		restrained, moderate, measured
	mesurer		to measure (out/up), weigh (up), assess, consider, gauge

	metacarpe		metacarpus (pt of hand between wrist and fingers)
	meteo		weather
avoir du	metier		to be experienced
	metier		trade, profession, craft, business
long	metrage		feature-length film
	mets (nm)		dish (food)
	metteur	en scene	director
se	mettre	a faire qch	to begin/start doing s.t
	mettre	de la vie dans qch	to liven s.t up
se	mettre	debout	to stand up
y	mettre	du sien	to contribute to (venture, biz)
se	mettre	en colere	to get angry
	mettre	qch en relief	to bring (s.t) out, set s.t off
	mettre	qn au courant	to put s.o in the picture, fill s.o in
	mettre	qn en defiance	to put s.o on (his) guard
	mettre	(q.ch) en bras	to get (s.t.) going
	mettre	en demeurre a payer	to give notice to pay
se	mettre	en jaune	to wear yellow
s'en	mettre	partout	to get it all over oneself
en	mettre	un coup	to give it all one's got
se	mettre	a poil	to strip off
se	mettre	au lit	to go to bed
se	mettre	en branle	to get started
se	mettre		to go, get, set to, start
	meuble (nm)		piece of furniture
	meubler		to furnish, fill (gaps in silence)
	meunier -ere		flour-milling
	meurtre		murder
	meurtrier -ere		murderous, deadly, lethal
	meurtriere (nf)		loophole
	meurtrir		to hurt, bruise, spoil, wound
	meute		pack (Fig), pack of hounds
	mi-		half-, medium-, mid-
	mi-trajet	du retour	half-way back
	miauler		to meow, mew
	miche		loaf

	miche (nf)		round loaf, roll
	mie (nf)		bread without the crusts
	mielleux -euse (adj)		honeyed, sugary
faire son	miel	de qch	to turn s.t to one's advantage
	miel		honey
les	miens		my family
	mieux		better, best, nicest, most attractive
s'attendre a	mieux		to expect better
il y a	mieux		it's nothing special
il y a un/du	mieux		There is an/some improvement
	mieux-etre (nm)		Improved well-being
	mieux-vivre		improved living standards
	mievre		sickly, soppy
	mignard(e)		sweet, dainty, twee
	mignasse		cute
	mileux -euse		seedy, shabby
	milice (nf)		militia
au	milieu		between, in the middle
	milieu (nm)		the middle, amid(st), surroundings, environment, middle course
les	milieux		social sphere, surroundings, environment
	militaire		soldier, military
	militant		activist, campaigner; militant (adj)
en	mille		in a nutshell
	mille		mile, thousand
	milliard (nm)		a 1000 million (billion)
	millier (nm)		a thousand or so
des	milliers		thousands
	million		million
	mimetisme		miniature
	minable		pathetic, lousy, petty, miserable
	minauder		to simper
	minaudiere		simperer
	mince		slender, thin, slim
	mine		appearance, look, mine, expression
	miner		to sap, undermine, wear away, mine
	minerai (nm)		ore
faire des	mines		to simper
	minet (nm)		pussycat, pretty boy

	minier		mining
	minutie (nf)		meticulousness
	minutieux -euse (adj)		meticulous, careful, detailed
	mioche (nf)		kid (coll)
ligne de	mire		line of sight
point de	mire		focus
se	mirer		to look at/admire oneself
	miroir (nm)		mirror
	misanthrope		misanthrop, misanthropist(e) (one who has no confidence in his fellow man)
	mise	en scene	production
	mise	en pages	lay-out
etre de	mise		to be proper, be appropriate
	mise (nf)		bet, stake
un	miserable (nm)		poor wretch, scoundrel, down and out
	misere (nf)		destitution, extreme poverty, squalor, misery, pittance
	misereux -euse (adj)		destitute, deprived
	mitrailler		to pelt, besiege, take photo after photo
	mitrailleuse (nf)		hail of bullets
	mobile (nm)		moving body, driving power, mobile
	mobilier		furniture
	moche		ugly, nasty, awful
	modeler		to mould, model, shape (s.o's destiny)
	moelle (nf)		marrow (bone)
	moelleux -euse (adj)		thick, soft, cosy, mellow, smooth, tender, mellifluous
	moellon (nm)		stone
	moeurs		customs, manners, morals, habits
	moignon (nm)		stump (sawn-off branch) (amputated limb)
	moindre		lesser
	moine		monk, friar
	moineau		sparrow
a	moins	que	unless...
au du	moins		at least
	moins		minus, less
	moisir		to mildew
	moisson (nf)	(de)	harvest, harvest time, haul (of)
	moite		muggy, sweaty, damp
de	moitie		half
	molecule		molecule
	mollement		half-heartedly
	mollet		softish
	mollir		to soften, abate, die down

	mome (nf)		kid, brat, girl
du	moment	que	seeing that
	momentane(e)		temporary, momentary
	momeries (nf)		childishness
	momie (nf)		mummy (Antiq)
	monceau (nm)		pile
conversation	mondaire		polite conversation
le grand	monde		high society
c'est un	monde		That's a bit much!
ainsi va le	monde		That's the way it goes
au	monde		on earth, in the world
il y a du	monde		there are a lot of people
	monde (nm)		people, world
	mondialement		throughout the world, universally
	monnaie		currency, change, coin, money
	monocorde		monotonous
	monstrueux -euse (adj)		colossal, hideous, monstrous
	montage		assembly, set-up, setting, mounting, putting up, connection
salle de	montage		cutting room (Cine)
	montagnard		mountain dweller
	montant		ascending, climbing
	montant (nm)		sum; upright, jamb, pillar, pole
	montee (nf)		rise, rising, climb, uphill pull, gradient, slope (up)
	monter	en grade	to be promoted
	monter	sur	to rise over, come up
	monter		to take (s.o/s.t) up, bring (s.o/s.t) up, raise, put (s.t) up, go up, climb, turn up (vol), turn, mount, cover
	monticule (nm)		mound, hillock
	montre		watch
se	montrer		to show oneself, appear
	montrer		to exhibit, display, shop, point out, show
par	monts	et par vaux	on the move
	monts		mountains
	monture		mount, frame (of spectacles)
(lunettes)	montures	en ecaille	horn-rimmed glasses/frames

se	moquer		de	to make fun of s.o
	moquerie (nf)			mockery, jeering, scoffing
	moquette			fitted carpet, wall-to-wall carpet
	moqueux -euse (adj)			mocking, making fun of
	moraine			fallen rocks?
	moralisateur -trice (adj)			moralistic, moralising
	morasse			foundry, proof
	morbleu			yikes! Zounds!
	morceau (nm)			bit, piece, lump (sugar)
il s'en	mord		les doigts	he bitterly regrets it
	mordant(e)			caustic, scathing; sarcasm (nm)
	mordicus			pig-headedly, stubbornly
	mordiller			to nibble at, chew
se	mordre		la levre	to bite one's lip
	mordre			to bite
	morgue (nf)			pride, arrogance, mortuary
	moribund			dying (man)
	morne (nm)		pierreux	a stony bleak
	morne (adj)			gloomy, dull
	morsure (nf)			a bite
	mortel -le			deadly, fatal, mortal
	mortier			mortar
avoir son	mot		a dire	to be entitled to one's say, have one's say
	moteur			action! (cine)
	motif			incentive, reason, motive, pattern, grounds for
	moto (nm)			(motor) bike
	motte			clod, turf, slab (butter), clump
	mou, mol, molle(s)			soft, gentle
	mouche (nf)			fly, bull's eye (target)
	moucher		son nez	to blow one's nose
	moucher			to snuff (out) (Fig), put s.o in his/her place
	moucheron (nm)			gnat, midge
	mouchoir			tissue, handkerchief
	mouette		rieuse	black-headed gull (Zool)
	mouette			gull (Zool)
	moufles (nf)			mittens
	mouflon			mouflon (wild, horned mountain sheep)
	mouiller			to moisten, wet, damp, drop anchor
	moulage (nm)			casting, moulding, cast

	moule		mould, matrix
	mouler		to mould, cast (statue)
	moulins		mills
	moulu		dead beat, fagged out, ground, powdered
	mouqere		Moukere (Algerian woman – linked to Algerian war)
	mourir		to die
	mouroir (nm)		twilight home, old people's home
etre dans la	mouscaille		to be flat broke (Coll)
	moussade		surly, sulky, sullen
	mousse (nf)		foam, lather, froth, mousse (Cul), moss (Bot), glass of beer
	mousse (nm)		ship's boy
	mousseline		muslin, chiffon
	mouton		sheep, mutton
	mouvoir [pp mu(e)]		to move, drive
	moyen -enne		middle, average, mean, medium
	muer		to moult
	muet -ette		dumb, mute
	mufle (nf)		muffle, muzzle, boor, lout
	muflerie (nf)		boorishness
	mugir		to bellow, roar, moo, low (cow)
	mugissements		bellowings, roarings, lowings
	muguet		thrush (Zool)
	mule (f) mulet (m)		mule
	munichois		from Munich
	munir	de	to supply, furnish, equip, provide (with)
	mur(e) (adj)		mellow, mature (mind, age), ripe (fruit)
	mur		wall
faire le	mur(s)		to go over the wall (escape)
	muraille (nf)		wall (high defensive)
	murer		to wall in, brick up (doorway)
	murette		low wall
	murissement (nm)		ripening, maturing, evolution
	murmurer		to whisper
les	murmures		grumbling(s), muttering
les	murs		premises
	musarder		to dawdle, linger, waste/kill time, go slow
	muscade (nf)		nutmeg

156

	muscadin (nm)	doormouse
	muscle(e)	powerful, strong, muscular, tough, competitive
se	muscler	to be more competitive, develop one's muscles
	museler	to muzzle
	museliere	muzzle
rat	musque	ground squirrel
	musulman(e)	Muslim
	mutin(e)	mischievous
	myope	Short-sighted (person), myopic (adj)
	mystification	hoax
	mythique	mythical
	mythomane	mythomaniac

N

	nacelle (nf)		basket, nacelle (of hot air balloon)
	nacre		mother-of-pearl, pearly (adj)
	nager		to swim, float, to be submerged (in liquid)
	naguere		not long since, formerly
	naif - naive		simple, gullible, artless, naïve
	naine (nf)		a dwarf, midget
	naissance		birth, base (of neck), root (hair/nail)
	nait		born
Je l'ai vu	naitre		I've known him since he was born
	naitre		to arise out of, be born of
	nantir	qn de	to provide s.o with, award s.t to s.o, pledge
	naphtaline		mothballs, naphthalene (chem)
	napper	de	to coat with (Cul), glaze
les	nappes		layers, cloths, covers
	naquirent		were born
	narguer		to taunt, flout
	narine		nostril
	narquois(e)		mocking
	nasarde		slap
	nasillard		nasal
	nattes		plaits, braids
	naufrage		shipwreck, sinking, collapse (biz)
	navette (nf)	(spaciale)	(space) shuttle
	navire (nm)		ship, vessel
	navrer		to upset
etre	ne		to be born
	neant		nothingness, emptiness
	nebuleux -euse		cloudy (sky), obscure, nebulous (ideas)
	negation (nf)		negative, negation
	neglige		neglected (wife), slovenly, slovenliness, neglige, slipshod
	negligent(e)		careless, casual, negligent
	negoce		trade
	negociant		merchant dealer
	negociateur -euse		negotiator
	neige		snow, cocaine

	neophyte (nmf)		neophyte (i.e a novice to a religious Order, proselyte)
avoir du	nerfs		to have stamina
avoir ses	nerfs		to have a fit of nerves
	nerfs		nerves
les	nervures		ribs (of vault), veins (of leaves)
mettre qch au	net		to make a fair copy of s.t
	net nette (adj)		clear, plain, neat, tidy, distinct
	nettement		clearly, distinctly, plainly
	nettete		sharpness
	nettoyer		to clean
	neurasthenie		depression, neurasthenia (Med)
	neutre (adj)		neutral
	neveu (nm)		nephew
	niais		simple, foolish, inane
	niaiserie (nf)		stupid/inane remark, stupidity, silliness
se	nicher		to nest, nestle
	nickeler		to nickle (-plate)
	nid	de pie	crows-nest (Naut)
	nid		nest
	nier		to deny (fact)
	nigand(e) (nmf)		(silly) twit (Pej)
les	nippes		togs, clothes
faire la	nique	a qn	to thumb one's nose at s.o
	niveau		level
	niveler	(je nivelle)	to level
	noble (adj)		of noble birth, aristocratic, worthy, natural, fine, delicate, prestigious
avoir ses lettres de	noblesse		to have an illustrious history
	noceur -euse		party-animal
	noctambule		night-time reveller, night owl
	noctambulisme		night-time revelling
	nocturne (adj)		late night, nocturnal
les	nodosites		chalky knobs, nodules (trees)
	noeud		knot
	noirceur		wickedness, blackness, darkness
	noirci(e) (adj)		blackened
se	noircir		to grow black, darken (sky)
	noisette		light brown, hazel; hazelnut (n)

	nombril (nm)		navel
	nominativement		by name
	nomme (nm)	(John)	the man named (John etc)
se	nommer		to be called
	nommer		to appoint, name, call
	normalise		standardised
	normand(e)		norman (French)
	nosse (nf)		nag (horse), meanie (Pej)
	notablement		significantly
	note		mark, note, annotation
	noter		to write/note/jot down, note, mark
	notion (nf)		idea, notion
	notoriete (nf)		fame, reputation, common knowledge, celebrity
les	notres		ours, our own (friends)
	noue		knotted, tied
se	nouer		to become knotty
	nounou (nf)		nanny, nurse
	nourrice (nf)		nurse
	nourricier -iere (adj)		nourishing
	nourrir		to nurse (infant), feed (people etc), foster (hatred), cherish (hope), keep (one's family)
se	nourrir		to eat, live, feed (on)
	nourrisseur		feeder, stockbreeder
	nourrisson (nm)		newborn baby, infant
grosse	nouvelle		big news
	nouvellement		lately, recently
	novateur		innovator, pioneer
	noyade (nf)		drowning
	noyau	de	stone, core of, pocket, nucleus, kernel
se	noyer		to drown, be drowned
	noyer		to drown
a	nu		bare, naked, exposed
	nuance		shade, nuance (kiv subtlety)
	nubile		marriageable
	nues		skies
les	nues (nfpl)		the heavens, clouds
	nuire		to harm, be harmful
	nuisible		harmful, injurious

	nuit	blanche	sleepless night
	nuitamment		by night
	nul nulle		not one, useless, no, not at all
	nulle	part	nowhere
	nullement		not at all
	nullite (nf)		worthlessness, nullity (Jur), invalidity, nonentity
	numeraire (nm)		cash
	numeration		notation
un	numero	de voltige	acrobatic act
quel	numero		what a character!
	numero		number, issue
	numeroter		to number
	nuque		nape (of neck)
	nyctalope(s)		night blind(s)

O

	objectif (nm)		aim, lens (adj) unbiased, objective
	objurgations		scoldings, reproofs
etre l'	oblige(e) (nmf)	de qn	to be indebted or obliged to s.o
	obscur(e)		dark, vague, obscure
	obscurcir		to overshadow, make (s.t) darken, blur, obscure, dim,
	obsedente		obssessive, haunting
	obseder		to haunt, obsess
les	obseques		funeral
	observateur		spotter (Mil), observer
	observation (nf)		remark, observation
fera-t-on-	observer		we will observe
	obstination		stubbornness, obstinacy
	obstinement		obstinately, persistently
s'	obstiner		to persist in (doing) s.t
	obus		(artillery) shell
	obusier		howitzer
	occasionner		to bring about, cause (delay), give rise to
l'	occident		the West
	occidental(e)		westerner
	occiput (nm)		occiput (back part of the head)
	occulter		to conceal
	occuper		to take up (time/space), live in, fill, hold, employ (workmen)
s'	occuper	de	to deal with, be interested in, attend to
l'	occurrence		case, instance, occasion
	ocre		ochre (yellowish)
	octroyer		to grant (s.o) s.t, allocate (s.o) s.t
l'	oculaire		eye-piece
	odeurs		prowlers
	odorant		Sweet-smelling
l'	odorat		sense of smell
a l'	oeil		for free, for nothing
	oeil (yeux pl)		eye(s)
	oeil (yeux)	bride(s)	slanting eye(s)
	oeillade (nf)		wink, glance
	oeillere		blinker, patch (eye)

plein comme un	oeuf		full to bursting
	officieux		unofficial
	officine		dispensary, pharmacy, organisation
s'	offrir	(a)	to treat oneself, buy oneself, present itself (to)
s'	offrir	en spectacle	to make an exhibition of oneself
	ogival		ribbed
	ogive		rib, ogive (Arch)
	oie		(silly) goose
	oignon		onion, bunion, fob watch
l'	oiseleur		bird-catcher
	oiseux -euse		trivial, pointless, trifling
l'	oisif		the idle(r), person of leisure
	oisivete		idleness
	olivier		olive tree
	ombrageux		nervous, shy (horse), easily offended (person), touchy
l'	ombre		shadow, dark
	omoplate		shoulder-blade
	onagre		evening primrose
	once		ounce, snow leopard (Zool)
	onction		unction, anointing
	onde	sonore	soundwave
	ondee (nf)		shower
	ondes		waves, water
	ondoiement (nm)		swaying, undulation, baptism (Rel)
	ondulation		swaying, curve, wave, undulation
	onduler		to curl, undulate, ripple, wave, roll up and down, corrugate, sway
les	ongles		nails (finger), claws
	opiner		to nod
	opiniatre		obstinate, headstrong, persistent
	oppobre		shame, disgrace
	opposition		contrast, conflict (of ideas), opposition
	opter		to opt for s.t, decide on s.t
	optique		optics, optical
	opuscule		pamphlet
	or		but, yet
	or (nm)		gold
	orage (nm)		(thunder)storm, (political) row

	oraison		prayer
	oranais(e)		s.o from Oran (NW Algeria – coastal)
	orbites		eye-sockets
	ordonnance		regulation, prescription, order, ruling (Jur), layout
l'	ordonnancement		scheduling, order, order to pay
	ordonne		well-ordered (life), tidy, orderly
	ordonner		to order, prescribe, ordain, put in order
l'	ordre		order, discipline, division, category, agenda
	ordure		filth, dirt, dung, rubbish, excrement, obscenity
	oreille		ear
	oreiller		pillow
d'	ores	et deja	already
	orfevre		goldsmith
	orfraie (nf)		sea eagle
	organe (nm)		organ, voice, spokesman, instrument (of govt)
	organiser		to organise
	orgue		organ
	orgueuil		pride, arrogance
l'	orifice	des puits	well openings
l'	origine		beginning, source, origin (of custom), derivation (word), birth
	ormeau		young elm tree
	ormes		elms
	ornament (nm)		decorative detail, embellishment, ornament
	ornee de		decorated with
	ornieres		ruts
	orographie		orography (branch of geography dealing with mountains)
	orpailleurs		gold-miners
	orphelin(e) (adj)		abandoned, orphaned
	orphelinat (nm)		orphanage
	orthographe		spelling
	orties		nettles
	oscillation (nf)		swaying, rocking, swinging, oscillation, fluctuation
	oser		to dare
l'	osier		wicker (work), willow
	ossements (nmpl)		remains

	ostensoir		monstrance
	oter		to remove, take away/off
le	ou		the or (alternative?)
	ou	en etes-vous	How's it going? Where have you got to?
	ouater		to pad, quilt
l'	oubli		neglect (of duty), oblivion, omission, forgetfulness
	oublier		to forget (about), leave s.t out, neglect
	oubliette		oblivion
	ouest (nm)		west, western
	ouir		to hear
	ouragan (nm)		hurricane, (political) storm
	ourle(nt)		hem
	ourler		to hem, sew up
	ourrieres		factory girls
les	ours		bears (Zool)
	outil		tool, equipment
l'	outillage (nm)		kit, set of tools, (factory) equipment
	outrager		to insult, offend, outrage, violate (morals)
a	outrance		in the extreme, to the utmost
(en)	outre		(besides, moreover) further, beyond, in addition to
	outre	mesure	unduly
	outre		exaggerated, excessive (praise), indignant, outraged
	outre-mer		overseas
	outrepasser		to exceed, overstep
	ouverture		opportunity, opening
l'	ouvrage		workmanship, product, book, piece of work
se mettre a l'	ouvrage		to set to work
	ouvreuse		usherette
s'	ouvrir	a qn	to open one's heart to s.o
	ovale (nm)		oval
	ovationner		to greet with wild applause
les	ovins		sheep
	oxyde	de carbone	carbon monoxide

	P		
	pacotille		junk
	page	de garde	end paper (of book)
	page (nf)		chapter (of history), page (book)
	pagode (nf)		pagoda
	paillasson		doormat, matting
	paille (nf)		straw
	paillette		speck, sequin, spangle, glitter, splinter (of rock)
	paillis		mulch
	paillote (nf)		grass hut
hors	pair		peerless, without peer
	pair (nm)		peer, peer (Lord), par, par value
	paisible (adj)		gentle, peaceful, calm, quiet, untroubled
	paitre		to graze
	palace (nf)		luxury hotel
	palais		sense of taste, palate, palace, law courts
	pale		poor (imitation), wan (smile), faint (light), pallid
	paletot (nm)		(knitted) cardigan
	palier		landing (stairs)
	palir		to turn pale, fade
	palissade (nf)		fence, hoarding
	pallier		to alleviate
	palme		palm, palm-leaf, prize, bar (Mil)
	palot(te)		rather pale
	palper		to feel (object), palpate
	palpitant		thrilling, exciting
	paludeenne		malarial, paludal (Geog)
se	pamer	de	to be ecstatic with (joy etc), swoon with (pleasure)
	pampre (nm)		vine branch
	pan (nm)		setcion, part, patch, side, bang! (Fig)
	panache		plume
	pancarte (nf)		sign, notice
	panegyrique		panegyric
	paniers		baskets
peur	panique	de qch	terror of s.t
	panne		failure, breakdown
tomber en	panne		to breakdown (mech), run out of inspiration (Fig)
	panneau		panelling, panel
	pans	de murs	sections of walls
	pansement		dressing (Med)

	panser		to muck out and feed, put a dressing on, feed
	pantelant(e) (adj)		panting, overcome, quivering
	pantin (nm)		a jumping jack (toy), puppet, stooge
	pantois		flabbergaster
	pantomine		mime, scene, fuss, mime show
	pantouffle		slipper
	paperasse (nf)		bumph, documents, paperwork
	papier	brouillon	scrap paper
	papier	peint	wallpaper
	papier		article, piece (writing), paper
	papillonner		to flit about, flirt incessantly
	papillotement (nm)		flickering
	papoter		to chatter
	paquebot		liner (boat)
	Paques (nmo		Easter
	paquet		bundle, parcel, packet, package, wad, heap (snow), sheet (rain)
	paquetage		pack (Mil)
	par	contre	on the other hand
	par		by
de la	par	de	on behalf of, from
	par-dessus		on, over, above, on top of
	par-devant	notaire	in the presence of a notary
	para		para (abbrev) (Mil) i.e parachutist
	paracher		to perfect, complete, finish
	parade		display, parry (sport), parade
	paraissait		appeared
	paraitre		to appear, be visible, show, seem
	parallele		parallel, similar, unofficial, sideline (Fig)
	parallelement		at the same time
	paralyser		to bring (s.t) to a halt, paralyse
	paralysie		paralysis
	parasitaire (adj)		parasitic(al)
	parasite		sponger, hanger-on
	paravent		screen
	parcelle (nf)		bit, scrap, fragment, plot (land)
	parchemin		bit of paper, parchment, diploma
	parchemine(e)		papery, shrivelled

	parcimonieux -euse		sparing, stingy, parsimonious
	parcourir		to examine, go over, travel through, browse
	parcours (nm)		distance covered, journey, run, route, course
	pardessus		overcoat
	pardi		of course!
	pardonner		to forgive, pardon
	pare-brise (nm)		windscreen (car)
	pare-feu (nm)		fire-break
pour moi, c'est	pareil		it's all the same to me
	pareil (nm)		equal, peer
	pareil, pareille		similar, same, identical
	parement		(facing) of stone
	parenthese		interlude, parenthesis ( ), digression
	parer	a	adorn s.t, steer clear of, ward off, fend off, parry, get s.t ready (Naut), deal with
	paresse		laziness, sluggishness
	paresseux -euse (adj)		lazy, idle, sluggish
	parfaire		to complete, perfect, make up
	parfois		sometimes
	pari (nm)		bet, wager
	parier		to bet (on/that)
	parieur -euse (nmf)		gambler, punter
	parigot		Parisian
	parjure		perjury, (false) oath, perjurer, faithless (person)
Je vous	parle	en ami	I speak to you as a friend
	parlementer		to negotiate, parley
	parler (nm)		way of talking, speech, dialect
	parmi		among
	parodie		mockery, parody
	parodier		to parody, mock, make fun of
	parodique		parodic
	paroi	du fond	the back wall
	paroi (nf)		partition (walls), wall (of rock), rock face, side (of car, ship), lining (stomach)
	paroisse		parish
prendre la	parole		to speak
	parole (nf)		the "floor" (priority to speak in meeting), speech

en	paroles	tout est facile	It's easy to talk
	paroxysm		crisis point, paroxysm (sudden anger, joy etc)
	parpaing		breeze-block
	parquet		flooring, (wooden) floor
	parrain		godfather, sponsor
	parsemer	de	to strew, sprinkle, scatter with
a	part	eux	apart from them
a	part		apart from, separately, to one side, aside
faire la	part	de qch	to take s.t into consideration
de	part	en part	through and through, right through
d'autre	part		moreover
pour une	part		to some extent
	part (nf)		slice, portion, helping share
faire recevoir qch en	partagager	qch a qn	to let s.o share in s.t
	partage		to be left s.t (in a will)
	partage		division, dividing, partition, share, portion, sharing, distribution
se	partager		to be divided, divide
	partager		to divide, share out
	partenaire		partner
en	partence	vers	(just) sailing, due to leave (train), heading for
	parterre		flower-bed, the pit
prendre son	parti	de qch	to make the best of it
Il a l'air	parti	pour reussir	He seems to be heading for success
C'est mal	parti		Things don't look too good
	parti (nm)		decision, choice, course of action
C'est	parti!		Here we go!
	partie		a part, party (to s.t), game (cards etc)
	parties	de campagne	outings (in the country)
faire	partir	(une tache)	to remove (a stain), fire (gun), start (engine)
a	partir	des chiffres	according to these statistics
	partir	fache/content	to go off/leave in a huff/happy
faire	partir	qn	to make s.o leave
a	partir	de 14 heures	from 4 o'clock...(onwards)
	partir	en vacances/ voyage	to go on holiday/a trip
	partir		to leave, go, go from, take off, start
	partisan (nm)		a follower, partisan, guerilla (soldier)
	partition (nf)		score (Mus)

	partout	ou	everywhere, all over
	parue		published
	parut		appeared
	parution		publication
	parvenait	s'entirer	managed to get away
	parvenir	a ses fins	to achieve one's aims
	parvenir		to reach, achieve (a purpose), manage to
	parvis (nm)		square (church), forecourt
de	pas		step by step
	pas (nm)		step, footstep, footprint, slip, blunder, pace, march, stride
faire le	pas		to take the step
faire le	passage		to overdo it
au	passage		on the way, in passing
	passage (nm)		way, crossing, passage (in book, music), passing (over, through, across) alley-way
	passager -ere		passing, temporary, passenger
	passant (nm)		passer-by, loop (of belt)
	passant(e) (adj)		busy
etre en	passe	de faire	to be well on the way to doing s.t
Ca	passe	cette fois	This time I'll let it go
Il est	passe	par la fenetre	He fell out of the window
Il ne me	passe	rien	He doesn't let me get away with anything
Il m'a	passe	son velo	He lent me his bike
le mois	passe		the past month
	passe (adj)		past, gone by, over
	passe (nm)		pass, thrust, channel, master-key, skeleton-key, the past
	passe-droit (nm)		preferential treatment
	passementerie		trimmings for dresses (passementerie)
	passer	au soleil	to fade in the sun
se	passer	de qch	to do without s.t
Il veut	passer	pour (un genie)	He wants to be seen as (a genius)
	passer	pour qn d'autre	to be taken for s.o else
pouvait se	passer		could happen
se	passer		to happen, take place, elapse, go by, cease
	passer		to spend, proceed, pass, go by, go on
	passer	qch a l'eau	to give s.t a rinse
	passer	un marche	to make a deal
	passer	une couche de peinture sur qch	to give s.t a coat/lick of paint
	passereau		sparrow (Zool)
	passerelle (nf)		footbridge, bridge (Naut), gangway

	passez	derriere moi	Follow me
	passionnant(e) (adj)		exciting, fascinating, gripping
se	passionner	de	to have a passion for s.t
	passionner		to thrill, fascinate
	pastis		pastis (French drink)
	patachon		the fast lane
	patatras		crash!
	pataud(e)		lumbering, clumsy
	pataugas (nm)		canvas, hiking boots
	patauger		to splash about, paddle, squelch, flounder
	pate		pastry, dough, mixture
	pate (nm)		block (of houses)
	patelin (nm)		village
	patente		licensed, authorised, established
	patente (nf)	de sante	health certificate
	paternel -elle (adj)		paternal, fatherly
	pateux -euse (adj)		mushy, thick, turgid
	pathetique (adj)		moving, pathetic (Anat), pathos
	patiemment		patiently
	patine (nf)		the patina
	patir	de	to suffer as a result of
	patissait		baked, suffered
	patour		pasture?
	patraque		woozy
	patrie (nf)		homeland, birth-place
	patrimoine (nm)		heritage, patrimony
	patron(ne)		boss, employer, proprietor, manager
	patronyme (nm)		patronomic, surname
	patte		paw, foot (bird), leg (insect), strap (clothing) flap (of pocket)
	patte-d'oie		junction, crow's foot
	paturage, pature		pasture
	paume(e) (adj)		lost, mixed up, out of it
	paume(e) (nmf)		misfit
les	paupieres		eyelids
	pavaner		to strut
jeter/ lancer un	pave	dans la mare	to set the cat among the pigeons
faire le	pave		to lay (s.t) with cobblestones, walk the streets
	pave		streets, cobblestone, pad, display
	paver		to dress, adorn
	pavillon		flag, colours, pavilion (of ear), detached house
	pavoiser		to deck with flags, dress ship (Naut.), rejoice

	pavot (nm)		poppy
	payer	de sa personne	to risk one's own skin
se	payer		to treat oneself to, get landed with (Fig), have to be paid for
	payer		to pay for, pay, settle
le	pays	du soleil	the land of sun
	Pays-Bas		Netherlands
	paysage		landscape, scene, scenery
	paysan (nmf)		small farmer, peasant
	peage		toll
	peau	d'agneau	sheepskin
	peaufiner		to refine, put the finishing touches to
	pecher		to sin
	pecheur		fisherman
	pectoral -aux		chest
	pecuaire		pecuary
	pedagogue (nmf)		pedagog, teacher, educationalist
	pedant		pedant (one who shows off his learning)
	pede		queer, gay, homosexual
	pedicule		pedicle (arch: a fetter for the foot)
(se)	peigner		to comb (out hair), thin out (article)
	peignoir (nm)		dressing gown, robe, cape
	peindre		to paint
faire de la	peine	a qn	to upset s.o, distress s.o
a	peine		barely
	peine	perdu	waste of effort
c'est a	peine	s'il repondit	he barely responded
	peine (nf)		pains, trouble, punishment, penalty, sorrow, difficulty
	peiner		to pain, distress, upset, toil, labour
	peintre (nm)		painter
	peinturlurer		to daub
	pelage		coat (Zool), plumage
	pele-mele		higgledy-piggledy
	pelerinage (nm)		pilgrimage
	pelle (nf)		shovel, spade, peel, French kiss (Fig)
	pelletee (nf)		shovelful, heap of
	pellicule		film (cine)
	pelos		clump/mass of hair
	pelote		ball (of wool)
	peloton (nm)		group (of people), platoon (Mil)
	pelouse		pitch, field, lawn
	peluche		plush, cuddly toy, fluff

	penaud(e) (adj)		sheepish
se	pencher	(sur)	to lean, bend down, look into, stoop
	pendaison		hanging (Jur), housewarming
	pendant (nm)	de	companion piece to, pendant
	pendantif		pendant (jewel)
	pendre		to hang
un vieux	pendu		an old hanged-man
	penetre		imbued, earnest, penetrated
se	penetrer	une idee	to get an idea firmly planted in one's mind
	penetrer		to soak into, seep into, penetrate, reach, fill, fathom, enter, get into
	penible		annoying, painful, distressing, laborious (task), irritating
	peniblement		with difficulty, painfully
	penombre		half-light, semi-darkness
	pensee (nf)		thought, pansy (Bot)
	penser	a	to think of/about, remember
	pension (nf)		boarding-school; boarding house, pension
	pensionnaire		resident, boarder, inmate
	pensum		imposition, chore, punishment
	pente (nf)		hill, slope
	pepier		to chirp
	pepin		slight problem, umbrella, pip
	pepiniere		nursery, cradle
	pepite (nf)		nugget
	percee		opening, glade, clearing
	percer		to wear a hole in, perforate, pierce
	percevoir		to collect, receive, appreciate, perceive, become aware of
	perche (nf)		a (thin) pole, perch
	percher		to perch, roost, stick s.t
	perdant (nmf)		loser
	perdre		to ruin, destroy, lose
se	perdre		to get lost, disappear, die out, get mixed up
	perdre	son temps	to waste one's time
	peregrinations		wanderings about
	perennite		permanence
	perfectionne		advanced, refined
	perfide		treacherous
	perforer		to perforate, bore (Hort)
	perigee		perigee [(opp to apogee): the point in the moon's orbit nearest to the earth]

	perihelie		perihelion (point where the planet or comet is nearest to the sun)
	perimer		to make (s.t) obsolete
se	perimer		to become old-fashioned, become dated, expire
	perinee (nf)		the perineum (anat)
les	peripeties		turns, adventures, ups and downs of life
ne saurait	perir		cannot perish
	perir		to be destroyed, die, perish
	perjurer		to perjure oneself
	perle		pearl, gem, bead
	perle(e) (adj)		polished, pearl
	perler		to appear
en	permanence		permanently
	permanent		constant, continuous, permanent
	permet	de	allows, lets
se	permettre		to allow oneself
en	permission		on leave (Mil)
	peroraison		peroration (the final part of an oration)
	perorer		to spout, hold forth, perorate
	perpetuel -elle (adj)		permanent, perpetual
se	perpetuer		to perpetuate itself, be perpetuated
	perplexe		puzzled, perplexed
	perron (nm)		flight of steps
	perroquet		parrot, hat-and-coat stand
	perruche		budgerigar, chatterbox (female – colloq)
	perruque (nf)		wig
	persienne		(slatted) shutter
	persifle	(persiflage)	the subject of idle banter (banter)
	personnage		character, image, figure
	personne		person, individual, anyone
grande	personne		grown-up (adult)
	personnel -elle (adj)		private, individual, confidential, personal, finite
	perspective	(de)	prospect (of), view, perspective
	perspicace		perceptive
	perspicacite		shrewdness, insight
en peu	perte		for nothing
	perte (nf)		ruin, destruction, loss
	pertinnement (adj)		perfectly well, pertinently
etre	perturbe		to be very disturbed
	perturber		to disrupt, interfere with, perturb
	pervertir		to corrupt
	pesant(e)		heavy, clumsy, ponderous

	pesanteur		gravity, weight, heaviness
	peser	sur	to hang over, weigh (s.o/s.t) down, influence
	peser		to weigh, be heavy, carry weight
	pestifere (adj)		plague-stricken, plague-infested
	pestilentiel -elle		pestilential, troublesome, deadly
	petaudier		scene of commotion and confusion
	pete-sec (adj)		abrupt
	peter		to break, bust, snap, go off, f*rt (Coll)
	peterades		backfiring
	petillant(e) (adj)		sparkling, bubbly
	petillement (nf)		cracking, twinkling, fizziness
	petiller		to fizz, crackle, sparkle
	petrir		to knead (dough)
	petrolifaire		oil, oil-bearing, oil-producing
	petulance (nf)		exuberance
pour	peu	que	if he's had anything (at all)...
a	peu	de chose	not much, very little
	peu		little, not very, un-, virtually, almost, practically (Fig), more or less, just about
ramures des	peupliers		branches of the poplars
	peurte		ruin, destruction
cela se	peut (pouvoir)		it may be, it could be, I may do
tout	peut (pouvoir)	arriver	anything could happen
Je n'y	peux (pouvoir)	rien	I can't do anything about it
	phaeton		coachman, phaeton (early type of motorised car)
	phalange (nf)		phalanx
	phare(s)		lighthouse, beacon; headlights
	philautie		philauty (an excessive regard for yourself, self-love)
	philosophe		philosopher, philosophical
	philosopher		to philosophize
	philtres		potions
	phlegme	habituel	usual composure
	photographe (nmf)		photographer
	phragmite	des joncs	sedge warbler (Zool)
	phrase (nf)		sentence, phrase
	phtsie (nf)		consumption, phthsis
	physicien		physicist
	physique (nf)		physical (appearance)
	piaffer		to stamp (horse)
	piano		softly (music), piano
	pianoter		to tinkle, tap in (Mus)

		piaule		room, pad (Fig)
		piauler		to bawl, chirp
	a	pic		sheer
		pic, pioche		pick-axe, peak, pick, mattock
		picoler		to booze, drink
		picorer		to forage, peck at, pick up
		piece		room, document, piece, part (mech), bit, fragment, place
		piece-jointe(s)		enclosure(s) (with letter/email)
		pied-bot		club-footed person
		Pied-noir		French colonial born in Algeria
		piege (nm)		a trap, snare, pit, pit-fall
		pierre	blanche	memorable event (quasi Biblical "What mean these stones?")
		pierre		stone
		pierreries		gems, precious stones
		pietinement		stamping, trampling
		pietiner		to trample, tread (foot), stamp
		pieton		pedestrian
		pieuvre		octopus
	faire des	piges		to do freelance work
		pigiste (nmf)		freelance
		pignon		gable, gearwheel, pinion, pine kernel
		pilastre		pillar, square column
		piler		to pound, crush, thrash
		piles		heaps, stacks, piles
		pilet		pintail (Zool)
		pilier		pillar, mainstay, stalwart, prop-forward (rugby)
		pilon		pestle
		pilule		pill
		pin		pine (tree)
		pince		pair of pliers, crowbar
		pince(e) (adj)		tight-lipped, thin, pinched
		pinceau(x)		brush
		pincee (nf)		pinch of (e.g. salt)
		pincer		to pinch, nip
		pinson (nm)		finch
		piocher		to dig (with pic), grind at, swot up (s.t – colloq)
	faire une	pipe	a qn	to give s.o a blow-job (Vulgar)
	casser sa	pipe		to kick the bucket (Fig), die
		pique		pike (Mil), spade, cutting remark, peak (hair)
	se	piquer		to take offence
		piquer		to prick, sting, offend, pique, stick, insert s.t into, mark s.t
		piquet		stake, peg, pole
		piqure (nf)	de rappel	booster (injection/vaccination)

			prick, sting, injection (med), puncture, shot, hole, speck, stain
	piqure (nf)		
	pire pis		worse
	pis-aller (nm)		lesser evil
	pisse-copie		hack journalist, hack writer
	pisse-vinaigre		groucher, grouser
	pistache		pistachio (nut)
	piste		trail, track, runway, dance-floor
	pistolet		gun
	pistonner		to pull strings for (s.o)
	pitie		pity, mercy
	piton		peg, peak (of mountain), eye(bolt), piton
	pituite		secreting phlegm or mucus (pituary)
	pivot		pin, axis, pivot
	PJ		(abbrev) police
	placard		cupboard, poster, clink (Coll for prison)
sur	place		on the spot, on/to the scene
	place (nf)		place, position, seat, spot, office, square
se	placer		to take one's seat/place, stand/sit next to
	placer		to put, place, seat, find a job for, invest, deposit
	placet (nm)		Writ and Statement of Claim (Jur), Petition (Jur)
	placeur -euse		usher -ette
	plafond		ceiling, roof
	plagier		to palagiarise
	plaider		to plead (a cause) (Jur)
	plaideur -euse		litigant
	plaidoirie (nf)		plea
	plaie (nf)		wound, sore, cut, scourge
	plaignant		litigant, complainant, plaintiff
de	plain-pied		single-storey, same level as
se	plaindre		to complain, moan, groan
	plaindre		to pity, begrudge
	plaine (nf)		plain
	plaire	a	to like, be attracted to
se	plaire	a faire	to enjoy doing
se	plaire		to please (kiv enjoy, like)
	plaisant		agreeable, funny, amusing, pleasant
	plaisant (nm)		the funny side
	plaisanter		to joke
	plaisanteries		jokes, pranks
	plaisantez-	-vous	are you kidding?

	plan			level, flat, plane (maths), plan, drawing, draft
	planche (nf)			shelf, board, plank, flowerbed, engraving, (printed) plate, boardwalk
	plancher (nm)			floor
	planer			to glide, hover, float, waft
	planque (nf)			hide-out, hidey-hole, cushy number (coll)
	planque (nm)			skiver (from Military duty)
	planquer			to stash
	plantation			patch, plantation
	planter			to drive in, knock in, plant, stick (Fig)
	plaque			plate (metal), block, slab, plaque, badge, patch (of ice, eczema)
	plat			dish (cuisine), course (dinner)
	plat(e) (adj)			flat, level, dull, insipid
	platane			plane tree
	plateau			tray, plateau, turntable, top, level, set (TV)
	platement			flatly, levelly
	playdoyer			defence, (speech for) the defence (jud)
a	plein		temps	full-time, the whole time
en	plein			in the middle of, full on
en	plein		coeur	right in the heart
en	plein		visage	full in the face
	plein(e) (adj)			full, plump, solid, rounded, complete, whole
	plenitude			fullness, ampleness, bliss
	pleurer			weep for, moan, cry, whine, sob, sigh, lament, exude sap (Arb)
	pleurnicher			to snivel
les	pleurs (nmpl)			tears, outcry
	pleutre (adj)			cowardly
	pleutre (nm)			coward
	pleuvoir			to pour in, rain, rain down, come in thick and fast (Fig)
	plexus (nm)			plexus (Anat)
	pli (nm)			a pleat, fold (curtain), envelope, cover, bend (of arm, leg)
	plier		bagages	to pack one's things and go
	plier		boutique	to shut up shop (Fig)
se	plier			to fold up, yield/submit oneself
	plier			to fold up, fold, bend, submit
les	plis			pleats, folds
	plisser			to fold, crease, pleat, wrinkle, be wrinkled
du	plomb			lead
	plonger			dive, plunge (down), immerse (s.o in s.t)

	plouc		uncouth, redneck (US), hick (US)
	ployer		to bow, bend, sag, buckle, give way
perdre ses	plumards		to lose one's hair, go bald
ecrire au fil de la	plume		to write as the thoughts come into one's head
	plume (nf)		feather, (pen) nib, quill
	plumitif (nm)		pen-pusher, hack (press), scribbler
	plupart	de	the most, mostly, majority, most of
8	plus	3 egale 11	8 plus 3 equals 11
deux fois	plus	de vin	twice as much wine
de	plus	en plus	more and more
au	plus	fort	at the height of
J'en ai	plus	qu'assez	I've had more than enough
Elle est	plus	que jolie	She's more than just pretty
Il travaille	plus	que moi	He works more than I do
Elle l'aime	plus	que tout	She loves him more than anything
au	plus		at the most, at best
les taxes en	plus		taxes not included/plus tax
ne	plus		any more, no more, no longer
sans	plus		that's as far as it goes, no more
	plus	ca va	as time goes on
	plus	d'un	more than one
en	plus	de cela	on top of that
deux fois	plus	longtemps que	twice as long as
une fois de	plus		once again, once more
Il a ete	plus	ou moins que poli	He wasn't particularly polite
de	plus		furthermore, moreover, what's more
tout au	plus		at the very most
	plusieurs		several
	plutot		rather
	pluvier		plover (Zool)
	pocher		to poach
	pochette (nf)		case, folder, pocket handkerchief, pouch
	poele (nf)		frying pan
	poele (nm)		stove, pall
	poesie		poem, poetry
	poetique (adj)		romantic, poetic
	poetiser		to poeticise
du	poids		load, burden, weight, heaviness
	poignard		dagger
	poignarder		to stab, knife

	poignee	(de main)	a handful, fistful (a handshake)
	poignee		handle (door)
	poignet		wrist cuff, wrist
a	poil		stark naked, starkers (coll)
de tout	poil		of all kinds
	poil (nm)		hair, fur
etre au	poil!		to be just the ticket (coll), be fantastic
	poindre		to dawn, come up, come out
	poing		fist
a	point		just right, just in time
	point		point, stage, degree, stitch, particular
	point	de	a touch of (music, ie just a bit)
mettre qch au	point		to perfect, work out, devise
Je n'en ai	point		I don't have any
etre au	point		to be well-designed/put together
	pointe	de terre	spit of land
	pointe		tip, head (arrow), peak (roof), point
de	pointe (nf)		advanced, state-of-the-art, high-tech, leading
se	pointer		to tick off, check, point, rise up
	pointer		to tick off, check, clock in/out, stick out, come up, point, open
	pointeur		checker, time-keeper, gun-layer, pointer
	pois		pea
	poison (nm)		pest, poison
	poisseux -euse		sticky, muggy, greasy
	poitrine (nf)		chest
	poivrer		to pepper
	poivriere (nf)		pepperpot
	polar (nm)		detective novel
	pole		pole (N, S)
	polemique		controversy, polemic
	polemiste		polemicist
	poli (nm)		polish, gloss
	poli(e) (adj)		polished, courteous, polite
	police (nf)		policy (ins), police
	policer		to civilise
	polichenelle		buffoon
	policier -iere (adj)		police, detective
	policier -iere (nmf)		detective film/novel, policeman, policewoman
	polissage (nm)		polishing
	polisson		little devil, naughty child

	polissonneries		naughty tricks
	politesse		politeness, decency, pleasantry
	pollu		hairy
	polonaise		Polish
se	poloser		to qrope each other
	poltronnerie		cowardice
	poltrons		cowards
	polype (nm)		polyp, sea anenome
	polyvalent		one who does several jobs, multi-functional
les	pomettes (nf)	saillantes	high cheek bones
	pommes	allumettes	potato straws
	pommier		apple tree
	pompier -iere		firefighter
faire le	pont		to make a long weekend of it, do the crab (gym)
	pont (nm)		link, bridge, deck (Naut), crab (gym)
	pont-levis (nm)		drawbridge
couper les	ponts		to break off all contact
	populaire		popular
	porc		pig, pork
	porceau (nm)		pig, swine
	porcelaine		china, porcelaine
	port		carriage, bearing, port, haven, harbour
	portail		gate, portal
bien	portant		good health
se	portassent	au devant	went ahead
	porte		door(way), gateway, doorstep, entrance
on se	porte	bien	we are doing well
	porte-avions (nm)		aircraft carrier
	porte-drapeau		standard-bearer
	porte-fenetre (nf)		French window
	porte-mine		propelling pencil
	porte-vue		view-holder
hors de	portee		out of reach
	portee		reach (of arm), range, scope, significance, bearing, implication (of words), span (of roof, bridge)
	portefaix (nm)		porter
	portemanteau		peg, hook, coat stand
se	porter	a merveille	to be in excellent health
se	porter		to be (ill, well etc), to be going (well, badly etc)

	porter		to carry, bear, produce, wear, take (s.t) somewhere
	porteur		bearer, carrier
	porteur -euse (nmf)		holder, bearer
	portfeuille		wallet
	portier (nm)		porter
	portiere		door (car), raft (Mil)
	portrait		description, picture, portrait
	posement		thoughtfully, carefully
se	poser	en qch	to claim to be s.t, present oneself as
se	poser		to settle, land, touch down, alight, ask oneself, arise
	poser		hang (curtain), fit (lock), pose (model), rest, lie (on s.t), show off, put, place, lay, set down s.t
des/les	positions		circumstances, posture, attitude, condition
se	posseder		to control oneself/one's temper
	poste	centrale	sorting office
	poste (nf)		position, job, post
se	poster		to position oneself
	posterieurement (adj)		subsequently, after
	postillon (nm)		the postilion (Hist: see English dictionary)
	postilloner		to spit (saliva)
	pot (nm)		pot, jug, jar
	potage (nm)		soup
	potager (nmo		kitchen garden
	potasser		to swot up on
	poteau (nm)		post, pole, stake
	potele(e)		plump, chubby
	poterne		back door, gateway, private (entrance), postern, rear
	potier -ere		potter
	potin		gossip
	pouce		thumb, inch (measure)
	poudreux -euse (adj)		powdery
	poudriere		powder keg
	poudroiement (nm)		shimmer
	pouf		ottoman, pouffe
	pouf(f)iasse (nf)		slut
	pouilleux(ses)		flee-ridden
	pouillot	fitis	willow warbler (Zool)
	pouillot	veloce	chiff-chaff (Zool)
	pouillot		warbler (Zool)
	poulain		colt, foal

	poularde (nm)		fattened chicken
	poule		hen, fowl, tart (slang)
	pouliche (nf)		filly
	pouls (nm)		pulse
	poumon		lung
	poupee	de chiffon	rag-doll
	poupee		doll
	poupin		chubby
	pour	que	however, although
	pourchasser		to pursue, hunt down (criminal)
	pouriture		rotting, rot
brule-	pourpoint		point-blank
	pourpoint		doublet (clothing; one of 2 words derived from same root)
des que je	pourrai (from pouvoir)		as soon as I can
	pourrir		to rot, decay, go bad
	poursuivre		to pursue, chase, continue (task)
	pourtant		however, (and) yet, nevertheless
etre	pourvu	de diplomes	to hold qualifications
bien	pourvu		well-off, well-endowed
	poussant		pushing
	pousse (nf)		shoot (Bot), growth, off-shoot
	pousse-boi		booster
	pousse-cafe (nm)		liqueur
	poussee (nf)		thrust, pressure, push, shove, eruption
	pousser	qn a bout	to exasperate s.o
	pousser		to push, shove
se	pousser		to move
	pousser	des cries d'orfraie	to scream blue murder (Coll)
	poussiere (nf)		dust
	poussin		chick (Zool)
	poutre (nf)		(wooden) beam, (metal) girder
les	poutrelles		joists
se	pouvoir		may do, might do, might happen, could be
	pouvoir		to be able to, can
	practicien -enne		(general) practitioner
les	prairies (nfpl)		meadow, prairies
	pratique (nf)		practice, experience, observance (Rel)
	pratiquer		to play, use, do, take part in, practise, pursue, make, carry out
aller sur le	pre		to fight a duel, do battle
	pre		meadow
	prealablement		first of all, beforehand

sans	preamble		with no forewarning
	preau		courtyard, playground (covered)
	prebende (nf)		income derived from a sinecure, prebend (Rel)
	precarite (nm)		precariousness, insecurity
	precaution (nf)		caution, precaution
	precedent		former, preceding, previous, precedent
	precepte		precept (maxim, rule of conduct)
	precepteur (nm)		(private) tutor
	precis		specific, definite, particular
	precisant		specifying
	preciser		to specify, clarify, add that, state (that)
	precomiser		to recommend, advocate
	preconiser		to advocate, recommend
	predire		to predict
	prefet (nm)	de police	police chief
	prejuge (nm)		prejudice, preconception
se	prelasser		to lounge
	prelat		prelate (Church dignitary e.g bishop)
	premonitoire		forewarned, giving notice
	premunir	qn contre qch	to caution s.o agains s.t
Ca leur	prend	souvent	Are they often like this?
Votre remarque	prend	tout sens	Your comment begins to make sense
	prendre	a gauche/ vers le nord	to go left/north
Je passe te	prendre	a midi	I'll come and pick you up at 12
s'en	prendre	a qch	to carry on about s.t
s'en	prendre	a qn	to lay the blame on s.o, take it out on s.o
	prendre	des forces	to build up one's strength
Je vais	prendre	mon Mercredi	I'm going to take Wednesday off
	prendre	que	to get the idea that
	prendre	un parti	to make up one's mind, make a decision
	prendre	un poisson	to catch a fish
se	prendre		to be caught, catch, take
Qu'est ce qui te	prendre		What's the matter with you?
a tout	prendre		all in all
	prendre	au plus court	to go/take the shortest route
	prendre	un conge	to take a vacation
	prendre	un nouveau patient	to take on a new patient
	prendre	un patient	to see a patient
	prendre	un voix grave	to adopt a solemn tone

Ne le	prends		pas mal	Don't take it the wrong way
Ca ne	prends		pas!	That won't wash! (Fig)
	prenom			first name, forename, Christian name
les	preparatifs			the preparations
se	preparer			to get ready (for), prepare (for)
	prepose (nm)			official, clerk, postman/postwoman
	prepuce			foreskin
	prerot			provost
cela	pres		que	except that
a peu	pres			a little close, almost, nearly
trop	pres			too close
	presager			to bode, portend, presage
	presence (nf)			influence, presence, attendance
a	present		que	now that
	presenter			to offer, present, table (motion)
se	presenter			to appear, go, come, introduce oneself
	presqu'ile (nf)			peninsula
	presque			nearly, almost, hardly, close to being
	press (nf)			the papers, the Press, press; magazines (pl)
	pressant(es)			urgent, insistent
	pressentir			to have a a premonition about
se	presser			to crowd, throng, crush
	presser			to squeeze, press, urge (s.o), hurry (s.o)
	pression (nf)			pressure
	prestation (nf)			benefit, allowance, fee, service, performance
	preste(ment)			quick(ly), sharp(ly), nimble(ly), alert(ly)
	prestidigitateur -trice			conjurer
	prestidigitation (nf)			magic, conjuring
	pret(e)			ready
	prete			loaned
	pretendant			pretender
	pretendre			to claim
	pretendu(e) (adj)			alleged, so-called, would-be
	pretendument			allegedly
	pretention			conceit, claim, pretentiousness
se	preter		a	to consent, agree to, lend itself to
	preter		main-forte	to lend a hand
	preter			to lend(ear), listen, loan, give (support), attribute, ascribe
	preter		a qch	to give rise to s.t

	preteur		lender
	pretre		priest
	preuve		evidence, proof
se	prevaloir	de	to take advantage of s.t
	prevenir		to anticipate, prevent, inform, forewarn
	prevention		predisposition, bias, prevention (of disease)
	prevenu		anticipated, prevented, averted
etre	prevenu(e)	de	to be accused of
	prevenu(e)		defendant (Jur)
	previsible		forseeable, predictable
	prevision (nf)		forecasting, prediction, forecast
	prevoir		to predict, forsee, anticipate
	prier		to beg, beseech, entreat, pray (to God)(for s.t), ask, request
	primer		to take precedence over, award a prize (to s.o for s.t)
	princier -iere (adj)		dazzling, princely
	principe		principle, rule, theory
se	prinoncer		to preach
	printanier -iere		spring-like, spring
	printemps (nm)		springtime, spring
a	priori		a priori (from the former; from cause to effect)
	pris (prendre)	de	overcome with
Je n'ai	pris (prendre)	pas assez de l'argent	I haven't brought enough money
Il en a	pris (prendre)	pour 20 ans	He got 20 years for it
On m'a	pris (prendre)	tres cher	I was charged a lot
une	prise		hold, grasp, grip, sample (of ore)
	prise (nf)		storming, capture, hold
	priser		to value, prize, hold in esteem
	prisonnier -iere (nmf)		prisoner
	prit	fin	ended
peine	privative	de liberte	custodial sentence
	prive (adj)		private, unofficial
	privee (nf)		private life, inside info, private
	priver		to deprive (s.o) of s.t
faire	prix		make, agree a price
	probe (adj)		upright, honest
	probite		integrity, probity
	procede (nm)		proceeding, dealing, conduct, process
faire le	proces	de qn	to criticise s.o
	proces		(legal) proceedings, action
	proces-verbal (nm)		(formal) report, minutes (of meeting), record (of evidence)

	processus (nm)			process, evolution (Med)
	prochaine			upcoming
	proche			close by, nearby
	proche (nm)			a relative, close friend, associate, nearest and dearest
	procuration (nf)			power of attorney, proxy (form)
se	procurer			to get (to/for itself), obtain
	procureur (nm)			the public prosecutor
	prodige (nm)			wonder, marvel, prodigy
	prodiguer			to be lavish, waste, be prodigal
	produire			to bring about (a result/effect), produce
se	produire			to take place, occur, happen, appear
	profession			occupation, profession, trade, business
se	profiler			to emerge, approach, stand out
	profiter	a qn		to benefit s.o, be of benefit to s.o
	profiter	de		to make the most of, take advantage of, enjoy (s.t)
	profondeur			depth
	profusion (nf)			abundance, wealth, profusion
	programmer			to schedule, plan, program
	progres			progress, improvement
faire des	progres			to make good progress/improvement
	progressiste			progressive
etre en	proie	de		to be tormented by
	proie			prey, quarry
	projection			discharge, projection (cine), showing, forecast
	projet (nm)			plan, scheme, rough draft (novel)
	prolix(e)			verbose, wordy
se	prolonger			to extend, continue, be prolonged
envoyer	promener	qn a bout		to send s.o packing
	promener			to take/lead s.o about, take s.o out for a walk/drive
	promeneur – euse			walker, stroller
	promettre			to show promise, promise
	promptitude (nf)			promptness, rapidity, speed, swiftness, suddenness
	proner			to extol, recommend
	proneur			endorser, one who recommends
se	prononcer			to decide, pronounce
	prononcer			to announce (verdict), deliver, pronounce
se	propager			to spread, reproduce
	propension			propensity
a	propos	de		in connection with, on the subject of

a tout	propos		about everything
les/des	propos		remarks
	propos		purpose, intention, subject, matter
se	proposer	de	to mean, propose to do s.t
	propre		neat (writing), clean, proper (meaning), in fact, appropriate, suitable, nature, attribute, own
	proprete (nf)		cleanliness, honesty
	propriete (nf)		ownership, estate, property, characteristic (of metal)
	proscrire		to prohibit, outlaw, ban, banish, proscribe
	prosodie		prosody (the science of versification)
se	prosterner		to bow down, prostrate oneself
	protecteur – trice		protector, guardian, patron
	protegait		protected
	protege(e)		protige, plastic (punched) pocket
	protestation		protest against, protest
	prouesse		feat, achievement, valour
	prouver		to demonstrate, prove
	provenir	de	to come from
	provisoire		temporary, provisional
	provocant(e)		provocative
	provocateur -trice		agitator, agent provocateur
	proxenete		procurer, pimp
	prunelle (nf)		pupil (of eye), sloe (bot)
	psalmodier		tp chant
	psychagogique		psychagogical
aurait	pu		could have
	puant		stinking, obnoxious
	puanteur (nf)		stench
	publier		to publish
ca ma mise la	puce	a l'oreille	that set me thinking
	puce		flea (Zool), pet (Fig), honey (Fig)
	pucelle		maid, virgin
	puceron		a greenfly
	pudeur (nf)		modesty, sense of decency
	pudi-bonderie		prudishness
	pudique		modest, chaste
	puer		to stink of
	pueril(e) (adj)		childish, puerile
	puis		besides, then, next
Que	puis-je (pouvoir)	pour vous	What can I do for you?
	puiser	a/dans	to draw (water) (from)
	puisque		since

	puits (nm)		a well, hole, shaft, pit (mining)
	pull (nm) (abbrev)		pullover, sweater, jumper
	pulsation (nf)		heartbeat, pulse, beating
	pulsion		impulse, urge
	pulverin		pulveriser (mechanism that pulverises s.t to fine dust/spray)
se	pulveriser		to crumble (into powder)
	pupitre		control panel, consol, desk, lectern
	pur		clean, pure, straight, unsullied
	purger		to drain, purify, bleed, purge, serve
	pusillanime		pusillanimous, combative(?)
	putain!		whore, slag, slut, f*!!, hell! (Expl)
	putain!		f*!>, f*!>ing hell (Expl)
	pute (nf)		whore, hooker, slut, s*!t (expletive)
	putsch		coup d'etat, uprising, putsch
	pyroxyle		pyroxylin (explosive substance e.g gun-cotton)

Q

	qu'en-dira-t-on (nm)		gossip
	quadrature		linked to quadrate (having 4 equal sides and 4 right angles, square)
	quai		wharf, quay, pier, embankment (river), platform (rail)
	qualifier		to style, term, qualify
en sa	qualite	de	in his capacity as
	quant	a	as for
	quartier		district, neighbourhood, quarters, quarter
	quasi		almost
	quasiment		practically
	que	ce qui (with verb)	let the one, let someone
	que	oui!	yes indeed! You bet!
	que		how, that, than, which, what, so (comparative), may, whatever
	quel	que	whoever
	quel(le)	qu'ait	whatever
	quelconque		nondescript, second-rate, poor, plain-looking, dull, whatever, any
	queleur -euse (nmf)		collector
	quelque	peu	somewhat, some little
	quemander		to beg for
tomber en	quenouille		to die out
se	quereller		to quarrel (over, about)
	querelleur -euse		quarrelsome
	questionnement		questioning
	queue (nf)		stem, stalk, cue, queue, tail, rear
	qui	que ce soit	whoever it is, anybody, whatever it is
	qui	que ce fut	whoever it was, anybody
	qui-vive		on the alert, who goes there
etre a	quia		to be left speechless
	quiconque		anyone
	quidproquo (nm)		misunderstanding
	quille (nf)		ninepin (skittles), skittle, leg, keel (of ship)
	quincaillerie (nf)		hardware, ironmonger's
	quinte (nf)		a fifth (music), coughing fit
	quinzaine		(about) 15, fortnight
	quittance (nf)		receipt, bill

	quitte		free, rid of, quit, quits
se	quitter		to part
	quoi	qu'il en soit	anyway, be that as it may
a	quoi	bon	what's the point?
C'est en	quoi		What's it made of?
	quoique		though, although
	quotidien		daily (paper), everyday

R

	rabacher		to repeat oneself, repeat endlessly
	rabais (nm)		reduction (in price), rebate, discount
	rabaisser		to belittle s.o, lower, reduce (price), disparage
	rabat		flap (of table, pocket)
	rabatteur -euse		beater
se	rabattre		to fall back (on), to fold (table)
	rabattre		to lower, shut down, fold back
se	rabbatait		rebuffed
	rable		sturdy, stocky
	raboleux		rough, uneven
	raboter		to scrape, plane
	rabrouer		to snub
	rabuter		to ransom, redeem, buy back, re-purchase, atone
	raccommodage (nm)		darning, repair, mending, reconciliation
	raccommoder		to darn, reconcile (2 persons), mend, repair
	raccompagner		to walk/drive s.o home
	raccord		join, connecting passage, link shot (Cine)
	raccordement		linking, connecting
se	raccorder		to join up, connect, link
	raccourcir		to shorten, curtail, cut short, grow shorter
	raccrocher	le combine	to put the phone down
	raccrocher		to put (s.t) down, hang up, pull in
	race		breed, stock, ancestry, descent, race
	race(e)		distinguished, thoroughbred, pedigree
	racine		root
se	racler	la gorge	to clear one's throat
	racler		to scrape against/away, clean, scrape off
marcher au	radar		to be on auto-pilot/cruise control
navire en	rade		ship in harbour
	radeau (nm)		raft
	radeur		scraper
	radieux -euse		radiant, beaming, brilliant, dazzling (sky)
	radis (nm)		radish
	radotage		drivel
	radoter		to talk drivel, ramble on
	radoucir		to calm, smooth (s.o) down, soften
	rafales		gusts, squalls, bursts (fire)
	raffiner		to refine, be fastidious
se	rafraichir		to become/get cooler, refresh oneself
	ragaillardir		to cheer s.o up, make (s.o) feel brighter
	rageur		furious

		ragot		malicious gossip
		raide		stiff (limb), taut, tight, unbending (character)
		raideur		stiffness
		raidillon (nm)		a rise (short, steep)
	se	raidir		to tense up, tighten
		raies		stripes
		rail (nm)		track, rail
		railler		to mock, make fun of
		raillerie (nf)		jib, mocking remark
		railleur		mocking
		rainure		groove, channel, rut
		raisonnement		reasoning, argument
		rajeunir		to give a new look to, modernise, update, make (s.o) look/feel younger, become a lot younger
	se	rajeunir		to make o.s look/out to be younger,
		rajeunissant(e)		rejuvenating
		rajouter	a	to add to
		rale (nm)		groan, death-rattle
		ralentir		to slow down, slacken
		raler		to moan, groan
		rallier		to rally (troops), win over, rejoin
		rallumer		to rekindle, switch on again
		ramage		song (of birds)
		ramasser		to gather
		rame	de papier	ream of paper
		rame (nf)		oar (Naut), ream, stake (Agric), train
		rameau (nm)		branch, bough
	se	ramener		to arrive, 'roll up'
		ramener		to bring (s.o or s.t) back (again), pull back (blanket)
		ramer	pour faire qch	to struggle to do s.t
	se	ramifier		to branch out, ramify
		ramoner		to sweep, back up
		rampait		crawled
		rampant		crawling, creeping, slimy
		rampe (nf)		banister, hand-rail, ramp, incline
		ramper		to creep, crawl, grovel
		ramure (nf)		antlers
		ramures		branches, foliage
		rancir		to go rancid
		rancoeur		resentment, rancour

	ranconter		(qch) par le menu	to relate (s.t) in detail
	ranconter			tell
sans	rancune			no hard feelings!
	rancune (nf)			spite, grudge, rancour
au	rang			row, line
	rang			rank
	range(e) (adj)			well-behaved
	rangee (nf)			row, line, tier (of seats)
	rangement (nm)			tidying up, putting away, storage space
	ranger			to put away, tidy away, arrange, rank
se	ranger			to draw up, line up, settle down, side with
	ranimer			to revive
	rapace			predatory, a grasping person
se	rapatrier			to send home
	rapetisser			to reduce, make s.t smaller
	rapiecee			patched
les	rapines			plunder
	rappel			recall, reminder, curtain call (Theatre)
se	rappeler			to remember
	rappeler			to call back, recall, call again, call s.o, call
par	rapport		a qch	in comparison with (s.t)
en	rapport		avec	related to
	rapport (nm)			return, yield, report, connection, account, relation
se	rapporter			to agree, tally with, refer, relate to
	rapporter			to bring back; add, join, give an account of s.t, yield, report
	rapporteur			tell-tale, reporter, recorder
	rapproche(e)			close together
	rapprochement (nm)			connection, link
les	rapprochements			comparing (of ideas), bringing together
se	rapprocher			to draw near(er)
	rapprocher			to bring (2) together, compare (facts), put together
rien qu'a s'en	rapprocher		de	just to get close to it
	rare			thin, sparse, rare
se	rarefier			to become scarce
	rarete			shortage, scarcity, rarity
	rarissime (adj)			extremely rare
au	ras		de	at the level of
	ras(e)			close-cropped, bare
	rasades			brim-full glasses (pub)

	rasant(e) (adj)		oblique, grazing (cattle), low, boring
	rasee		shaved
	raser		to shave (off), bore s.o, raze (building), graze, brush, skim (over)
	rassasier	de	to stuff with (food), be replete with
se	rassasier		to eat one's fill of
	rassemble		gathered
se	rassembler		to assemble, gather
se	rasseoir		to sit (s.o) down again
se	rasserener		to calm down, clear (sky)
	rasserener		to reassure, calm
que l'on se	rassure		set your mind at rest
	rassurer	qn	to reassure s.o, put s.o's mind at rest
se	rassurer		to reassure oneself
	ratait		backfired, failed, miscarried
	ratatine		shrivelled (fruit), written off
	rate (nf)		spleen
	rateau (nf)		rake
	ratelier (nm)		false teeth (pl), hayrack (Agric)
	rater		to fail, flunk, miss
nous nous sommes	rates		we missed each other
	rattacher		to bind, be connected with, fasten, link up with
	rattraper		to catch up with, recapture, make up for (lost time)
	raturer		to cross out, correct
	rauque		husky, harsh
les	ravages		devastation
	ravaler		to clean, renovate, reface, swallow (pride)
	raviner		to gully, furrow
	ravir		to delight
	ravissement (nm)		rapture
	raviver		to revive (memory, fire), brighten up (colour)
	rayer		to scratch, score, rule, line, delete (name), strike out
	rayon		ray, shelf, radius, radiation, section, department (in store, biz), concern (interest)
ce n'est pas mon	rayon		that's not my concern, it's not (really) my line
	rayonnage (nm)		shelves
	rayonnant(e)		beaming
	rayonnement (nm)		influence, radiation
	rayonner		to radiate
	rayure (nf)		stripe, streak, groove

	raz-de-maree		tidal wave
	reaction (nf)		response, reaction
	reagir	a	to respond to, react to
	realisable (adj)		workable, feasible
	realisation		production (film, TV etc), achievement, carrying out, fulfilment
	reanimateur -trice (nmf)		member of an intensive care team (Med)
	rebelle (adj)	(a)	rebellious, stubborn, unruly, obstinate, resistant (Med)
se	rebequer		to rebel
	rebondir		to bounce, rebound, pick up, take a new turn
	rebord		edge, border, rim
	rebours		against the grain, the wrong way
	rebrousser		to retrace one's steps
	rebuffade		rebuff
	rebut		rubbish
	rebuter		to dishearten, discourage
	recalciter		to show strong objection to, oppose, recalcitrate
	recapitulons		let's recap
se	recaser		to redeploy, find another job for (s.o)
	receler		to harbour (criminal), conceal, receive (stolen goods)
	recepteur-diffuser		receiver-distributor/broadcaster
	recette (nf)		takings, receipts, formula, recipe, acceptance
	rechange		spare, alternative
se	rechauffer		to warm (o.s) up
	reche (adj)		rough
sans	recherche		carelessly, without thought
	recherche (nf)		research, search, pursuit, meticulousness
	rechercher		to seek after, search for, seek, inquire into (causes)
	rechigner		to balk at
	rechuter		to have a relapse, fall again
	recidiviste		habitual offender, backslider (Rel), recidivist
	recipient (nm)		container, receptacle
	recit		narrative, account, story, recital
	recitatif		recitative (a type of composition)
	reclamation		complaint, objection, claim
	reclamer		to protest, lay claim to, complain
	recoin		nook, recess
	recolte (nf)		the harvest

	recolter		to harvest, reap, collect, dig up, win
se	recommander	par	to be well-known for
	recommander		to advise
	recomposer		to reconstruct, reconstitute, reset (TV)
	reconduire	qn	to see (s.o) out, take s.o home (chez lui)
	reconforter	qn	to comfort, cheer (s.o) up
avoir de la	reconnaissance	pour qn	to be/feel grateful to s.o
	reconnaissance (nf)		acknowledgement, recognition, admission
	reconnaissant(e) (adj)		grateful, thankful
se	reconnaitre		to get one's bearings, reconnoitre, to recognise each other, know where one is, recognise oneself
	reconnaitre		recognise
	reconquete (nf)		regaining, winning back
	reconstitution		reforming, reconstruction, re-constituting of
(se)	reconvertir		to redevelop, adapt, convert
se	recoucher		to go back to bed
	recouler		to retreat, draw back
	recourir		to call on (s.o), to turn to (s.o), resort to
	recouverts	de	covered with
	recouvrer		to regain, collect, recover
	recouvrir		to cover (with), hide, conceal, re-cover (chair)
	recracher		to spit out
se	recrier		to protest
(se)	recroqueviller		to huddle up, shrivel up
	rectiligne		straight-lined, rectilineal -ar
	recu (nm)		receipt
	recueil (nm)		collection (poems), miscellany, anthology
	recueiller		to collect, gather, pick up, catch
se	recueillir		to meditate, collect one's thoughts
	recul	de	recession of (waters)
	recul		drop/decline, detachment, backing up, backing down, retreat, recoil (of cannon)
	recule (adj)		distant, remote
	reculer		to retreat, move back, postpone
	recuperer		to get back, claim, salvage, recover
se	recuser		to decline to give an opinion
	recuser		to challenge (a witness)
	redacteur -trice		author, writer, draftsman, editor (press)
	redaction (nf)		editing, essay, wording, drafting (of docs), writing, editorial staff
	reddition		surrender
etre	redevable	de	to be indebted to s.o
	redevance (nf)		dues, royalties, rental

		redevenu		became again
		rediger		to draw up, draft (docs), write, edit
	en	redingote		frock-coat, fitted coat
		redite (nf)		(useless) repetition
		redoubler		to increase (efforts, dose), redouble
		redoutable		formidable, commanding
		redoute (pp)		feared, dreaded
		redouter		to dread, fear
		redressement		recovery, straightening out/up, rectification
	se	redresser		to stand up (straight) again
		redresser		to set upright, erect
		redresseur		rectifier, redresser of wrongs
		reduire		to reduce, lower (price)
	se	reduire	en poussiere	to crumble to dust
		reduit (nm)		cubby-hole
		reel reelle		actual, real
		reexpedier		to re-direct, forward (post)
	se	refaire		to recuperate, recover one's health, change one's way, retrieve one's losses
	en	referer	a	to consult, refer to
	se	refermer		to close (door)
		refiler		to pass, palm s.t off (on s.o)
		reflechi (adj)		thoughtful, (well-)considered, deliberate, reflective
		reflechire	a sur	to ponder (on s.t), reflect (light), realise that
	a la	reflection		when you think about it (colloq), on second thoughts
		reflet		reflection, image
		reflexion		thought, reflection, remark
		refluer		to ebb, flow back, surge (crowd)
		reflux (nm)		surging away, decline, ebb tide
		refouler		to force/drive back, suppress (feelings), force back (tears)
		refouloir		repressor
		refractaire		insubordinate, fireproof
		refranchement		entrenchment (Mil)
		refroider		to cool (engine), chill (air, water), cool (off) enthusiasm, cool down
		refugie		refugee
		refugier		to take refuge
		refus		refusal
	se	refuser	a qn	to set one's face v s.t, shut one's eyes to s.t
		regagnent		regain
		regagner		to regain, recover, get back to (a place)

a son	regard		in his eyes
	regard (nm)		look, eyes, expression, eye, opinion, spyhole (Tech)
	regardant		fussy, particular
Tu ne m'as pas	regarde		You must be joking!
	regarder		to look at, look, watch, check, concern, overlook
a l'abri des	regards	indiscrets	away from prying eyes
	regenerer		to regenerate, reactivate
	regie (nf)		state control, local government control
	regime (nm)		diet, system, regime, regulations, scheme, object, (running) speed
	regir		to govern, rule
	regle		steady, well-ordered, ruled (paper)
	regler		to settle, pay for, pay, sort out, decide on, fix, arrange, organise
	reglisse (nm, nf)		liquorice
	regorger		to overflow, abound
	regressif -ive (adj)		regressive
	regret (nm)		regret
mille	regrets		I'm terribly sorry
	regretter	d'avoir fait	to regret doing
	regretter		to regret, miss
	rehabiliter		to reinstate, rehabilitate, renovate (building)
les	reins		loins, back
les	reins		the small of the back
	reintegrer		to reinstate (s.o), return to
	rejeter		to throw/fling s.t back, transfer, throw up, reject, turn down
se	rejoindre		to be simililar, be in agreement, meet (up)
	rejoindre		to meet up, catch up with, join, return to, get back to
	rejoton		shoot, sucker, kid (colloq)
	rejouissant		heartening, delightful, amusing
	relacher		to relax, loosen, release, set (s.o) free, let (s.t) go
passer le	relais	a qn	to hand over to s.o
	relais		intermediary, restaurant, relay
	relancer		to throw back, revive, restart
	relayer		to relieve, take over from, relay (TV signal)
	relent		stench, smell
	releve		summary, (gas/elec) meter reading (adj) raised, erect (head), exalted (position), noble

	relever		to raise again, lift up again, erect
	relief		relief (Geog), depth, raised pattern, landscape
	relier		to link, connect, join
	reliquaire (nm)		reliquary
	relire		to read over, proof-read, re-read
	reluquer		to stare at, eye, check out/over (oggle)
	remarque		comment, remark
faire	remarquer		to point out
	remarquer		to notice, remark, observe
	rembarquer		to go back on board (ship), reload, re-embark, resume
	rembarrer		to send packing (coll)
	remerciement		thanks
se	remettre		to resume (doing s.t)
	remettre		to replace, put (s.t) back again, remit, hand over, deliver (letter)
	remise		ransom, presentation, shed, ceremony, discount, remission
	remontant		dating back
se	remonter		to recover one's strength
	remonter		to ride up, rise, go back (in time), go up, climb up again, reassemble, re-stock (shop)
	remontrance		reprimand, remonstrance
	remontrer		to show, demonstrate
	remontrerer		to go over again, reassemble
	remords		self-reproach, remorse
	rempart		battlements, rampart
	rempart (nm)		rampart
	remplacement		replacement, temporary role, temp work
	remplir		to fill up, perform, fulfil, occupy
	remporter		to win (victory), carry off (prize), achieve (success), take (s.t) back/away
	remuant		stirring
	remuer		to move, stir up, shift, stir
	renaitre		to be born again, return, re-appear
	renard		fox
	rencherir		to make (s.t) more expensive, put (s.t) up
	renconger		to fall back
	rencontre (nf)		a meeting, encounter
	rencontrer		to meet, encounter
	rendez-vous		appointment, meeting
	rendormir		to put (s.o) back to sleep
	rendre	compte de qch	to account for s.t, yield, produce, give
	rendre		to give back, return, restore, yield, bring up, vomit, give up, render
se	rendre		to give in, give oneself up, surrender

se	rendre	compte de qch	to realise (something)
	rene		rein
	renfermait		contained
	renferme		withdrawn
se	renfermer		to become withdrawn
	renfermer		to contain, hold, lock (s.t) away
	renflement		bulge
	renfler		to puff out, bulge
	renfonce		recessed
	renforcer		to strengthen, reinforce, confirm (stmt), intensify (effort)
	rengaine (nf)		corny old song
se	rengorger		to strut, swagger
	renier		to renounce, disclaim, disown
se	renier		to go back on everything one has stood for, go back on one's opinions
	renifler		to sniff (out), smell
	renomme (adj)		renowned, famed, famous, reputation
	renommer		to re-appoint
	renoncer	a qch	to give up s.t, renounce
	renouveau (nm)		revival, regeneration, rebirth, springtime (Lit)
se	renouveler		to recur/be renewed
	renouveler		to renovate, renew
	renseignements		pieces of information, enquiries
	renseigner		to give information to/about
	rentes		income, pension, allowance, annuity
	rentrant		retractable, reflex (angle – Maths)
	rentre(e)		suppressed, held in, sunken
	rentree (nf)		return, home-coming, re-opening (school)
	rentrer	au logis	to get home
venait de	rentrer		had just returned
	rentrer	en soi-meme	to withdraw within oneself
	renversant		astounding, staggering
	renverser	la tete en arriere	to tilt/tip one's head backward
	renverser		to overturn, upset, spill, reverse, knock over, invert (image, proposition, chord), go back on one's decision
	renvoyer		to reflect (heat), send back, return, put off (meeting)
	repaire		den, haunt (of criminals), lair

se		repandre		to spill, spread, run over
		repandre		to pour out, spread, give out, spill, shed (blood)
		repandu		widespread, prevalent
		reparer		to rectify, redress, restore, mend
		repartie (nf)		rejoinder (come-back-at-you remark)
		repartir		to set out again, go back, retort, start again, leave again
		repassage (nm)		ironing, sharpening
		repecher		to fish out, allow to qualify (sport)
		repercuter		to reverberate, reflect, echo, pass on, send back
		repere		landmark, marker, reference point, criterion
		repere (nm)		mark, landmark, marker, reference point
		reperer		to locate, spot, pinpoint, mark
		repertir		to divide, distribute, share out, apportion
		repetition (nf)		rehearsal, coaching, repetition
		replier		to fold up, turn down, fold (s.t) back/over, evacuate (civilians) (Mil)
		replique (n)		retort, rejoinder, cue (to act), replica
	les	replis		bends, meanders, coils
		replonger		to dive again, sink back into, plunge again
se		repointer		to turn up again, clock in again
		repomper		to pump (up, out) again
		repondre	a	to answer, meet, fulfil, come up to, fit, deal with, respond to, reply to
		repondre	a cote	to miss the point
se		repondre		to match, call to each other, answer each other
		reportage		report, story (Journ)
se		reporter	a	to refer to
se		reposer	sur qn	to rely on s.o
		reposer		to put s.t down (again), rest, ask (s.t) again
se		reposer		to have a rest, rest
		repoussant(e) (adj)		revolting, hideous
		repousser		to push (s.t) back into, push back/away/to, repel, dismiss, turn down, decline, revolt, put (s.t) back, grow again, grow back
		reprendre	haleine	to get one's breath back
		reprendre		to resume, take back, recapture, recommence
		represailles		retaliations, reprisals
		representation		performance (theatre)
se		representer		to imagine, crop up again, arise again
		repression (nf)		suppression
		reprimer		to repress, suppress

	reprise (nf)		resumption, renewal, recapture, retaking, darn (sew), mend, repossession, return, part-exchange, taking back, takeover (Comm), acquisition (Comm), round (fight)
	reprocher		to reproach
	reprouve(e)		outcast
	reptation (nf)		crawling
	republique (nf)	des lettres	collected body of literary/learned men
	repugner	a	to disgust, be repugnant to, be averse (to)
	repugner	a faire qch	to be loathe to do s.t
	repus		replete
	requete (nf)		petition (Jur), request
les	rescape(e)(s)		survivor(s)
	reseau (nm)		network, system
	reserve		reservation, guard, reserve
	residu (nm)		remnant, waste, residue
se	resigner		to resign oneself
	resistance (nf)		strength, resistor, resistance
	resolu		determined (person), resolute
	resonner		to ring out, clash, resound, echo
se	resoudre	a faire	to make up one's mind to do s.t, resolve
	resoudre		to resolve, terminate, annul, clear up
	respectacle (adj)		respectful
	respiration		breathing, breath
	respirer		to breathe in, smell, radiate, exude, breathe
les	responsables		leader, manager, person in charge, those to blame
	ressaisir		to grip again, recapture
	ressasser		to brood over, dwell on
se	ressembler		to be alike
se	ressentir		to feel, experience (effects of)
	ressentir		to feel
	resserre		narrow, confined
	resserrer		to contract, narrow, tighten
	ressort (nm)		spring, elasticity, resilience, province, scope, competence (jur)
	ressortir		to come/go out again, be evident
les	ressources		means, resources
	restau		(abbrev of) restaurant
	restauration (nf)		restoration (Arch, Hist), catering, Restoration (period)
	restaurer		to feed, restore (Hist Art)
de	reste		spare, left over(s)
du	reste		besides
	reste (nm)		balance, remainder, rest

	rester		to remain, be left, stay
	restituer		to restore, reproduce, recreate
(se)	restreindre		to restrict, limit, cut down (expenses)
	resultat (nm)		outcome, result
(se)	resumer		to summarise, sum up
	retable		altar piece
	retaper		to patch up, do up, fix (car)
en	retard		late
de	retard		behind schedule
	retard (nm)		delay
	retardataire		latecomer
a	retardement (adj)		belated, delayed action
se	retenir		to stop oneself, control oneself
	retenir		to keep, detain (s.o), hold (back), contain, suppress, reserve, be left with, accept, uphold
	retentir	sur	to have an impact on
se	retentir		to feel
	retentir		to sound, ring, echo, reverberate
	retenu		retained (n); discreet (adj)
	retenue (nf)		restraint, detention, inhibition
	reticence		reluctance, non-disclosure, reticence
	retif		restive
	retirer		to take away, get, derive, withdraw
se	retirer		to withdraw, retire, subside, recede
	retomber		to fall down again
	retorquer		to retort
de	retour	a	back (at) (e.g home, our table)
	retour		turn, return, reversal (opinion, fortune), going back
en	retour	sur	back on(to)
	retourner	qn comme un gant	to make s.o change their mind completely
se	retourner		to turn (around)
se tenir en	retrait		to stand back
	retraite		shelter, refuge, withdrawal (Mil), retirement, retreat, lair
	retraite (nmf)		retired person
se	retrancher		to entrench oneself
	retrancher		to cut off (s.o from s.t)
se	retrecir		to contract, narrow, shrink (garment)
	retribuer		to pay (labour, service)

		retribution		payment
		retroactif -ive (adj)		back-dated, retrospective
		retrousser		to turn up, roll up (sleeves)
		retrouvailles (nfpl)		reunion, reconciliation
	se	retrouver		to meet up, meet again, find oneself, be found, follow (Fig)
		retrouver		to find, rediscover
		retroviseur		rear-view mirror, wing mirror
	se	reunir		to meet, gather together
		reunir		to unite, join/bring together
		reussir		to turn out (well, badly), succeed, thrive, make a success of s.t
		reussite		success
	en	revanche		on the other hand, in return
		revanche (nf)		revenge
		revasser		to (day-)dream
		revasserie		Day-dreaming
faire une		reve		to have a dream
a mon/son		reveil		on waking
		reveiller		to wake, wake (s.o) up, bring (s.o) round, revive, awaken, arouse
		reveilloner		to celebrate Christmas, see the New Year in
		revelateur -trice (adj)		revealing, telling
	se	reveler		to make one's name/mark, be revealed
		reveler		to reveal, disclose, make s.o known, give away, show
	les	revenants		ghosts
		revendeux -euse		second-hand dealer, stockist
		revendication		demand, claim
		revendiquer		to claim, demand, assert (rights)
		revendre		to sell off (parts etc), sell on, retail, sell s.t
	s'en	revenir	(de)	to come back to, return (from)
		revenir	de	to abandon/get over (illness)
		revenir		to come back, come again, return (to)
Puisse-t-il		revenir	sur sa decision	We can only hope that he goes back on his decision
		rever	a qch	to ponder over s.t, dream
	a	reverbere (nm)		street lamp, light
		reverence (nf)		bow, curtsey, reverence
		reverie (nf)		daydreaming, daydream, reverie
		reverra		will see again
		revers (nm)	de la medaille	the other side of the picture/medal/coin

	revers (nm)			the other side, back (of the hand), lapel (of coat), reverse (of fortune)
	revetement			facing (wall), coating, covering, lining
	revetir			to assume, take on, put on, hold, have (character)
prix de	revient			cost price
	revient			return
	revint		sur	went back on (word)
	revirement			change (sudden), reversal (feeling)
	reviser			to revise, review, redraw, overhaul
	revivre			to go over, live through again, come alive again, be reborn/revived
	revoila!			there he/it is again!
	revoir			to see (s.o/s.t) again, check through, review, go over
	revolte (nf)			rebellion, revolt
	revolter			to appal
se	revolter			to rebel, be appalled
	revue			magazine, journal, revue (spectacle)
	revulse(e)			contorted
	rewriter			redactor, reviser, rewriter
	rez-de-chaussee			ground floor, ground floor flat
	rhume			cold
suivre le	rhythme			to keep up (the pace)
	rhythmer			to put rhythm into, give rhythm to
	riant(e) (adjo			pleasant, happy
	ribambelle			flock, host, string of, whole series of
les	Ricains			Yanks (Slang)
	ricaner			to giggle, snigger
	ricaneur -euse (adj)			sniggering
	richard(e)			well-heeled person
	richesse (nf)			wealth, riches
	rictus (nm)			grin
	ride (adj)			wrinkled, lined
	ride (nf)			wrinkle, ripple
	rideau			curtain (of trees), screen
	ridicule			absurd, ridiculous, ludicrous, ridiculously low, pathetic
	rien		n'y fut	it was all to no avail
il n'en etait	rien			it wasn't anything
	rien		que	just
il n'en est	rien			nothing of the kind!
	rieur -euse (adj)			cheerful, laughing
	rigole			channel, drain, rivulet

	rigoler		to have fun, laugh
	rigoreux -euse (adj)		severe, harsh, strict, rigorous
Il ne t'en tiendra pas	rigueur		He won't hold it against you
a la	rigueur		at a pinch, if absolutely necessary..., may well be...
de	rigueur		obligatory, essential
	rigueur (nf)		harshness, severity, strictness
	rimer		rhyme
	rimmel (nm)		mascara
	ripailler		to feast
	riposte		Counter-attack, counter, return, retort
	riposter		to counter, answer back, retort
	rire	dans sa barbe	to laugh up one's sleeve
	rire		to laugh
	risee		derision, scorn
	risque (nm)		risk
	risquer		to venture, risk, chance
	rite (nm)		ritual, rite
	rivage (nm)		the bank of the river, shore
	rive (nf)		shore
	riviere	de diamants	diamond necklace
	rixe (nf)		brawl
	riziere (nf)		paddy-field, rice field
	robespierriste		follower of Robespierre (French revolutionary)
	robinet (nm)		tap, faucet
	rocailleux -euse		stony, rocky
	roche		boulder
	rocher, roc		rock
	roder		to prowl, wander the streets, lurk
	rodomontades		rantings
	rogatoire (adj)		letters (Jur), rogatory
	rogner		to trim, dip, whittle away (Econ)
	roi		king, tycoon, master of
	romain(es)		Roman
	roman	d'anticipation	science-fiction novel
	romancier -ere		novelist
	romanesque		worthy of a novel, romantic
se	rompre		to snap/break in/break off
	rompre		to break up, snap, break, end, disrupt, interrupt
	rompu(e)		broken

		ronces		brambles
n'avoir plus un		rond		to be broke
		rond(nm)		circle, slice, round
		rondement		bluntly, briskly
		rondouillard		tubby, podgy
		ronfler		to snore, roar, hum, purr (engine)
		ronge(e)	de	corroded with
	se	ronger	les ongles	to bite one's nails
		ronger		to nibble, gnaw
		ronronnement		purring
		roquer		to castle (chess)
		rosace (nf)		rosette, rose window
		rose(e)		pale pink, rosy
		roseau(x)		reed (Bot)
		rosee		dew
		rosier		rose-bush
		rossignol		nightingale
		rotie (nf)		piece of toast
		rotin		rattan (furniture)
	se	rotir		to scorch, roast (get sunburnt)
		rotisseur -euse		steakhouse owner
		roue (nf)		wheel
		roue(e) (adj)		cunning, sly
		rouer		to beat
		rouerie (nf)		cunning, trickery
		rouet		a spinning wheel
		rougeaud		ruddy, ruddy-faced, ruddy-cheeked
		rougi		reddened, blushed
		rougir	de qch	to be ashamed of s.t
		rouille (nf)		rust
		rouleau		roll (of notes)
		roulement (nm)	a billes	ballbearing
	se	rouler	par terre	to fall about laughing
	se	rouler		to turn over and over, roll (up)
		rouler		to roll (along, up, out, s.t into a ball), go (vehicular), drive, rumble (thunder)
		roumains		Romanians
		rouspeter		to grumble (at/about)
		roussir		to turn/go brown or red, singe
		routinier -ere (adj)		stuck in a rut, set in one's ways, routine
		routinier -ere (nmf)		creature of habit
	se	rouvrir		to open (again), open up (again)

		rouvrir	to turn (s.t) back on, re-open, resume
		roux	auburn, red-head, russet, ginger, red
		royal	regal, lofty, fit for a king, majestic, royal
		ruban	ribbon, band
		rubicard (nm)	almost perfect
		rubiconde	ruddy, florid, flushed
		rubrique	section, category, rubric (Rel)
		ruche	(bee)hive
		rude	rough, stiff, hard, harsh, severe (blow), arduous (task), brusque
		ruelle (nf)	back street, alleyway
	se	ruer	to rush (for/towards/down)
		ruer	to kick
		rugissement	roar, howl
		rugosite	ruggedness, roughness
		rugueux -euse (adj)	rough, rugged, bumpy
		ruisseau	brook, (small) stream, flood (of tears)
		ruisselent	trickle down
		ruisseler	to stream, drip, run, flow
		rumeur	rumour
		rupture	break-up, breakdown, fracture, breaking off, rupture
	la	ruse	cunning, trick, ruse
		ruse	crafty, sly, cunning
		ruser	to use cunning, trickery
		rushes (nmpl)	rushes (Cine), final burst, attack (sport)
		russe	Russian
		rutiler	to gleam
		rythmer	to put rhythm into, give rhythm to

S

	sabir		mumbo-jumbo
	sable		sand
	sablier	d'or	golden hourglass
	saborder		to scuttle, scupper, sink
	sabot		clog, boot, shoe
	saboter		to sabotage
	sac	a papier	nitwit (Pej)
	sac		bag, sack, sackful
	saccade (adj)		jerky
	saccade (nf)		jerk, jolt
par	saccades		by fits and starts
	sachant	que	knowing that
Pas que je	sache (savoir)		Not that I know
	sacre(e)		sacred, holy; damn! Blasted..., hell of a...
	sacrifier	a	to conform to (custom), give away, slash, sacrifice, sell (s.t) off cheap
	sacristie (nf)		vestry, sacristry (Rel)
	sacro-saint		sacrosanct
	sage		wise, sensible, sober, restrained, moderate, reasonable
	saignant		rare (meat) (Cul), sensationalism (Press)
	saignant(e) (adj)		raw, bleeding, savage, sensationalist
	saigner		to bleed
	saillant(e) (adj)		prominent, bulging, salient
	saillie		projection (jut), flash of wit
	sain		sound, sane, healthy, wholesome
Je n'en	sais (savoir)	rien	I don't know
	saisir		to grip, grab, seize, snatch (s.t) up, jump at (Fig), distrain (Jur)
Tu	sait (savoir)	bien expliquer	You are good at explaining things
Il ne	sait (savoir)	rien de moi	He doesn't know anything about me
	salamalec(s)		unctuousness (i.e insincere emotion)
	salaud!		bas!!xrd (Expl); rotten (adj)
	sale		dirty, filthy, nasty, rotten
	sale(e)		salty
	salement		seriously, badly, messy
	salete		dirtiness, junk food, dirt
	salle (nf)		room, chamber, ward, audience, auditorium
	salon		lounge, living room, salon, exhibition, show, fair
	saloperie		muck, gunge, junk food, junk, damn (coll)

	saltimbanque		entertainer, street acrobat
	saltpetre		saltpetre (potassium nitrate)
	saluer		to greet, welcome, say goodbye to
	salut		hello, greeting, salvation, salute
	salutaire		wholesome, beneficial
	salvateur -trice (adj)		saving
	sanctionner		to punish, give official recognition to, sanction
bon	sang		for g*d's sake (Pej)
	sang (nm)		blood, lineage, race, kinship
	sang-froid (nm)		coolness, composure, freedom from agitation
	sanglante		bloody
	sangle	dans	sqeezed into
	sangliers		wild boars
	sangloter		to sob
	sans-culotte		sansculotte (Hist), a ragged fellow
	sans-facon		bluntness, informality, off-hand manner
	sans-gene		inconsiderate(ness)
	sans-logis		homeless
	saoul(e), soul(e)		drunk
	sapiniere		fir plantation
	sapins		trees
	saquer (slang)		to mark (s.o) down
	sarabande		racket, bedlam
	sarcelle		teal (bird)
	sarclage (nm)		hoeing
	sarigue		opossum
	sarment		vine shoot
	sas		sieve, airlock, lock
	satellite		satellite, bevel pinion
	satisfaire		to fulfil, satisfy
	sauf		except, save that, but
	saugrenu		absurd, preposterous
	saule		willow
	sauliller		skip
	saupoudrer	de	to sprinkle (with), give (s.t) sparingly
Il ne	saurait (se savoir)	en etre question	It's completely out of the question
ca se	saurait (se savoir)		People would know about that
au sens	saussurien		the known sense

faire un	saut	a (location)	to make a flying visit to (place)
faire le grand	saut		to kill oneself
	saut		leap, jump, vault, waterfall
	saut-de-loup		Ha-ha (Arch) (fence or wall, usually on one side which keeps a clear view of the landscape beyond the other side)
	saute-risseau(x) (nm)		errand-boy
	sauter	aux yeux	to be obvious
	sauter		to jump, leap, explode, blast (rock)
	sautereaux		grasshoppers
	sautiller		to hop, skip along, jump up and down
	sautoir (nm)		long necklace/chain, baby-bouncer
	sauvage		wild (plant, animal, person), unsociable, shy, unauthorised (hist: Indian-savage)
	sauvegarder		to back s.t up, safeguard
	sauver		to save, salvage, rescue
	sauveteur		rescuer
	sauveur (nm)		saviour (Rel)
On la	savait (savoir)	riche	She was known to be rich
	savamment		learnedly, skilfully, eruditely
	savant		learned, clever, scientist, scholarly, erudite, complicated
	savoir		to know
se	savoir		to get to know (about)
va	savoir		who knows?!
	savoir	ecouter	to be a good listener
allez	savoir		who knows?!
	savoir (nm)		knowledge, learning
	savon		soap
les	saxifrages		saxifrages (rock plants)
	saynete (nf)		playlet
les	sbires		henchmen, bent coppers (colloq)
	scabieuses		scabby, rough
	scander		to scan, chant, declaim, accentuate
	sceau		mark (of genius), seal, stamp
	scelerat(e)		wicked, scoundrel
	sceleratesse		wicked deed, wickedness
	sceller		to seal, ratify, confirm
	scenario		screenplay, script
	scenariste		scriptwriter
mettre en	scene		to stage/direct (a play)
	scene (nf)		stage, scene

	schema (nm)		diagram, outline, pattern
	scie (nf)		saw, bore (person), hit tune
	sciemment		knowingly
	scier		to saw (wood/stone), amaze s.o
	scier		to saw, stun, numb
les	scievies		sawmills
	scintillaient		twinkled
	scintillement		sparkling, twinkling
	sclerosant(e) (adj)		mind-numbing
	scolaire (adj)		educational, academic, school
	scorie		dross, slag (Geol), scoria
	scotcher		to sellotape
	scrupule		(conscientious) doubt, scruple
	scruter		to scan, search, scrutinise
	scuire	(de bois)	sawdust
	séance	tenante	immediately
	séance (nf)		meeting, session, show, performance (cinema)
	seau		bucket(ful), pail
	sec		dry, sharp, curt, incisive
	seche		dried, cigarette/fag, dry
	sechement		curtly, tartly
	secher		to dry up, dry
	secher	sur pied	to wilt
	seconder		to back s.o up, forward s.o's plans, second
	secouer		to shake (s.o up), rouse, shake off
	secouer	le joug	shake off the yoke
	secourir		to help, aid
	secousse		shock, jolt, shake
	secreter		to foster, hatch, secrete, exude
	seculaire		age-old
	seducteur		seducer
	seduction (nf)		charm, enticement, seductiveness
	seduire		to captivate, charm, fascinate, seduce, attract s.o
	seduisant		attractive, appealing
bout de	sein		nipple (Anat)
au	sein	de	within
	sein		breast/bosom
	sejour (nm)		stay, abode
	sejourner		to stay, remain, lay (fluid)
mines de	sel	gemme	Rock-salt mines
	selenite		lunar
	selle (nf)		a saddle

ses	sembables			his fellows, fellow-men
	semblable			similar, alike, fellow, counterpart
	semblant		de	pretense of, semblance of
	semee		de	strewn with, scattered
les	semelles			soles (shoe)
	semoule (nf)			semolina
	sempiternel -elle			endless, perpetual
	senatororie (nf)			senatorial election
un journal a	sensation			tabloid newspaper
	sensation			feeling, sensation
	sense			sensible (person)
	sensement			sensibly
	sensibilite			sensitivity, sensiblity
	sensible			sensitive, sentient, tangible
	sensiblerie (nf)			sentimentality
	sensualite			sensuality
	sente (nm)			a path
	sentier (nm)			beaten track, trail, (foot)path
	sentiment			sensation, consciousness, feeling
	sentinelle (nf)			sentry (Mil.)
	sentir			to feel, sense, appreciate, smell, smack of, be conscious of
se	sentir			to feel
	seoir (il sied)			to suit
	sequelle (nf)			consequence, after-effect, repercussion
	sequestre (nm)			sequestration (Jur)
	serac			serac (see English dictionary)
ce	serait			it would be
	serenite (nf)			calmness, equanimity, severity
	sergent-chef			staff sergeant, flight sergeant
	serie			set, series
	serier			to classify
	serin			canary
	seriner		qch a qn	to drum s.t into s.o
	seriner		qch a qn	to drum s.t into s.o
	serment (nm)			oath
	serpent		a sonnette	rattlesnake
	serpilliere (nf)			floorcloth

		serre(e)		tight, close, hard, strict, thick, crammed
	se	serrer		to crowd, sit/stand close together, tighten up
		serrer		to press, squeeze, tighten, clench, keep close to, grip
		serrure (nf)		lock
		sert	de	serves as
		serveur -euse		waiter, dealer, server
		serviable		helpful
	se	servir	de qch	to help oneself, use s.t, make use of s.t
		servir		to be useful
		serviteur		servant
		servitude		constraint
		sesame (nm)		sesame
	au	seuil	de	at the beginning on, on the threshold of
		seuil (nm)		threshhold, doorstep, doorway, bank (Geol)
		seul(e)		alone, on one's own, single-handedly, lonely, by oneself, only
		seve		sap (plant)
		severe		strict, harsh, severe
		sevir	contre qn	to deal ruthlessly with s.o, rage (war, epidemic)
		sezigue		her/him (personal pronoun)
		sideen, sideene (nmf)		AIDS sufferer
		sideral(aux) (adj)		sidereal (measured by the apparent motion of the stars)
	il s'en	sied (from seoir)		it is appropriate, it is right and proper
		siege (nf)		seat, centre (of learning), chair
		sieger		to be seated
		sifflant		whistling, wheezing
		siffler		to whistle, wheeze, hiss, boo
	canard	siffleur		widgeon (Zool)
		sigle		acronym
		signaler		to point out, report s.t, indicate
		signalisation(s)		signalling, sign(s)
		signe		indication, sign, symbol, mark, gesture, token (of friendship)
	se	signer		to cross oneself (genuflex)
		signer		to sign (document)
		signet (nm)		bookmark
		signification (nf)		meaning, importance, notification (Jur)

	signifier	qch a qn	to notify s.o of s.t
	signifier		to mean
	silhouette		figure, shape, outline, silhouette
	sillage (nm)		wake, vapour, trail, slipstream
	sillonne		furrowed, crossed, criss-crossed
	sillonner		to furrow, cut across, cross
	sillons		furrows
	simagree		play-acting
	simarre		scarf, woman's long dress
	similitude		similarity
	simple		ordinary, common, plain, simple, easy
	simulacre		pretence, show, semblance
	simuler		to feign, sham
	sincerite (nf)		honesty, sincerity, genuineness
	singe		ugly person, horror, monkey/ape
	singeries		antics, clowning
	singularite		peculiarity, singularity
	singulier(e) (adj)		remarkable, odd, curious, singular, peculiar
	sinon		otherwise, except, else, apart from, not to say
	sinuosite		winding/meandering
un triste	sire		a nasty bit of work (coll)
	sire		lord
	siroter		to sip
	sitot	que	as soon as, so soon
	situer		to locate, place, situate
	slave		Slav, Slavonic
	sobriete		moderation, restraint, temperance, sobriety
	societaire (nf)		member
	socle		plinth, base, stand, pedestal, platform (Geol)
	soi		self, oneself, himself, herself
	soi-disant		so-called, self-styled
en	soie		in silk
il va de	soie		it's obvious
	soif		thirst
	soigner		to heal, take care over, treat, look after
	soin		care
	soit	qu'il	whether it's, be it that
	soit		suppose, for instance, whether
	soixantaine		about 60
	sol		ground, earth, soil, floor
	solaire		sun, solar system, solar energy, sun-cream
	solder		to settle the balance of, sell off, clear
	solderie (nf)		discount shop

	soleil			sun, sunlight
	solennel -elle			official, formal, solemn
	solennite (nf)			solemnity
	solidaire			jointly, interdependent, united (kiv J&S guarantee)
	solidarite			solidarity, common ground, common cause
	sollicitation (nf)			entreaty, appeal
	solliciter			to request, beg for, appeal to s.o
	solliciteur -euse (nmf)			supplicant
	sollicitude			concern, solicitude
	sols			French currency (antiq)
	somatiser			to have a psychosomatic reaction to
	sombre			dark, gloomy, dull (sky), dim (light), dismal (thoughts)
	sombrer			to sink (ship), founder (empire), sink into
en	somme			in short, on the whole
	sommeil			sleep/slumber
	sommer		qn	to command s.o (to do s.t), summons s.o
	sommet			top, crest
	somnambulisme			sleep-walking
	somnifaire			sleeping pill
	somnolence (nf)			drowsiness, lethargy
	somnoler			to be sleepy, be lethargic, drowse
	son			sound; his, her
	sonde (nf)			probe, drill (mining), sounding line, plummet
	sonder			to probe, sound (s.o) out, examine, test, investigate
n'y eut	songe			hadn't thought
n'y	songeait			didn't think about it
	songer			imagine, think, dream, muse
	songeur -euse			pensive
	sonnailler			sounding, signalling
	sonne(e) (adj)			groggy, shattered
	sonner		a toute volee	to set all the bells ringing
	sonner			to ring out, strike (clock), ring for, make (s.o) dizzy, knock (s.o) out, sound, ring
	sonnerie (nf)			chimes, ringing, bells
les	sonnettes			small bells, (house) bells
	sonore (adj)			resonant, resounding, acoustic(al), high sounding
	sonorite			tone, sound, quality
	sophisme			sophism (clever but unsound reasoning, fallacious reasoning)

	sorcier (nm)			wizard, sorcerer
	sorcilleuses			eyebrows
	sort (nm)			condition in life, lot, destiny, fate, chance, fortune
de	sorte	a		so as to, in order to
faire en	sorte	que		to make sure...
	sorte (nf)	(de)		manner, way; sort of, kind of
	sortie (nf)			outburst, tirade, exit, departure
	sortileges			spells
	sot (nm)			a fool, idiot
	sot(te)			silly/stupid/foolish
	sottise (nf)			foolish remark/act, stupidity
	souche			vine stock, founder (family), stump (tree)
	souchet			shoveler (Zool)
	souci (nm)			worry, problem, care, thought
se	soucier	de		to be concerned/worry about s.o or s.t
	soucieux -euse (adj)			worried
	soucoupe			saucer
	soudain			suddenly
	soudee	par la rouille		welded by rust
	souder			to bind together, weld, solder
	souffle			breath, explosion
etre a bout de	souffle			to be out of breath
	souffle(e) (adj)			blown (out), flabbergasted, souffleed
	souffler			to blow (out), whisper, suggest, huff, blast, take a breather, flabbergast, pinch (job) puff
	souffler (nm)			prompter (Theatre), glass-blower
	soufflet			bellows, slap in the face
	souffleter			to slap in the face
	souffleur			Bottle-nosed dolphin (Zool)
	souffleur -euse			prompter (Theatre), blower
	souffrance (nf)			suffering
	Souffre-douleur (nm)			punchbag
	souffrir			to endure, undergo, suffer, feel pain, be damaged (by s.t), bear (pain, loss, fatigue)
	soufre			sulphur

	souhaiter		to wish (for)
	souilers		shoes
	souiller		to dirty, soil, pollute, sully
tout son	soul		as much as one wants
	soul(e) (adj)		drunk
	soulager		to relieve, soothe, alleviate (pain, grief)
se	souler		to intoxicate, get s.o drunk
	soulerie		bender, drinking spree
	soulever		to raise, lift up, rouse, stir up
les	souliers		shoes
	soupcon		suspicion/inkling/hint
	soupconner		to suspect
	soupir		to sigh
	soupirail (nm)		cellar window
	soupirant		suitor
	soupirer		to sigh, pine for
	souplesse		suppleness, flexibility, versatility
	source (nf)		spring, source
	sourcil		eyebrow
	sourciller		to frown, 'raise an eyebrow', 'bat an eyelid'
	sourd(e)		deaf, dull, muffled, hollow (voice), secret (desire), veiled (hostility)
	sourdement		in an underhand manner, dully
	sourdre	de	to seep out, rise (from), well up (from)
	sourire		to smile, smile on, appeal to
	sournois(e) (adj)		sly, underhand, insidious
	sous		under
	sous-entendre		to imply
	sous-entendu		innuendo
	sous-jacent(e)		underlying, subjacent
	sous-louer		to sub-let, sub-lease
les	sous-oeuvres		foundations
	sous-seing (nm)		private agreement, private contract
	sous-sol		basement, sub-soil (geol)
	soustraction		removal
	soustraire	a	to subtract, take away from, shield (s.o) from
se	soustraire	a	to escape from, hide from, shy away from, avoid
se	soutenir		to last, continue, stand
	soutenir		to support, keep, defend (theory), uphold, sustain

	soutenu		firm, bold (colour), steady, sustained
	souterrain		underground/tunnel/subway
	soutien		support
	soutien-gorge		bra
	soutirer		to decant (wine), extract (money from s.o), squeeze s.t out of
	souverain		supreme (happiness), sovereign (power/prince)
	soyeux -euse		silky
	spartiale		Spartan
	spatule	blanc	common/Eurasian spoonbill
	specialise		specialised
	spectacle (nm)		show, entertainment, play, show biz, sight, scene
	spirituel -elle (adj)		witty, spiritual
	spontane(e)		spontaneous
	sportif -ive		lively, heated, sporty, athletic
	squelette		skeleton
	stade		stadium, stage
	stagiaire (nm)		trainee
	stagner		stagnate
	stationner		to park, station (Mil)
	statufier		to erect a statue to, transfix
	statut (nm)		status, regulation, statute
	steno		short-hand typist, stenographer, short-hand
	stereotype (nm)		cliché, stereotype
	sterile (adj)		unproductive, sterile, fruitless, barren, childless
	stipendier		to hire
faire du	stop		to hitch(hike)
	stopper		to halt, stop, mend
	strabisme (nm)		squint, strabismus
	strict(e) (adj)		plain (truth), bare (essential), exact, strict (person)
	strictement		absolutely, strictly
	strier		to make grooves in, streak (with)
	strophe (nf)		stanza
	stupefaction		amazement
	stupefait(e) (adj)		dumbfounded, astounded
	stupide		stunned (lit), stupid, foolish, silly
dans le	style	du Palais	in legal parlance
	style		style, kind, speech form (ling)
	stylo (nm)		pen
au	su	de qn	to s.o's knowledge
Ca c'est	su (from se savoir)	toute de suite	Word immediately got round

	suave		sweet, smooth, mellifluous, exquisite, suave
	suavite		sweetness
	subalterne		junior, subordinate
	subir		to undergo (trial), submit to
	subit(e)		sudden, unexpected
	subitement		suddenly
	subjuguer		to subdue, captivate, subjugate, enthral
	sublimer		to sublimate
	submerger		to flood, overwhelm, submerge
	subodorer		to detect, suss
	subrepticement		surreptitiously
	subtil		shrewd, subtle
	subtilite		subtlety, fineness
	suc		sap, essence, juice
	succession (nf)		stream, succession, series, inheritance, estate (Jur)
	succion (nf)		suction, biting
	succomber	(a)	to die, give way, yield, succumb (to)
	sucoter		to suck
	sucrer		to sweeten, put sugar in s.t, cancel (permission)
	sue		sweat
	sueur		sweat, perspiration
	suffire		to be enough, suffice
	suffisamment		enough, adequately
	suffisance (nf)		arrogance, self-importance
	sufflet		whistle, hiss, wheezing
	suffoquer		to choke, suffocate
	suffrage (nm)		vote
	suggerer		to suggest
Je n'y	suis	pas	I don't get it
il s'en	suit		it follows
comme	suit		as follows
par	suite	de	on account of, due to
a la	suite	de qn	as a result of, behind s.o, one after the other
la	suite		continuation, consequence, result, suite (mus), sequence, succession (of events), retinue
a la	suite	de	after
par la	suite		later, afterwards
par	suite		consequently
	suivant	le temps	depending on the weather

	suivi(e)		sustained, coherent (reasoning), connected (speech) consistent, popular
	suivre		to follow, accompany, come after, run alongside, hug, follow the progress of, keep pace with
se	suivre		to be in order, be consecutive, happen one after the other, be coherent
vif du	sujet		to the point
	sujet		ground, reason, cause, subject, theme, topic
	sulfureux -euse		fiendish (Fig), sulphurous
	superbement		haughtily, superbly
	superbenefice (nm)		surplus profit
	supercherie		deception, fake, hoax
	superflu		vain, unnecessary, useless, superfluous
	superieure		upper, top, higher, bigger, superior
	superposer		to stack (up), superimpose
	suppleer		to deputise for (s.o), take the place of
le dernier	supplice		capital punishment
	supplice		torture, torment, agony, severe punishment
	supplier		to beseech, implore, entreat
	supporter		to bear, prop, hold up, support (theory), endure, withstand (pain, heat)
	supposer		to postulate, assume, suppose, presuppose
un dangereux	suppot	de la subversion/ reaction	a dangerous subversive/reactionary
	supprimer		to suppress, remove (difficulty), omit, delete (word), abolish (law/tax)
	supputer		to calculate, work out
voir	supra		(see) above
	sur		about, concerning, on, towards, over, above
	sur-le-champ		right away
	sur(e)		safe, secure, sure
	sur(e) (adj)		(slightly) sour
	suranne		outdated
	surbaisser		to lower
	surcharger	de	to overload (with)
de	surcroit		moreover
	surcroit (nm)		increase
	surdoue		gifted
	sureau		elder (tree)
	surete		safety, security, soundness
	surexcitation		Over-excitement
	surface		area, surface
	surfaire		to exaggerate, overrate
	surgir		to rise, come into view, arise, crop up (difficulties)
en	surimpression	a	superimposed on
	surlendemain (nm)		2 days later

	surmonter		to overcome, be surmounted with
	surmultiplication		overdrive
vitesse	surmultiplie(e)		overdrive
faire du	surplace		to be stuck, be getting nowhere
	surplace (nm)		stuck (traffic)
	surplomber		to overhang, jut out over
au	surplus		in addition, what's more, besides
	surprenant		astonishing, surprising
	surprendre		to overhear, intercept, surprise
	sursaut (nm)		sudden burst, flash
	sursauter		to give a jump, start(fear)
	sursis (nm)		deferment of military service, respite
	surtout		mostly
	surveillant(e)		supervisor, invigilator, store detective
se	surveiller		to watch oneself/yourself
	surveiller		monitor
	survenir		to occur, happen
	survie (nf)		survival, afterlife, survivorship (Jur)
	survoler		to do a quick review of, skim through, fly over
	sus		in addition to
	susciter		to give rise to (difficulties), arouse (hostility), cause (astonishment)
	susdit(e)		aforesaid
	suspect		doubtful, suspicious
se	suspendre	a par	to hang from...by
	suspendre		to defer, postpone, suspend
	susurrer		to murmur, whisper
	symbiose		symbiosis
	symbolique (adj)		symbolic, notional, token
	symbolique (nf)		symbolism
	symetrie		symmetry
	sympa		nice
	sympathique		friendly
	synchronisme		synchronism (concurrence of events in time)
	syndicat		trade union, union, association, syndicate
	synthese		summary, synthesis
	systeme		scheme, way, dodge, system

T

	tabac	blond	Virginia tobacco
	tabatiere (nf)		snuff-box
	tableau		board, picture, painting
	tablette (nf)		bar, shelf, stick, tablet (Med)
les	tablettes (nfpl)		annals, agenda, diary
	tablier		apron, pinnafore, overall
	tabou (nm)		taboo (Rel), sacred, untouchable
	tabouret		footstool, stool
repondre du	tac	au tac	to snap back, reply tit-for-tat
	tache		stain, spot, flaw, bruise
	tache		task, job
	tacher		to stain, spot, sully (reputation)
	tacher		to endeavour, try
	tadorne		shelduck (Zool)
	taie (nf)		corneal opacity, (pillow) case
	taiga (nf)		taiga (swampy coniferous forest around Siberia)
	taille		waist, size, shape, waistline
	tailler	les plumes	trim the feathers
	tailler		to cut, prune, trim
	taillis		copse, coppice
	taire		to hush up, keep (s.t) to o.s
se	taire	(Ils se turent)	to hold one's tongue, be silent (They stopped talking)
	tais-toi		be quiet, don't talk to me about that
	talentueux -euse		talented, gifted
	talloner		to follow closely/spur on
	talon		heel
	talus		slope, embankment ankle-bone
	tambour (nm)		drum, barrel, cylinder drummer
	tambourinement		drumming, hammering (door)
	tamis (nm)		sieve
	tampon		plug, stopper, waste plug (bath), swab, rubber stamp, postmark, (inking) pad
	tan-sad		side-car (motorbike)
	tandit	que	while, whereas
	tangage		pitching (Naut.)
	tangible (adj)		tangible
	tanner		to make s.t leathery, tan

	tant	et si bien que	so much so that
	tant	mieux	so much the better
	tant	qu'a moi	as for me
en	tant	que chanteur de blues	as a blues singer
en	tant	que tel	as such
	tant	que tu y est	while you're at it
	tant	s'en faut	not by a long shot
	tant		so much, so many, as much, as well (as)
a	tant	l'heure	so much time
	tant	pis pour eux	too bad for them
	tant	que ca?	That many? That much?
	tant	de	so many, so much
	tant	et plus	a great deal, a great many
	tant	que	as long as (time)
	tantot	...tantot	now this....now that
	tantot		sometimes
	tapage		din, racket, fuss, hype, scandal
	tape (nf)		slap, pat
	taper	sur qn	to bad-mouth s.o, slag s.o off (coll)
	taper		to hit, type
se	tapir		to hide, crouch
	tapis		cloth/covering/cover
	tapissent	les murailles	line the walls
	tapisser		to line, spin (web)
	tapisserie (nf)		tapestry
	tapoter		to tap, pat
	taquiner		to tease, bother
	taraud (nm)		screw-tap
	tarauder		to tap, screw
sur le	tard		late in life
	tarder		to be a long time coming
	tardivement		rather belatedly, late
se	targer	de qn	to pride oneself on s.t
	tarir		to dry up (spring, tears, jokes)
	tartine (nf)		slice of bread and butter
	tas		heap, pile
	tatant		touching, testing
	tater		to feel, touch, try, test

	tatonnement	(par)	by trial and error
	tatonner		to grope (in dark)/proceed cautiously
a	tatons		grope, feel
	taupe		mole
	taureau (nm)		bull
	taxer	(de)	to accuse (of), to surcharge (letter), tax, impose tax on (s.o or s.t)
	teindre		to tint, stain, dye
avoir le	teint	pale	to look pale
	teinte		tint, shade, colour
	teinte		stained, dyed
	teinter		to tint, stain, dye
	tel	est cet	this is the case
	tel	que	as, as it is
	tel	quel	as it is
un(e)	tel(le)		so-and-so
	telescopage (nm)		collision, overlap
	tellement		to such a degree, so (much/little)
	temeraire		rash, reckless
	temerite		rashness, reckless action, temerity
	temoignage		evidence, testimony, statement
	temoigner		to testify/give evidence/show
	temoin		witness
	tempe (nf)		temple (anat)
	temperament		disposition, constitution, temperament
	temperer		to moderate, temper
	tempestif -ive (adj)		untimely, misplaced
	tempete		storm, hurricane
les	tempins		the times
	tenace		tenacious, obstinate, stubborn
	tenailler		to gnaw (away), rack with (guilt), eat away
	tendance		inclination, propensity, tendency
se	tendre		to become taut/strained
	tendre		to stretch, bend, hold out, keep (promise)
	tendre (adj)		tender, soft, delicate, fond, affectionate, loving, tend, lead
	tendresse		affection, tenderness, affectionate gesture
	tendu		taut
les	tenebres		darkness, gloom

	tenebreux -euse		dark, obscure
	tenez		there you are (take it)
s'en	tenir	a	to keep to, stick to
	tenir	le coup	to make it, to hold on, to last out, cope
se	tenir	les cotes	to split one's sides with laughter
se	tenir	les coudes	to stick together
se	tenir	pour	to consider oneself to be
en	tenir	pour qn	to have a crush on s.o
se	tenir		to hold, hold on, fit/hold together, behave, be held
	tenir		to keep, have, hold
	tentateur -trice (adj)		tempting
	tentateur -trice (nmf)		tempter/temptress
	tentative (nf)		an attempt, endeavour, bid
	tenter		to attempt, try, tempt
	tenu (nf)		bearing, behaviour, sitting, clothes
	tenue		keeping, managing, running (shop), sitting
	tergivisation (nf)		equivocation
	terme (nm)		end, term
	terne (adj)		dull, lifeless, dingy, lacklustre
	ternir		to tarnish, dull
	terrain		ground, soil, terrain, land
	terraquer		to ground up
prix en	terrasse		price for outside table (service)
	terrasse (nf)		flat roof, large balcony, roof garden
	terrasser		to lay (s.t) low/crush/overthrow
	terrau(x)		compost
par	terre		on the ground, on the floor
	terre-neuve		newfoundland dog
	terre-plein (nm)		terrace/earth platform
se	terrer		to hide, go to ground, disappear into its burrow
	terreux		earthy, muddy, grubby, gritty
	terreux -euse		muddy, gritty, earthy, full of dirt
	terrier	de lapin	rabbit-hole
	terrier		hole, terrier (dog)
	tertre		hillock, mound
	testamentaire		(clause/disposition) of a will
	tetanie		tetany (Med), spasmodic twitching
	tetanique		lockjaw

		tetaniser		to paralyse, tetanise
a tue-		tete		at the top of one's voice
		teter		to suckle, suck (I.e baby)
		tetons		breasts
		tetu		stubborn, pig-headed
		texte		subject, topic, text
		thaler (nm)		thaler (old silver coin from C18th)
		thermoplongeur		coiled heater, immersion heather
		thon (nm)		tuna
		tibia (nm)		shin, shinbone, tibia (Anat)
		tic		habit, mannerism, tic (med)
		tiede		lukewarm, tepid, warm, mild
qu'a cela ne		tienne		never mind!
la, le		tienne, tien		yours
a la		tienne!		cheers! Best of luck (irony)
		Tiens	donc!	Fancy that!
		tiens...		Oh...
un		tiers tierce		one third (1/3)
		tige		stem, trunk, shaft (of column), rod
		tignasse (nf)		mop of hair, hair
		tigre (nm)		tiger, tiger-skin, monster
		tilleul		lime tree, lime blossom
		timbale (nf)		metal drinking cup, kettledrum
		timbre		bell, timbre (voice), stamp (on doc or envelope)
		timide		shy, bashful, timid
		timore		timorous, over-scrupulous
		tintamarre		din, racket
		tinter		jingle
		tintinnabulement		tinkling
		tir		shooting, gunnery, fire, firing, shooting gallery, rifle range
		tirage		draw, circulation (Jour), impression (print)
		tirailler		to pull (s.o, s.t) about, to tug at
en		tirailleur		skirmisher (Mil.) in skirmishing position
une		tire-ligne		a ruling-pen
		tire(e) (adj)		pulled, drawn, haggard, peaked
se		tirer	d'affaire	to manage
s'en		tirer		to come through difficulties, cope

se	tirer		to get out of, escape, be off, clear off
	tirer		to stretch, pull out, pull, tug, shoot, incline to
	tiret (nm)		dash (-)
	tireur		marksman/markswoman, gunman, striker (sport)
	tiroir (nm)		drawer
	tisonner		to poke (the fire)
	tisser		to weave, spin
	tisserand(e)		weaver
	tissu (nm)		fabric, string, textile, texture
	titi		urchin, scamp
	titiller		to tickle, titillate
en	titre		on the staff, regular
	titre		title, heading, deed (Jur), status
	titulaire		incumbent (e.g. an installed personage)
	titulariser		to confirm s.o in a post
	tocsin		alarm bell
	tohu-bohu (nm)		the hustle and bustle
	toile		canvas
	toilette		grooming, wash, state of appearance
	toise		fathom (ie 6 foot)
	toison		fleece, mane, abundant growth (of hair)
a	toit	pointe	a peaked roof
	toit		roof
	toiture		roofing/roof
	tole		sheet metal
	toler		to work into sheet metal
	tolerer		to turn a blind eye to (s.t), put up with (s.t), tolerate
se	tolerer		to tolerate each other
	tombe		gravestone, grave
Laisse	tombe		Forget it! Give it a rest!
	tombeau		tomb, monument
	tomber	amoureux	to fall in love
	tomber	au ciel	to come out of the blue
	tomber	des nues	to be thunderstruck
laisser	tomber	qn	to give up, drop, let s.o down
	tomber		to fall, crash, sag, drop, come down, hang, be announced, vanish subside, die out/down
faire	tomber		to bring down, topple, collapse, remove, eradicate
	ton (nm)		tone, intonation, breeding, pitch, accent

	tonalite			key, tone, tonality
	tonicite			tone, bracing effect
	tonneau			cash, barrel
	tonnerre (nm)			the thunder
	tonnoire(s)			barrels
	tonte			mowing
	toquer			to knock
Je m'en	torche			I don't give a s!*t (Expl)
	torcher			to wipe, dash off (Fig), cobble (s.t) together (Fig)
	torchon (nm)			cloth, floor cloth, tea-towel
	tordant(e) (adj)			hilarious, very funny
se	tordre			to writhe, twist, wring
	tordre			to twist, wring (hands/clothes)
	torpeur			numbness/torpor/mental inertia
	torpilleur			torpedo boat
	torrefier			to roast (coffee, chestnuts, etc)
	torrent			mountain stream, torrent
	torride			scorching (heat)
	tors			twisted
	torsader			to twist
a	tort	et a travers		wildly
	tort			wrong, error, fault, injury, harm, tort (legal)
a	tort			wrongly
	tortillee(s)			twisted
se	tortiller			to wriggle, writhe, squirm
	tortiller			twist up, twist, wiggle
	tortionnaire (nmf)			torturer
	tortueux -euse (adj)			winding, convoluted, tortuous, devious
	torve			menacing
le plus	tot	possible		as soon as possible
	tot			early, not long, soon
	touche (nf)			touch, stroke, key, button, dash, bite (fishing), hit (fencing), key (piano, keyboard, pc), fret (guitar)
	touche, coule!			hit and sunk
	toucher			to move s.o, touch s.o, affect s.o, concern, meddle, tamper with
	toucher (nm)			touch, feel
	touffe			tuft (of hair/straw), clump (trees)
	touffu			bushy, thick
	touiller			to stir, toss (salad)

C'est	toujours	ca de pris	That's s.t at least
	toujours		nevertheless, ever, all the same, always
	toupet (nm)		quiff, nerve, (the) cheek
	tour		course, direction (of biz), round, rotation, trip, trick, feat, circumference, circuit, tour, (potter's) wheel
	tour (nf)		tower
	tourbillon (nm)		whirlwind, whirlpool, eddy, whirl, hustle n bustle (life)
	tourelle (nf)		turret
	tourillon		swivel pin, king pin (USA)
	tourmenter		to torture, harrass, torment
	tournage		shooting (Cine), filming (Cine), set (Cine)
	tournant		rotating, revolving, staggered (Pol); turning (n); point (n)
	tournebouler		to upset
	tournebouler		to upset
	tournee (nf)		a round (of drinks), tour, beating
	tourner	autour de	to be around/about (£), somewhere in the region of
	tourner		to get round, turn, stir (sauce), spin, go sour, go round, shoot (Cine), phrase, make a movie (Cine), tour
se	tourner		to turn (round)
	tourner et retourner	qch	to turn s.t over and over
les soie sur ma	tournette		the (strands) of silk on my spinner
	tourneur		turner (artisanal skill), thrower
	tournoyer		to fly around in circles, wheel, swirl around, whirl
	tournure		turn, shape, course of events, figure (lady)
	tourtourelle (nf)		turtle dove
	tous	les combien?	How often?
	tous	les dix minutes	every 10 minutes
	tousser		to cough, splutter
	toussoter		to cough slightly, splutter
en	tout		in every respect
	tout	a coup/ d'un coup	all at once, suddenly
que	tout	aille	let everything go
C'est	tout	aussi cher	It's just as expensive

en	tout	et pour tout	all told
Ca m'en a	tout	l'air	It looks very much like it to me
	tout	pret	Ready-made
du au	tout		completely
	tout	bien compte	all in all
	tout	de meme!	Really! Honestly!"
	tout	le monde	everybody
sur	tout		mostly
	tout	a fait	quite, entirely
	tout	ce qui compte	all that matters
	tout	de go	straight out
c'est	tout	le contraire	it's the very opposite, quite the contrary
	tout		everything, anything, all, quite, whole, every, while, however, although
le	tout		everything, the lot
former un	tout		to make up/form a whole
le	tout-venant		all and sundry
	tout(e), tous		any, every, all, quite, the whole
a	toute	age	at any age
	toute	la fortune	all the luck
de	toute	nature	of any kind
	toutefois		however, nevertheless
	toux		cough
avoir le	trac		to feel nervous, have stage fright
	trac (nm)		stage-fright, nerves
	tracas (nm)		worry, bother, trouble
	tracasser		to worry, bother, plague s.o
	trace (nf)		trail, track, footprint
	trace (nf)		trail, track, mark, scar
	tracer		to lay out, map out, outline, trace
	traction		tension, traction, push-ups
	traducteur – trice (nmf)		translator
	traduire		to translate, express (feeling/idea), represent
	trafiquant		dealer, trafficker, 'pusher' (coll)
	trahir		to give away a secret, betray, reveal
	trahison		betrayal, treachery
etre en	train	de faire	to be doing
etre en	train		to be full of energy

	train		line (of vehicles), mood, train
a font de	train		at top speed
mise en	train		warming up
	trainailler		to take ages, loaf about
	trainasser		to take ages, loaf about
	traineau (nm)		sleigh, sledge
se	trainer		to crawl along, go on one's knees
	trainer		to lug, drag along, drag (s.t) across the floor
	trait		arrow, beam (of light), trait, stroke, mark, act, deed of courage/kindness
	trait (nm)		line, dash, stroke, feature
	traite (nf)		treatise, treaty
	traiter		to treat, negotiate, deal (with a subject), discuss, handle (biz), entertain
	traiteurs		caterers
	traitre		a traitor, villain, treacherous
sous les	traits	de	in the guise of
	traits (nmpl)		features
	trajet		journey, drive, ride, flight, crossing
	trajet		journey, crossing, route
	trame (nm)		framework (of novel), thread (of existence), woof, weft
	tranchant		sharp
	tranchant (nm)		sharp edge, side, cutting edge
	tranchee (nf)		trench, drain
	trancher	net	to bring to a firm conclusion
	trancher		to slice (bread), cut short (chat), cut off, slice
etre	tranquille		to be/feel easy in one's mind
	tranquille (adj)		quiet, calm, peaceful, tranquil
	transferer		to pierce, go through, go right through
	transformer	en	turn into
	transfuge		renegade
un amoreux	transi		a bashful lover
	transiger		to compromise
se	transir		to chill to the bone, paralyse (with fear)
	translation		miraculous moving to Heaven without death, translation
	transmettre		to pass on (message), transmit

		transparaitre		to show through
		transparent		open, clear, transparent, limpid
		transport		outburst of feeling, rapture, transport
		transsudation		sweat
		transvaser		to decant (drink)
		transversalement		crosswise, transversely
		trapu(e) (adj)		stocky, thick-set, squat, tough, brainy (Coll)
		travailler		to work (on), train, cultivate
		travee		now
	a/au	travers	que	through s.t
	de	travers		askew, wrong, wrongly
		travers		across, crosswise
		travers (nm)		failing, bad habit, fault, breadth
		traverse (nf)		cross-piece, cross-bar, sleeper, strut, side street
		traversee (nf)		the passage
		traverser		to cross, go/pass through, go across, live on through
		travestir		to misrepresent, distort, dress (s.o) up
		trebucher		to stumble, slip up
	le	trefonds	de	the very depths of
		treillis (nm)		fatigues (Mil dress)
		treleau(x) (nm)		trestle
		treleau(x) (nm)		trestle
		tremble (nm)		aspen (Arb)
		tremblement		tremor, trembling, shaking, wavering, quivering
		trembler		to shake, quake, quiver, shiver, waver, tremble
		tremper		to soak, seep, mix
		trepaner		to trepan (med: use a cylindrical saw to remove a piece of bone from skull)
		trepignement (nm)		stamping (of feet)
		trepigner		to jump up and down, stamp one's feet
		tressaillir		to give a start, shudder (with fear), leap (for joy)
		tresser		to weave, plait, braid
		treuil (nm)		winch, windlass
		treve (nf)		respite, truce
		treve (nf)		truce (Mil), respite

	tri		sorting (post etc)
	tribun (nm)		great orator, tribune (Hist)
	tricher		to cheat, cut corners (Fig)
	tricot		knitting, knitwear, sweater, jumper
	trier		to sort out, select
	trifouiller	dans qch	to rummage through s.t, tinker with
	trimbaler		to lug (s.t) around, drag (s.o) around
	trimestriel -elle		quarterly
	trinquer		to toast, booze
rendre	tripes	et boyaux	to be as sick as a dog, to spew up
	tripes (nfpl)		guts, innards
c'etait pas	triste		it was quite something
	triste (adj)		sad, dreary, gloomy, depressing
	triton (nm)		tritone (musical – see English dictionary)
	troc (nm)		exchange (in kind), barter
	trogne (nf) (tronche)		mug, face
	trois-o-mats (nm)		three-master ship
	trois-pieces		3-roomed flat
	trombe	(de vent)	water-spout (whirlwind)
	tromblon		blunderbuss, grenade adaptor
Tout le monde peut se	tromper		Anyone can make a mistake
se	tromper		to be mistaken, make a mistake
	tromper		to deceive, cheat, betray, disappoint, mislead, be wrong
	tromperie (nf)		deceit
	trompette		trumpet (player), bugler
	trompeur		deceiver, misleading (appearance), deceitful
	trompeur -euse (adj)		deceptive, misleading
	tronc		trunk, shaft
	tronche		mug, face
	troncon (nm)		section (e.g railway)
	troner	sur	to have pride of place on
	tronquer		to truncate, cut down (words), curtail
	trop-plein (nm)		excess, over-abundance, overflow
	troquer		to crunch, munch, sketch
	trotter		to trot, scamper (mice)
	trottinette (nf)		scooter
	trottoir (nm)		pavement
	trou	de serrure	keyhole
	trou (nm)		hole, gap, deficit, shortfall, prison/"nick"
	trouant		piercing

	trouble			confusion, disorder, agitation, uneasiness, confused, embarrassment, cloudy, dim
	trouer			to perforate, make a hole
	troufignon			arsehole (Vulgar)
	troufion			soldier, squaddie
	troupeau			flock, herd
	troupier (nm)			squaddie, soldier, stand-up comic
	trousseau (nm)	de clefs		bunch of keys
	trousseur	de jupons		womanizer
	trouvaille			find, invention, innovation
se	trouver			to be, find oneself, feel, find
	truander			to con (s.o), cheat
	trublion (nm)			troublemaker
	truc			knack, thing, thingy, what's-it, special effect (cine), trick; what's his name
	trucage			special effect, doctoring, rigging, fixing
par le	truchement	de qch		through s.t
	truchement (nm)			interpreter
	truculent(e) (adj)			earthy
	truelle (nf)			trowel
	truie			sow
	truite			front
	tsiganes			gypsies (Hungarian)
	tubage			(well) casing, intubation (Med: insert tube thru larynx)
a	tue-tete			at the top of one's voice
se	tuer			to commit suicide, kill oneself, get killed, flog oneself to death (Fig)
	tuer			to kill, slaughter (animals)
	tuerie (nfpl)			killings
	tuile (nf)			tile, blow (Fig)
	tulipier			a tulip tree (Bot.)
	tulle			(fine silk net used for dresses) tulle
	tumefier			to make (s.t) swell up
	tumulte (nm)			hubbub, uproar, commotion, turmoil (of passions)
	turc turque			Turkish
	turpitude			lewdness, revolting, baseness, infamy
	tutelle (nf)			guardianship, tutelage
	tuteur – trice (nmf)			guardian (Jur), tutor

	tutoyer		to address using 'tu' form, be on familiar terms with
	tuyau	(en cuivre)	hose, pipe (copper pipe), tube, 'tip-off' (coll)
	tuyau	de cheminee	flue
	TVA		VAT (tax a la valeur ajoutee)
	tympan (nm)		eardrum, pinion (clock)
	tympaniser		to tympanise (maybe 'drum'; 'blow out' gas)
	type		example, guy (Coll), chap, typeface, type, kind, sort of
	typer		to portray (s.o) as a type, play (s.o) as a type
	typique		typical

U

	ubiquite		omnipresent, being everwhere
	ulcere		sickened, revolted
	uni		close, united, smooth, level, even
	uniformite		monotony, uniformity
	unijambiste (nmf)		one-legged person
s'	unir		to join (together), combine, unite
l'	unite		unity, one (maths), unit, oneness (of God)
	univoque		unequivocal, specific, pathognomonic (Med)
	untel -le		Mr/Mrs So-and-so
	urgence		urgency, emergency
l'	usage		custom, practice, employment, usage, use, practice, experience
	use(e)		Well-worn, worn-out
	user	de	to use, exercise, take, exploit
s'	user		to wear oneself out, wear out
l'	usine		factory, (gas) works, (steel) works
	usite		used, current, in use
	ustensile (nm)		utensil
	utilite		usefulness, use

V

N'y	va	pas	Don't go
un	vacarme		din, racket, row
	vache		nasty, mean
	vache (nf)		cow, b!!s**d (Expl for man), b*?/h (Expl for wom)
	vacherie		meanness, nastiness
	vacillement		flickering, swaying, waving, faltering
	vadrouiller		to wander around
	vagabond(e)		vagrant
	vagabond(e) (adj)		wandering, stray, roving, volatile (mood)
	vagabonder		to wander, stray
	vague	a l'ame	melancholy
	vague (adj)		some sort of, vague
	vague (nf)	de froid	cold spell
	vague (nf)		wave
	vague (nm)		space; indefinite, vague (adj)
etre	vaillant		to be in good health
	vaillant		valiant, brave, courageous
	vaille	que vaille	somehow or other
	vaille		worth, value
	vainqueur (nm)		victor, conqueror, winner
	vaisseau (nm)		vessel (anat), ship
	vaisselle (nf)		dishes, crockery
	val (vaux), vallon(s)		valley(s)
	valaque		Wallachian
	valet	de chambre	valet, manservant
	valeur (nf)		worth, merit, validity, securities (pl), stocks (pl), value
	valise (nf)		suitcase
	vallon		valley
	vallonnement (nm)		hills and valleys
	valse (nf)		waltz, constant succession
avait	valu		was worth
eut	valu		had been worth
	vanite (nf)		futility, vanity, emptiness, conceit
	vaniteux -euse		vain/conceited person
	vanne (nf)		valve
	vantail		leaf (of door)

se	vanter		to boast, brag
	vanter		to speak highly of, praise
a	vapeur		(powered by) steam
	vaporeux -euse (adj)		hazy, steamy, vaporous, filmy
	vaquer	a ses affaires	to go about one's business
	vaquer		to attend to (s.t)
	vareuse		tunic, (sailor's) jersey
	vasiere		mud-flat
	vasistas		louvre window
	vasouiller		to flounder
	vasque		basin (of fountain)
	vaste		immense, vast, spacious, huge, great (joke)
	vaudeville		light comedy, vaudeville
	vaurien		good-for-nothing
etre toujours par monts et par	vaux		to always be on the move
	vecu		real life, actual, personal experiences
	vecut		lived
	veille (nf)		vigil, eve, staying up (at night), preceding day, wakefulness, lookout (naut)
	veiller		to sit up, keep awake, see to, watch over
	veinard (nm)		lucky, jammy devil
	velin		vellum (paper)
	velleite (nf)		vague desire, vague attempt
	velours		velvet
	veloute(e)		velvety, smooth, mellow
	velu (adj)		hairy
	vendement		yield
se	vendre	(a)	to be sold, sell out (to), sell oneself to
	veneneux -euse (adj)		poisonous
maladie	venerien - enne		venereal disease
	vengeance		revenge
se	venger		to take revenge on s.o for s.t
	venger		to avenge
	venin		venom
en	venir	a	to come to
en	venir	a	to come to
	venir	de faire qch	to have just done s.t.
faire	venir	le medicin	to call the doctor

etre dans le	vent		to be trendy
rafale/ coup de	vent		gust of wind
	vente		sale
	venter	(les merites)	to blow; (sing the praises)
a plat	ventre		flat on his/her belly
	ventre		abdomen, belly
	ventre	a terre	at full speed
	ventru		bulbous
	venue		visit
	vepres		evensong
	ver		worm, grub, larva, maggot
	verbe		language, verb
	verdatre		greenish
	verdoyant		green, verdant
	verdure		greenery
	verge (nf)		penis (anat), rod
	verger		orchard
sans	vergogne		shamelessly, straight out
	vergue (nf)		yard (Naut.)
	veridique		truthful, authentic
	verifier		to prove correct
toute	verite	n'est pas bonne a dire	some things are better left unsaid
	verite (nf)		truth, realism
enoncer des	verites	premieres	to state the obvious
	vermeil (nm)		vermeil (gold money)
	vermiculaire		vermiform (having shape of a worm)
	vermisseau (nm)		small earthworm
	vermouler		worm-eaten
	vernir		to varnish, glaze, apply nail varnish
	verole (nf)		the pox
	verole(e)		pox-ridden, rotten
on	verra		we'll see
	verre		glass
	verrou (nm)		bolt, deadlock
	verrouille(e)		bolted, locked
	vers		towards
	vers (nm)		verse, line of poetry
	verser		to overturn, pour out, tip (out/in), shed (tears/blood)
au	vert		for recuperation
	vert(e)		green, unripe, spicy, risque, sharp, stiff, verdant, spritely (older person)

	vertige (nm)		dizziness, giddiness,
	vertigineux -euse (adj)		dizzy, giddy (height), breathtaking (speed), staggering (rise in price)
	vertu		quality, virtue, property
	verve (nf)		animation, verve
	veste (nf)		jacket
	vestiaire (nm)		changing room, cloakroom
	vestige		trace, remains, remnant, relic
	vestimentaire		clothing
	veston (nm)		(man's) jacket
	vetu		dressed
	vetuste (adj)		run down, dilapidated, out-dated
	veuf, veuve		widower, widow
	veuille		willing/will
	veuille	bien	please
ne m'en	veuillez	pas	don't be angry with me
Ca (ne)	veut	pas	Ain't gonna happen (coll)
Je	veut!		you bet!
	veuvage (nm)		widowhood
Je n'en	veux	pas	I don't want it/them/any
	vexer		to offend, upset, annoy
	viager -ere (adj)		for life, life
	viager (nm)		life annuity
	viande		meat
	viatique (nm)		viaticum (Rel): portable altar; communion (Rel); support, comfort
	vibration (nf)		vibration
	vibrer		to vibrate, thrill, quiver
	vicaire		curate (of parish)
	vicient		vitiate
	vicier		to corrupt, spoil, pollute, vitiate, contaminate (air)
	vicissitude(s)		change of circumstances/fortune, the ups and downs of life
	vide (adj)		blank, vacant
	vide (n)		empty space, void, vacuum, space
	vide (nm)		space, vacuum, gap, void, emptiness
	vider		to empty, drain (glass)
mettre de la	vie	dans qch	to liven s.t up
etre en	vie		to be alive
prendre	vie		to come to life
ainsi va la	vie		that's the way it goes

faire la	vie		to live it up
	vie (nf)		life
	vieil, vieille, vieux		old, shabby (hat), stale (news)
les	vieillards		the elderly, old people
	vieillir		to grow old
	vieillissant		aging
	vieillissement		aging
	viellesse		old age, agedness, oldness
J'ai du	viellir		I must've grown (gotten) old
J'en	viens		I've just come from there
J'y	viens		I'm coming to that point
la	Vierge		the Virgin (Mary)
mon	vieux		old boy, chap (coll)
	vif	du sujet	to the point
(pris) sur le	vif		thumbnail, candid, on the spot, live
	vif, vive		lively, vivacious, alive, bright, vivid
	vigie (nf)		look-out
	vil		vile, base
a	vil	prix	dirt cheap
	vilain		nasty, bad, unpleasant, sordid, wretched
	villemorienne		antiquated music theatre (Villemorien)
	vindicte		condemnation
	viol		rape, violation
	violemment		violently
	violence		violence, force
	violer		to infringe, desecrate, rape, violate
	violoncelle (nm)		cello
	virage (nf)		bend, curve, change of direction, colour change (Cine)
	virer		to transfer, fire, sack (Fig), expel, remove, turn (around)
	virevolter		to twirl
en	virgule		comma, point (Math), comma-shaped
	viril		male, virile
	vis		screw
	vis-a-vis		person opposite, person who lives opposite, opponent, meeting, encounter, vis-a-vis, tete-a-tete
en	vis-a-vis		opposite each other
	visage		face
	visceral(e) (adj)		deep-rooted, visceral
	viscere (n)		internal organ
	viser		to (take) aim, aim at, aim for
	visible		available, visible

	visiere (nf)		peak, visor, eye-shade
	visionner		to view
la peine d'etre	visite		worth being visited
	visiter		examine, inspect, visit
	vison (nm)		mink, mink coat
	visser		to treat s.o severely, screw (on, in, down, up)
	vital(e)(aux) (adj)		essential, vital
les	vitesses		gears (car)
	vitrail -aux		Stained-glass window
	vitre		glazed
	vitree		glazes
	vitres		pane (of glass), window (pane)
	vitrier		glazier
	vitriere		window
	vitrine (nf)		display cabinet, glass case, shop window, showcase
	vivace (adj)		perennial, enduring
	vivant (nm)		living being
	vivant(e) (adj)		lively, vivid, vivacious, living, alive
les	vivats		cheers
	vivement		briskly/suddenly/sharply
	vivifiant		bracing, invigorating
	vivre	comme un coq en pate	to live like a cockerel in clover
	vivre	(pp: vecu)	to live through, go through, experience, cope with, live, last
se laisser	vivre		to take things easy
les	vivres		supplies, provisions
	vivres		food, supplies
	vocable (nm)		term
	vocable (nm)		term
	vociferer		to shout, vociferate
	voeu(x)		vow(s)
	voie	de garage	siding (Rail)
	voie (nf)		way, track, means, channel, lane, road, route
	voila	tout	that's all
	voila		there/here it is!
en	voila		here you are, there you are, there you go then
me	voila		here I am!
	voile	noir	blackout
	voile (nf)		sail, sailing boat

	voile (nm)		veil, cloud, fog, shadow (Med.), mist (eyes)
	voilee	par	veiled by
	voiler		to veil, conceal, mist, buckle, warp, cover
	voir	les choses au jour le jour	to take each day as it comes
se	voir		to realise, see oneself, show, see each other, be seen
	voire		not to say, even, indeed
Je n'y	vois	rien	I can't see a thing
	voisinage		proximity/vicinity/neighbourhood
ca se	voit	vite	it shows quickly
	voiture (nf)		carriage, cart (horse-drawn), vehicle, car
	voix	de chantre	rich and powerful voice
a mi-	voix		under one's breath, in an undertone
saisir au	vol		to grasp
	vol		flight, flying, flock, theft, robbery
	volage		fickle, flighty
	volaille		poultry, fowl
	volant		steering wheel
	volatil(e)		volatile
	volcan		volcano
de haute	volee		first rate
	volee (nf)		flight, shower (of blows), flock, volley (missiles), band (of girls)
	voler		to fly, steal
	volet (nm)		shutter, panel, section, constituent (part)
	voleter		to flutter
	voliere (nf)		aviary
	volontaire		deliberate, determined, voluntary
	volonte		willingness, will, will-power
	volontiers		gladly, willingly
	voltiger		to flit, flutter about
	voltigeur		light infantryman (Hist Mil)
	volume (nf)		bulk, mass, tome, volume
	volumineux -euse		thick, bulky, voluminous, ample
	volupte (nf)		(sensual) pleasure
	volute		curl of smoke
	vomissement		vomitting
le	votre		yours
	voue	a l'echec	doomed to failure

	voue(e)		doomed
	vouer		to dedicate, consecrate, vow
ou	voulez-	vous en venir	Where are you coming from? Where are you going with this (idea)?
en	vouloir	a qn	to bear s.o a grudge, be determined on s.t, admit, allow
	vouloir	dire	to mean
s'en	vouloir		to regret, be cross with o.s
se	vouloir		to like to think of o.s as, try to be, meant to be
	vouloir		to want, will, desire, require, need, demand (of thing)
en	vouloir		to want to get on (Motivation)
	vouloir (nm)		will (Philos)
	voulu		intended, deliberate
	voute		arched/vaulted, round-shouldered
	vouvoiement (nm)		using the 'vous' (polite) form
	voyager		to travel
	voyance		clairvoyance
	voyant(e)		loud, showy, ostentatious
	voyou		lout, yobbo, rascal, hoodlum (US)
en	vrac		unpackagaged, higgledy-piggledy
	vrac		bulk, loose
	vrai		in truth…
il est	vrai	que tant	It's a well-known fact that…
	vraisemblablement		probably
	vraisemblance		probability, likelihood
	vrille		spiral, tailspin, tendril (Bot)
	vu		openly, publicly
	Vu?		"Get it?" "Understood?"
	vulgariser		to popularise

W

un	wagon-lit		a sleeping-car (rail stock)

X and Y

	xyloidine		xyloidine (explosive compound by action of nitric acid on starch or woody fibres)
il	y	a, ait	there is to do, be done
qu'il	y	ai	that there is
Il n'	y	en a plus/pas	There are none left/none
	y		there, it, of it, about it (y is not always translated!)
Il n'	y	a plus rien	There's nothing left
Je ne m'	y	fait pas	I can't get used to it
ah j'	y	suis	ah, I've got it! Ah, I'm with you
entre quatre	yeux		face-to-face
sous les	yeux		before my (very) eyes
	youyou		dingy, ululation

Z

	zebre		bloke (Fig)
	zebree		zebra
il y a du	zef		it's windy
	zele (adj)		enthusiastic, zealous
	zele (n)		enthusiasm, zeal
	zero	heure	midnight
	zezaiement		lisp
	zezayer		to lisp
	zinc		counter, bar, zinc, 'plane
	zob		penis (anat), px%!k (Vulgar)
	zona (nm)		shingles
	zone		area, zone
	zou	allez	hurry up; get out!; go on
	zouare		clown, comedian
	zozotement		lisp
	zozoter		to lisp

(c) 2022 John E Wright

Printed in Great Britain
by Amazon